DIABETIC AIR FRYER COOKBOOK

1700 Days Of Tasty And Super Easy Recipes, Low Fat, Low Carb and Low Sugar. Delicious air fryer meals for diabetic diet | 30 Days Meal Plan.

IVORY WALLAKER

Introduction

In the pages of this book, you'll discover a delightful collection of recipes designed specifically for those managing diabetes. Say hello to the "Diabetic Air Fryer Cookbook" - your guide to delicious and healthy meals made effortlessly in the air fryer.

With a focus on flavor, nutrition, and convenience, this cookbook is here to revolutionize your cooking experience. Embracing the power of the air fryer, you'll embark on a culinary adventure filled with mouthwatering dishes that will satisfy your cravings while keeping your blood sugar in check.

From crispy favorites like cinnamon apple rings to guilt-free indulgences like chocolate-dipped bananas, every recipe is carefully crafted to provide you with wholesome ingredients and fantastic taste. Get ready to enjoy a variety of dishes, from appetizers to desserts, all prepared with love and consideration for your well-being.

Whether you're new to the world of air frying or a seasoned pro, this book is your go-to resource for diabetic-friendly meals that never compromise on taste. So let's embark on this flavorful journey together, discovering a world of possibilities as we embrace the power of the air fryer in our kitchens.

Get ready to savor every bite without worries. Let's dive into the "Diabetic Air Fryer Cookbook" and make healthy eating a joyous experience.

©Copyright by IVORY WALLAKER. All rights reserved.

This document provides exact and reliable information regarding the topic and issues covered. The publication is sold with the idea that the publisher is not required to render accounting, officially permitted, or otherwise qualified services.

A practiced professional individual should be ordered if advice is necessary, legal, or professional. From a Declaration of Principles which was accepted and approved equally by a Committee of the American Bar Association and a Committee of Publishers and Associations. In no way is it legal to reproduce, duplicate, or transmit any part of this document in either electronic means or printed format. Recording this publication is prohibited, and any storage of this document is not allowed unless written permission from the publisher. All rights reserved.

The information provided herein is stated to be truthful and consistent in that any liability, in terms of inattention or otherwise, by any usage or abuse of any policies, processes, or directions contained within is the solitary and utter responsibility of the recipient reader. Under no circumstances will any legal responsibility or blame be held against the publisher for reparation, damages, or monetary loss due to the information herein, either directly or indirectly. Respective authors own all copyrights not held by the publisher. The information herein is solely offered for informational purposes and is universal.

The presentation of the information is without a contract or guarantee assurance. The trademarks used are without any consent, and the trademark publication is without permission or backing by the trademark owner. All trademarks and brands within this book are for clarifying purposes only and are owned by the owners, not affiliated with this document.

Font design by Vernon Adams, photo by Bruna Branco, Victoria Shes, Tim Toomey. Layout and cover design by Yuliia Diiuk.

Contents

Chapter 1: Demystifying Diabetes: Exploring the Basics
The Role of Diet in Diabetes Control **8**

Chapter 2: Unleashing the Power
of the Air Fryer for Diabetes-Friendly Cooking **9**

Chapter 3: Breakfast **10**

Veggie Quiche	11	Sweet Potato Hash	13
Spinach Egg Muffins	11	Zucchini Fritters	14
Herbed Omelette	11	Salmon Roll-Ups	14
Apple Pancakes	12	Banana Bread	14
Blueberry Muffins	12	Quinoa Bowl	15
Avocado Toast	12	Turkey Skewers	15
Veggie Burritos	13	Eggplant Bake	15
Yogurt Parfait	13		

Chapter 4: Lunch and salads **16**

Chicken Salad	17	Tuna Salad	25
Salmon with Lemon-Dill	17	Turkey Kabobs	25
Quinoa Veggie Salad	17	Stuffed Bell Peppers	26
Greek Salad	18	Shrimp Caesar Salad	26
Shrimp Avocado Salad	18	Lentil Salad	26
Spinach Strawberry Salad	18	Noodle Salad	27
Caesar Salad	19	Watermelon Feta Salad	27
Black Bean Salad	19	Baked Cod	27
Tofu Stir-Fry	19	Chicken Lettuce Wraps	28
Caprese Salad	20	Caprese Skewers	28
Tuna Lettuce Wraps	20	Greek Orzo Salad	28
Sesame Chicken Salad	20	Falafel Salad	29
Chickpea Salad	21	Zucchini Pad Thai	29
Zucchini Falafel	21	Southwest Quinoa Salad	29
Stuffed Peppers	21	Stuffed Chicken Breast	30
Cauliflower Rice Bowl	22	Thai Beef Wraps	30
Kale Quinoa Salad	22	Mediterranean Pasta Salad	30
Teriyaki Salmon Salad	22	Sesame Tofu Salad	31
Chicken Pita Wraps	23	Shrimp Avocado Salad	31
Shrimp Lettuce Cups	23	Turkey Taco Wraps	31
Beet Goat Cheese Salad	23	Eggplant Mozzarella Stack	32
BBQ Chicken Salad	24	Quinoa Stuffed Peppers	32
Mushroom Spinach Salad	24	Grilled Chicken Salad	32
Thai Beef Salad	24	Zucchini Noodle Salad	33
Mexican Quinoa Bowl	25	Southwest Quinoa Bowl	33

Chapter 5: Dinner 34

Grilled Balsamic Chicken 35	Mediterranean Tuna Salad 43
Lemon-Dill Salmon 35	Turkey Veggie Skewers 43
Roasted Veggie Quinoa 35	Stuffed Bell Peppers 44
Greek Feta Salad 36	Grilled Shrimp Caesar 44
Shrimp Avocado Wraps 36	Lentil Tahini Salad 44
Strawberry Spinach Salad 36	Asian Chicken Noodle Salad 45
Light Caesar Chicken 37	Watermelon Feta Salad 45
Black Bean Corn Salad 37	Lemon-Caper Baked Cod 45
Tofu Stir-Fry 37	Chicken Lettuce Wraps 46
Caprese Skewers 38	Caprese Skewers 46
Tuna Lettuce Wraps 38	Greek Orzo Salad 46
Sesame Chicken Salad 38	Air-Fried Falafel Salad 47
Chickpea Cucumber Salad 39	Zucchini Pad Thai 47
Zucchini Chickpea Fritters 39	Southwest Chicken Salad 47
Stuffed Bell Peppers 39	Spinach Stuffed Chicken 48
Mexican Cauli Bowl 40	Thai Beef Lettuce Wraps 48
Kale Butternut Salad 40	Mediterranean Pasta Salad 48
Teriyaki Salmon Bowl 40	Asian Tofu Salad 49
Chicken Pita Wraps 41	Grilled Shrimp Salad 49
Air-Fried Shrimp Cups 41	Turkey Taco Lettuce Wraps 49
Beet Goat Cheese Salad 41	Eggplant Mozzarella Stack 50
BBQ Chicken Ranch 42	Quinoa Stuffed Peppers 50
Mushroom Spinach Salad 42	Lemon Herb Grilled Chicken 50
Thai Beef Salad 42	Zucchini Noodle Salad 51
Mexican Chicken Bowl 43	Southwest Quinoa Bowl 51

Chapter 6: Poultry and meat 52

Grilled Lemon Chicken 53	Honey Sriracha Salmon 57
Roasted Turkey Breast 53	Grilled Chicken Breast 57
Balsamic Glazed Salmon 53	Sesame Beef Stir-Fry 58
Grilled Shrimp 54	Balsamic Pork Chops 58
Mediterranean Chicken 54	Teriyaki Turkey Meatballs 58
Teriyaki Beef Skewers 54	Grilled Pork Tenderloin 59
Roasted Chicken Thighs 55	Greek Grilled Chicken 59
Cajun Grilled Chicken 55	Grilled Chicken Drumsticks 59
Air-Fried Chicken Wings 55	Lime Grilled Shrimp 60
Honey Mustard Pork Tenderloin ... 56	Roasted Turkey Legs 60
Grilled Lamb Chops 56	Glazed Pork Belly Slices 61
Spicy Shrimp Skewers 56	Grilled Sirloin Steak 61
Parmesan Chicken Tenders 57	

Chapter 7: Snacks and appetiserz 62

Air-Fried Zucchini Fries 63	Buffalo Cauliflower Poppers 69
Buffalo Cauliflower Bites 63	Quinoa Stuffed Zucchini 70
Baked Parmesan Wings 63	Asian Beef Skewers with Sesame Seeds ..70
Mediterranean Stuffed Mushrooms 64	Chicken Bites with Garlic and Parmesan....70
Roasted Chickpeas 64	Mediterranean Cucumber Roll-Ups 71
Caprese Skewers 64	Spicy Edamame 71
Spicy Tofu Wraps 65	Greek Yogurt Veggie Dip 71
Spinach Artichoke Dip 65	Air Fried Mozzarella Sticks 72
Zucchini Pizza Bites 65	Teriyaki Tofu Skewers 72
Teriyaki Turkey Meatballs 66	Caprese Salad Skewers 72
Smoky Eggplant Dip 66	Zucchini Nachos 73
Lemon Pepper Shrimp 66	Roasted Red Pepper Dip 73
Quinoa Sushi Rolls 67	Turkey Bacon Asparagus 73
Roasted Red Pepper Hummus 67	Baked Buffalo Cauliflower 74
Turkey Lettuce Wraps 67	Quinoa Stuffed Mushrooms 74
Baked Sweet Potato Fries 68	Greek Lamb Kebabs 74
Cilantro Lime Shrimp Skewers 68	Avocado Shrimp Ceviche 75
Spinach Feta Mushrooms 68	Baked Sweet Potato Chips 75
Greek Chicken Meatballs 69	Asian Sesame Tofu Skewers 75
Avocado Egg Salad Wraps 69	Spinach Feta Phyllo Cups 75

Chapter 8: Fish and seafood 77

Lemon Herb Air-Fried Salmon 77	Spicy Buffalo Air-Fried Shrimp 82
Spicy Cajun Shrimp Skewers 77	Coconut Crusted Air-Fried Shrimp 83
Garlic Herb Air-Fried Tilapia 77	Herb-Marinated Air-Fried Mackerel 84
Lemon Pepper Air-Fried Cod 78	Panko Crusted Crab Cakes 85
Teriyaki Glazed Air-Fried Salmon 78	Balsamic Glazed Air-Fried Salmon 85
Blackened Air-Fried Catfish 78	Parmesan Herb Air-Fried Scampi 85
Herb-Crusted Air-Fried Halibut 79	Soy-Glazed Air-Fried Salmon 86
Chili Lime Air-Fried Shrimp 79	Garlic Herb Air-Fried Scallops 86
Mediterranean Herb Air-Fried Swordfish...79	Lemon Basil Air-Fried Snapper 86
Parmesan Crusted Air-Fried Scallops . 80	Cajun Catfish Nuggets 87
Dijon Mustard Glazed Air-Fried Trout . 80	Mediterranean Herb Air-Fried Trout 87
Sesame Ginger Air-Fried Tuna Steaks 80	Teriyaki Glazed Shrimp Skewers 87
Greek Air-Fried Sea Bass 81	Lemon Pepper Air-Fried Sole 88
Cajun Shrimp Po' Boys 81	Spicy Sriracha Air-Fried Calamari 88
Lemon Garlic Air-Fried Mahi-Mahi 81	Herb-Crusted Red Snapper 88

Chapter 9: Vegetarian recipes ... 89

Crispy Tofu Nuggets ... 90
Zucchini Feta Fritters ... 90
Stuffed Portobello Mushrooms ... 90
Eggplant Parmesan ... 91
Air-Fried Veggie Spring Rolls ... 91
Mediterranean Stuffed Peppers ... 91
Cauliflower Buffalo Bites ... 92
Air-Fried Falafel ... 92
Sweet Potato Veggie Burgers ... 92
Caprese Stuffed Avocado ... 93
Quinoa Stuffed Bell Peppers ... 93
Crispy Zucchini Chips ... 93
Spinach Feta Stuffed Mushrooms ... 94
Greek Stuffed Tomatoes ... 94
Crispy Parmesan Asparagus ... 94
Caprese Skewers ... 95
Sweet Potato Fries ... 95
Chickpea Vegetable Curry ... 95
Air-Fried Vegetable Tempura ... 96
Mediterranean Eggplant Bake ... 96
Quinoa Stuffed Peppers ... 96
Air-Fried Brussels Sprouts ... 97
Stuffed Portobello Mushrooms ... 97
Sweet Potato Buddha Bowl ... 98
Crispy Onion Rings ... 98

Chapter 10: Dessert ... 99

Cinnamon Apple Rings ... 100
Air-Fried Strawberry Shortcake ... 100
Chocolate-Dipped Bananas ... 100
Mixed Berry Crumble ... 101
Cinnamon Sugar Tortilla Chips ... 101
Lemon Poppy Seed Donuts ... 101
Pumpkin Spice Energy Balls ... 102
Air-Fried Peach Crisp ... 102
Raspberry Chocolate Chip Muffins ... 102
Coconut Macaroons ... 103
Blueberry Almond Turnovers ... 103
Vanilla Chia Pudding ... 103
Baked Cinnamon Raisin Apples ... 104
Air-Fried Pineapple Rings ... 104
Chocolate Avocado Pudding ... 104
Caramelized Banana Slices ... 105
Almond Flour Cookies ... 105
Berry Frozen Yogurt Bites ... 105
Air-Fried Coconut Shrimp ... 106
Mixed Berry Parfait ... 106

Chapter 11: Week-meal plan 30 days ... 107
Chapter 12: Measurement conversion ... 108
Chapter 13: INDEX ... 109
Chapter 14: Conclusion ... 112

Chapter 1: Demystifying Diabetes: Exploring the Basics The Role of Diet in Diabetes Control

What is Diabetes? Diabetes is a chronic medical condition characterized by high blood sugar levels. It occurs when the body either does not produce enough insulin (a hormone that regulates blood sugar) or cannot effectively use the insulin it produces. There are primarily two types of diabetes: type 1 and type 2.

Type 1 Diabetes: Type 1 diabetes is an autoimmune disease that typically develops in childhood or adolescence. People with type 1 diabetes require insulin injections or an insulin pump to control their blood sugar levels. While diet plays a crucial role, medication is necessary for managing this type of diabetes.

Type 2 Diabetes: Type 2 diabetes is the most common form of diabetes, usually occurring in adulthood. It is often associated with lifestyle factors such as obesity, sedentary behavior, and poor dietary choices. Unlike type 1 diabetes, type 2 diabetes can often be managed through a combination of healthy eating, regular physical activity, and, in some cases, oral medications or insulin therapy.

The Importance of Diet in Diabetes Control: Diet is a cornerstone of diabetes management, regardless of the type. Making informed food choices helps regulate blood sugar levels, maintain a healthy weight, and reduce the risk of complications associated with diabetes. A balanced diet rich in whole grains, lean proteins, healthy fats, and a variety of fruits and vegetables is recommended for individuals with diabetes.

Carbohydrates and Blood Sugar: Carbohydrates have the most significant impact on blood sugar levels. Understanding how different carbohydrates affect blood sugar is crucial. Foods with a high glycemic index, such as white bread or sugary drinks, can cause blood sugar spikes. On the other hand, foods with a low glycemic index, like whole grains and non-starchy vegetables, have a milder impact on blood sugar levels.

Glycemic Load: Glycemic load (GL) takes into account both the quality and quantity of carbohydrates in a food. It provides a more accurate assessment of how a particular food affects blood sugar. Choosing foods with a low glycemic load can help maintain stable blood sugar levels.

The Role of the Diabetic Air Fryer: The air fryer is a versatile kitchen appliance that can be a valuable tool for individuals with diabetes. By using significantly less oil, air frying allows for healthier cooking while still achieving delicious and crispy results. The recipes in this cookbook have been specially crafted for the air fryer, providing diabetic-friendly options that prioritize taste and nutrition.

Chapter 2: Unleashing the Power of the Air Fryer for Diabetes-Friendly Cooking

Reduced Oil Consumption: One of the significant benefits of air frying is the ability to cook with significantly less oil compared to traditional deep frying. This reduction in oil consumption is particularly beneficial for individuals with diabetes, as excessive intake of unhealthy fats can lead to weight gain, insulin resistance, and other complications. Air frying allows you to enjoy crispy and flavorful foods with minimal oil, promoting a healthier diet.

Lower Fat Content: In addition to reducing oil, air frying also helps reduce the overall fat content in your meals. Excess fat intake can contribute to weight gain and increase the risk of cardiovascular issues, which are often associated with diabetes. The air fryer's cooking method allows excess fat to drip away from the food, resulting in a lower fat content while maintaining desirable textures and flavors.

Improved Glycemic Control: The air fryer's ability to cook food quickly at high temperatures promotes better glycemic control. The shorter cooking time helps retain more nutrients in the food, including fibers that can slow down the absorption of sugars. By using the air fryer to prepare diabetes-friendly meals, you can minimize blood sugar spikes and maintain more stable glucose levels.

Versatile Cooking Options: The air fryer is a versatile appliance that can be used for various cooking techniques, including frying, baking, roasting, grilling, and more. This versatility allows you to prepare a wide range of diabetes-friendly recipes without needing multiple kitchen gadgets. From crispy vegetable chips to succulent chicken breasts, the air fryer can handle it all, providing you with endless culinary possibilities.

Mastering the Air Fryer: Tips and Techniques

Preheating: Preheating the air fryer is essential for achieving optimal cooking results. Most air fryers require a few minutes to heat up before you start cooking. Preheating helps ensure even cooking and crispy textures.

Use Parchment Paper or Silicone Liners: To prevent food from sticking to the air fryer basket, you can line it with parchment paper or silicone liners. These non-stick options make cleanup easier while preserving the food's crispy exterior.

Shake and Flip: To ensure even cooking, shake the air fryer basket or flip the food halfway through the cooking process. This allows for uniform browning and crispy textures on all sides.

Avoid Overcrowding: Overcrowding the air fryer basket can impede proper air circulation, resulting in uneven cooking. To achieve the best results, cook food in a single layer or in batches if necessary.

Adjust Cooking Times and Temperatures: Every air fryer model may have slightly different cooking times and temperature settings. It's essential to familiarize yourself with your specific appliance and make adjustments as needed to achieve the desired results. Consult the manufacturer's instructions and recipe guidelines for recommended settings.

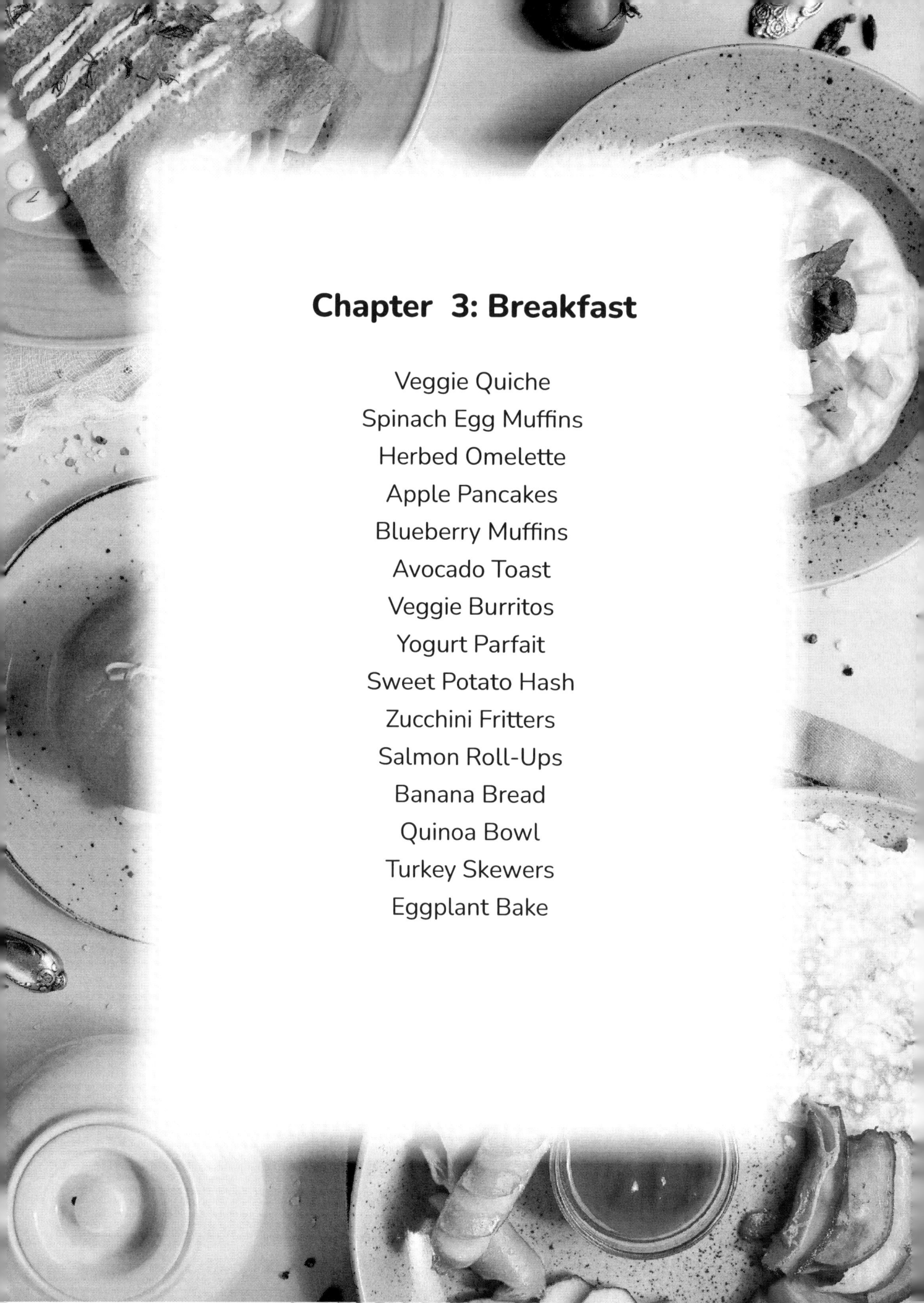

Chapter 3: Breakfast

Veggie Quiche

Spinach Egg Muffins

Herbed Omelette

Apple Pancakes

Blueberry Muffins

Avocado Toast

Veggie Burritos

Yogurt Parfait

Sweet Potato Hash

Zucchini Fritters

Salmon Roll-Ups

Banana Bread

Quinoa Bowl

Turkey Skewers

Eggplant Bake

Chapter 3: Breakfast

Veggie Quiche

INGREDIENTS:

(Calories: 180 / Carbs: 8g / Proteins: 14g / Fats: 10g)

- 1/2 cup chopped mixed vegetables (such as bell peppers, onions, zucchini)
- 2 large eggs
- 1/4 cup unsweetened almond milk
- Salt and pepper to taste
- 1 tablespoon grated Parmesan cheese (optional)

Cooking time: 25 minutes / servings: 1
Preparation time: 10 minutes

INSTRUCTIONS FOR COOKING:

- Preheat your air fryer to 350°F (175°C).
- In a mixing bowl, whisk together the eggs and almond milk. Season with salt and pepper.
- Add the chopped vegetables to the egg mixture and stir well to combine.
- Grease a small oven-safe dish that fits inside your air fryer basket.
- Pour the vegetable and egg mixture into the dish.
- Place the dish in the air fryer basket and cook for 20-25 minutes or until the quiche is set and slightly golden on top.
- Remove from the air fryer and let it cool for a few minutes before serving.
- Optional: Sprinkle grated Parmesan cheese on top before serving.

Spinach Egg Muffins

INGREDIENTS:

(Calories: 120 / Carbs: 4g / Proteins: 12g / Fats: 6g)

- 1/2 cup chopped spinach
- 1/4 cup sliced mushrooms
- 2 large eggs
- 1 tablespoon diced onions
- Salt and pepper to taste

Cooking time: 15 minutes / servings: 1
Preparation time: 15 minutes

INSTRUCTIONS FOR COOKING:

- Preheat your air fryer to 350°F (175°C).
- In a mixing bowl, whisk the eggs until well beaten.
- Add the chopped spinach, sliced mushrooms, diced onions, salt, and pepper to the beaten eggs. Mix well.
- Grease a silicone muffin mold or line a muffin tin with silicone liners.
- Pour the egg and vegetable mixture into the muffin cups, filling each about three-quarters full.
- Place the muffin mold or tin in the air fryer basket and cook for 12-15 minutes or until the egg muffins are set and slightly golden on top.
- Remove from the air fryer and let them cool for a few minutes before removing from the mold or tin.
- Serve warm or refrigerate for later consumption.

Herbed Omelette

INGREDIENTS:

(Calories: 160 / Carbs: 5g / Proteins: 12g / Fats: 10g)

- 2 large eggs
- 2 tablespoons chopped fresh herbs (such as parsley, basil, or chives)
- 1/4 cup diced bell peppers
- 1/4 cup diced tomatoes
- Salt and pepper to taste
- Cooking spray

Cooking time: 10 minutes / servings: 1
Preparation time: 5 minutes

INSTRUCTIONS FOR COOKING:

- Preheat your air fryer to 350°F (175°C).
- In a bowl, whisk the eggs until well beaten. Season with salt and pepper.
- Spray a small oven-safe dish that fits inside your air fryer basket with cooking spray.
- Pour the beaten eggs into the dish.
- Add the chopped fresh herbs, diced bell peppers, and diced tomatoes to the egg mixture. Stir gently to combine.
- Place the dish in the air fryer basket and cook for 8-10 minutes or until the omelette is set and slightly puffed.
- Remove from the air fryer and let it cool for a few minutes before serving.

Apple Pancakes

INGREDIENTS:

(Calories: 220 / Carbs: 15g / Proteins: 8g / Fats: 16g)

- 1/2 cup almond flour
- 1/2 teaspoon baking powder
- 1/2 teaspoon ground cinnamon
- 1/4 cup unsweetened almond milk
- 1/4 teaspoon vanilla extract
- 1 small apple, peeled and finely chopped
- Cooking spray

Cooking time: 25 minutes / servings: 1
Preparation time: 10 minutes

INSTRUCTIONS FOR COOKING:

- Preheat your air fryer to 350°F (175°C).
- In a mixing bowl, whisk together the almond flour, baking powder, and ground cinnamon.
- Add the almond milk and vanilla extract to the dry ingredients. Mix well to form a smooth batter.
- Fold in the finely chopped apple.
- Lightly coat the air fryer basket with cooking spray.
- Drop spoonfuls of the pancake batter onto the greased basket, forming small pancakes.
- Cook for 4 minutes, then flip the pancakes and cook for an additional 4 minutes or until golden brown.
- Remove from the air fryer and serve warm.

Blueberry Muffins

INGREDIENTS:

(Calories: 180 / Carbs: 8g / Proteins: 14g / Fats: 10g)

- 1/4 cup almond flour
- 1/4 teaspoon baking powder
- 1 tablespoon unsweetened applesauce
- 1 tablespoon almond milk
- 1 tablespoon honey or sweetener of choice
- 1/4 teaspoon vanilla extract
- 1/4 cup fresh blueberries

Cooking time: 25 minutes / servings: 1
Preparation time: 10 minutes

INSTRUCTIONS FOR COOKING:

- Preheat your air fryer to 350°F (175°C).
- In a mixing bowl, whisk together the eggs and almond milk. Season with salt and pepper.
- Add the chopped vegetables to the egg mixture and stir well to combine.
- Grease a small oven-safe dish that fits inside your air fryer basket.
- Pour the vegetable and egg mixture into the dish.
- Place the dish in the air fryer basket and cook for 20-25 minutes or until the quiche is set and slightly golden on top.
- Remove from the air fryer and let it cool for a few minutes before serving.
- Optional: Sprinkle grated Parmesan cheese on top before serving.

Avocado Toast

INGREDIENTS:

(Calories: 160 / Carbs: 5g / Proteins: 12g / Fats: 10g)

- 1 slice of whole grain bread, toasted
- 1/2 ripe avocado, mashed
- 1 small tomato, sliced
- Salt and pepper to taste

Cooking time: 0 minutes / servings: 1
Preparation time: 5 minutes

INSTRUCTIONS FOR COOKING:

- Toast the slice of whole grain bread until golden brown.
- Spread the mashed avocado evenly onto the toasted bread.
- Top with slices of fresh tomato.
- Season with salt and pepper to taste.
- Serve immediately.

Veggie Burritos

INGREDIENTS:

(Calories: 280 / Carbs: 29g / Proteins: 18g / Fats: 9g)

- 1 whole wheat tortilla
- 2 large eggs, beaten
- 1/4 cup diced bell peppers (any color)
- 1/4 cup diced onions
- 1/4 cup diced tomatoes
- 1/4 cup diced zucchini
- Salt and pepper to taste
- Optional toppings: salsa, avocado, low-fat cheese

Cooking time: 10 minutes / servings: 1
Preparation time: 15 minutes

INSTRUCTIONS FOR COOKING:

- Preheat your air fryer to 375°F (190°C).
- In a non-stick skillet, sauté the bell peppers, onions, tomatoes, and zucchini until softened.
- Season the beaten eggs with salt and pepper, then pour them into the skillet with the sautéed vegetables.
- Cook the eggs and vegetables, stirring occasionally, until the eggs are fully cooked.
- Warm the whole wheat tortilla in the air fryer for about 1 minute to make it pliable.
- Spoon the cooked egg and vegetable mixture onto the center of the tortilla.
- Add any optional toppings such as salsa, avocado, or low-fat cheese.
- Fold the sides of the tortilla over the filling, then roll it up into a burrito.
- Place the burrito in the air fryer basket and cook for 5-6 minutes, or until the tortilla becomes crispy and golden.
- Remove from the air fryer and let it cool slightly before serving.

Yogurt Parfait

INGREDIENTS:

(Calories: 180 / Carbs: 16g / Proteins: 18g / Fats: 6g)

- 1/2 cup plain Greek yogurt
- 1/4 cup mixed berries (such as strawberries, blueberries, raspberries)
- 1 tablespoon chopped nuts (such as almonds, walnuts)
- 1/2 tablespoon honey (optional)

Cooking time: 0 minutes / servings: 1
Preparation time: 5 minutes

INSTRUCTIONS FOR COOKING:

- In a glass or bowl, start by layering half of the Greek yogurt.
- Add half of the mixed berries on top of the yogurt.
- Sprinkle half of the chopped nuts over the berries.
- Repeat the layering process with the remaining yogurt, berries, and nuts.
- Drizzle honey on top if desired for added sweetness.
- Serve immediately or refrigerate until ready to eat.

Sweet Potato Hash

INGREDIENTS:

(Calories: 140 / Carbs: 30g / Proteins: 3g / Fats: 0g)

- 1 medium sweet potato, peeled and grated
- 1/4 small onion, grated
- 1 tablespoon whole wheat flour
- 1/2 teaspoon garlic powder
- 1/2 teaspoon paprika
- Salt and pepper to taste
- Cooking spray

Cooking time: 15 minutes / servings: 1
Preparation time: 10 minutes

INSTRUCTIONS FOR COOKING:

- Preheat your air fryer to 375°F (190°C).
- In a bowl, combine the grated sweet potato, grated onion, whole wheat flour, garlic powder, paprika, salt, and pepper.
- Mix well until all the ingredients are evenly combined.
- Divide the mixture into two equal portions and shape each portion into a flat patty.
- Lightly coat the air fryer basket with cooking spray to prevent sticking.
- Place the sweet potato patties in the air fryer basket and cook for 12-15 minutes, flipping them halfway through, until they are crispy and golden brown.
- Remove from the air fryer and let them cool slightly before serving.

Zucchini Fritters

INGREDIENTS:

(Calories: 180 / Carbs: 22g / Proteins: 9g / Fats: 6g)

- 1 medium zucchini, grated
- 1/4 small onion, grated
- 2 tablespoons crumbled feta cheese
- 1 tablespoon chopped fresh herbs (such as parsley, dill, or basil)
- 1/4 cup whole wheat breadcrumbs
- 1 large egg, beaten
- Salt and pepper to taste
- Cooking spray

Cooking time: 12 minutes / servings: 1
Preparation time: 15 minutes

INSTRUCTIONS FOR COOKING:

- Preheat your air fryer to 375°F (190°C).
- In a bowl, combine the grated zucchini, grated onion, crumbled feta cheese, chopped fresh herbs, whole wheat breadcrumbs, beaten egg, salt, and pepper.
- Mix well until all the ingredients are evenly combined.
- Shape the mixture into small fritters, about 2-3 inches in diameter.
- Lightly coat the air fryer basket with cooking spray to prevent sticking.
- Place the zucchini fritters in the air fryer basket and cook for 10-12 minutes, flipping them halfway through, until they are crispy and golden brown.
- Remove from the air fryer and let them cool slightly before serving.

Salmon Roll-Ups

INGREDIENTS:

(Calories: 120 / Carbs: 2g / Proteins: 13g / Fats: 7g)

- 2 slices of smoked salmon
- 2 tablespoons cream cheese
- 1 tablespoon chopped fresh dill (optional)
- Fresh lemon juice, for garnish
- Salt and pepper to taste

Cooking time: 0 minutes / servings: 1
Preparation time: 10 minutes

INSTRUCTIONS FOR COOKING:

- Lay the smoked salmon slices flat on a clean surface.
- Spread the cream cheese evenly on each slice.
- Sprinkle the chopped fresh dill (if using) over the cream cheese.
- Season with salt and pepper to taste.
- Roll up the slices tightly into a cigar shape.
- Slice the roll-up into bite-sized pieces.
- Squeeze a little fresh lemon juice over the roll-ups for added freshness.

Banana Bread

INGREDIENTS:

(Calories: 190 / Carbs: 15g / Proteins: 6g / Fats: 11g)

- 1 ripe banana, mashed
- 2 tablespoons coconut flour
- 1 large egg
- 1/2 teaspoon baking powder
- 1/4 teaspoon ground cinnamon
- 1/4 teaspoon vanilla extract
- 1 tablespoon chopped walnuts (optional)
- Cooking spray

Cooking time: 30 minutes / servings: 1
Preparation time: 15 minutes

INSTRUCTIONS FOR COOKING:

- Preheat your air fryer to 325°F (160°C).
- In a bowl, combine the mashed banana, coconut flour, egg, baking powder, ground cinnamon, vanilla extract, and chopped walnuts (if using). Mix well until all the ingredients are combined.
- Lightly coat a small oven-safe dish with cooking spray.
- Pour the banana bread batter into the dish and spread it evenly.
- Place the dish in the air fryer basket and cook for 25-30 minutes until the banana bread is cooked through and golden on top.
- Remove from the air fryer and let it cool slightly before slicing.

Quinoa Bowl

INGREDIENTS:

(Calories: 220 / Carbs: 34g / Proteins: 9g / Fats: 6g)

- 1/4 cup quinoa
- 1/2 cup water
- 1/2 cup mixed berries (such as strawberries, blueberries, and raspberries)
- 1 tablespoon chopped almonds
- 1 tablespoon unsweetened Greek yogurt
- 1/4 teaspoon cinnamon
- 1/4 teaspoon vanilla extract
- Optional: Stevia or sweetener of choice to taste

Cooking time: 15 minutes / servings: 1
Preparation time: 5 minutes

INSTRUCTIONS FOR COOKING:

- Rinse the quinoa under cold water to remove any bitterness.
- In a small saucepan, combine the rinsed quinoa and water. Bring to a boil.
- Reduce the heat to low, cover, and simmer for about 15 minutes until the quinoa is tender and the water is absorbed.
- Fluff the cooked quinoa with a fork and transfer it to a bowl.
- Add the mixed berries, chopped almonds, Greek yogurt, cinnamon, and vanilla extract to the bowl. Mix well.
- Sweeten with Stevia or your preferred sweetener if desired.
- Enjoy the quinoa breakfast bowl warm or chilled.

Turkey Skewers

INGREDIENTS:

(Calories: 320 / Carbs: 12g / Proteins: 25g / Fats: 19g)

- 2 turkey sausage links
- 1/2 bell pepper, cut into chunks
- 1/2 zucchini, sliced
- 1/4 red onion, cut into chunks
- 1 tablespoon olive oil, 1/2 teaspoon dried oregano
- Salt and pepper to taste

Cooking time: 12 minutes / servings: 1
Preparation time: 10 minutes

INSTRUCTIONS FOR COOKING:

- Preheat the air fryer to 400°F (200°C).
- Cut the turkey sausage links into bite-sized pieces.
- In a bowl, combine the turkey sausage pieces, bell pepper chunks, zucchini slices, red onion chunks, olive oil, dried oregano, salt, and pepper. Toss until the ingredients are well coated.
- Thread the turkey sausage pieces and vegetables onto skewers.
- Place the skewers in the air fryer basket and cook for 12 minutes, turning halfway through, until the turkey sausage is cooked through and the vegetables are tender.
- Remove the skewers from the air fryer and serve hot.

Eggplant Bake

INGREDIENTS:

(Calories: 140 / Carbs: 10g / Proteins: 7g / Fats: 8g)

- 1 large eggplant, sliced into 1/2-inch rounds
- 1 cup sugar-free tomato sauce
- 1 cup part-skim mozzarella cheese, shredded
- 2 tablespoons olive oil
- 2 cloves garlic, minced
- 1 teaspoon dried basil
- 1 teaspoon dried oregano
- Salt and pepper to taste
- Fresh basil leaves, for garnish

Cooking time: 25 minutes / servings: 4
Preparation time: 15 minutes

INSTRUCTIONS FOR COOKING:

- Preheat your air fryer to 375°F (190°C) for 5 minutes. In the meantime, lay the eggplant slices on paper towels and sprinkle a little salt over them. Let them sit for 10 minutes to remove excess moisture. Pat them dry with a paper towel.
- In a bowl, combine olive oil, minced garlic, dried basil, dried oregano, salt, and pepper. Brush both sides of the eggplant slices with this mixture.
- Place the seasoned eggplant slices in a single layer in the air fryer basket. Cook for 8-10 minutes, flipping them halfway through, until they are tender and slightly golden.
- Remove the eggplant from the air fryer. In a baking dish, spread a thin layer of sugar-free tomato sauce. Place a layer of eggplant slices on top. Sprinkle a portion of mozzarella cheese over the eggplant. Repeat the layers until you've used all the eggplant and cheese, finishing with a layer of cheese on top.
- Place the baking dish back into the air fryer and cook at 375°F (190°C) for an additional 10-12 minutes, until the cheese is melted and bubbly.
- Garnish and Serve: Once cooked, remove the dish from the air fryer and let it cool slightly. Garnish with fresh basil leaves before serving.

Chapter 4: Lunch and salads

- Chicken Salad
- Salmon with Lemon-Dill
- Quinoa Veggie Salad
- Greek Salad
- Shrimp Avocado Salad
- Spinach Strawberry Salad
- Caesar Salad
- Black Bean Salad
- Tofu Stir-Fry
- Caprese Salad
- Tuna Lettuce Wraps
- Sesame Chicken Salad
- Chickpea Salad
- Zucchini Falafel
- Stuffed Peppers
- Cauliflower Rice Bowl
- Kale Quinoa Salad
- Teriyaki Salmon Salad
- Chicken Pita Wraps
- Shrimp Lettuce Cups
- Beet Goat Cheese Salad
- BBQ Chicken Salad
- Mushroom Spinach Salad
- Thai Beef Salad
- Mexican Quinoa Bowl
- Tuna Salad
- Turkey Kabobs
- Stuffed Bell Peppers
- Shrimp Caesar Salad
- Lentil Salad
- Noodle Salad
- Watermelon Feta Salad
- Baked Cod
- Chicken Lettuce Wraps
- Caprese Skewers
- Greek Orzo Salad
- Falafel Salad
- Zucchini Pad Thai
- Southwest Quinoa Salad
- Stuffed Chicken Breast
- Thai Beef Wraps
- Mediterranean Pasta Salad
- Sesame Tofu Salad
- Shrimp Avocado Salad
- Turkey Taco Wraps
- Eggplant Mozzarella Stack
- Quinoa Stuffed Peppers
- Grilled Chicken Salad
- Zucchini Noodle Salad
- Southwest Quinoa Bowl

Chapter 4: Lunch and salads

Chicken Salad

INGREDIENTS:

(Calories: 290 / Carbs: 12g / Proteins: 34g / Fats: 12g)

- 4 oz (113g) boneless, skinless chicken breast
- 2 cups mixed salad greens
- 1/4 cup cherry tomatoes, halved
- 1/4 cup cucumber, sliced
- 1/4 cup bell peppers, sliced
- 1 tablespoon balsamic vinegar
- 1 tablespoon olive oil
- Salt and pepper to taste

Cooking time: 15 minutes / servings: 1
Preparation time: 15 minutes

INSTRUCTIONS FOR COOKING:

- Preheat the air fryer to 400°F (200°C).
- Season the chicken breast with salt and pepper.
- Place the chicken breast in the air fryer basket and cook for 12-15 minutes, or until the internal temperature reaches 165°F (74°C) and the chicken is cooked through.
- Remove the chicken from the air fryer and let it rest for a few minutes. Slice it into thin strips.
- In a large bowl, combine the mixed salad greens, cherry tomatoes, cucumber, and bell peppers.
- In a small bowl, whisk together the balsamic vinegar, olive oil, salt, and pepper to make the dressing.
- Drizzle the dressing over the salad and toss to coat.
- Top the salad with the sliced grilled chicken breast.
- Serve immediately.

Salmon with Lemon-Dill

INGREDIENTS:

(Calories: 280 / Carbs: 10g / Proteins: 30g / Fats: 14g)

- 4 oz (113g) salmon fillet
- 1 tablespoon lemon juice
- 1 teaspoon fresh dill, chopped
- Salt and pepper to taste
- 1 cup mixed vegetables (broccoli, carrots, cauliflower), steamed

Cooking time: 15 minutes / servings: 1
Preparation time: 10 minutes

INSTRUCTIONS FOR COOKING:

- Preheat the air fryer to 400°F (200°C).
- Season the salmon fillet with salt, pepper, and lemon juice.
- Place the salmon fillet in the air fryer basket and cook for 12-15 minutes, or until the salmon is cooked through and flakes easily with a fork.
- In a small bowl, mix together the lemon juice, fresh dill, salt, and pepper to make the lemon dill sauce.
- Remove the salmon from the air fryer and drizzle the lemon dill sauce over it.
- Serve the air-fried salmon with steamed mixed vegetables on the side.

Quinoa Veggie Salad

INGREDIENTS:

(Calories: 350 / Carbs: 40g / Proteins: 10g / Fats: 18g)

- 1/4 cup quinoa
- 1 cup mixed vegetables (such as bell peppers, zucchini, and eggplant), chopped
- 1 tablespoon olive oil, Salt and pepper to taste
- 2 cups mixed salad greens, 1 tablespoon lemon juice
- 1 tablespoon tahini, 1 clove garlic, minced
- Fresh herbs (such as parsley or basil), chopped (optional)

Cooking time: 20 minutes / servings: 1
Preparation time: 15 minutes

INSTRUCTIONS FOR COOKING:

- Cook the quinoa according to the package instructions.
- Preheat the air fryer to 400°F (200°C).
- In a bowl, toss the mixed vegetables with olive oil, salt, and pepper.
- Place the seasoned vegetables in the air fryer basket and cook for 15-20 minutes, or until they are tender and lightly browned.
- In a separate bowl, whisk together the lemon juice, tahini, minced garlic, salt, and pepper to make the dressing.
- In a serving bowl, combine the cooked quinoa, roasted vegetables, mixed salad greens, and fresh herbs (if using).
- Drizzle the lemon-tahini dressing over the salad and toss to coat.
- Serve the quinoa and roasted vegetable salad immediately.

Greek Salad

INGREDIENTS:

(Calories: 180/ Carbs: 9g / Proteins: 6g / Fats: 14g)

- 2 cups mixed salad greens
- 1/4 cup cherry tomatoes, halved
- 1/4 cup cucumber, sliced, 1/4 cup red onion, thinly sliced
- 2 tablespoons kalamata olives, pitted
- 2 tablespoons crumbled feta cheese
- 1 tablespoon olive oil, 1 tablespoon lemon juice
- 1/2 teaspoon dried oregano, Salt and pepper to taste
- Fresh herbs (such as parsley or dill), chopped (optional)

Cooking time: 0 minutes / servings: 1
Preparation time: 10 minutes

INSTRUCTIONS FOR COOKING:

- In a large bowl, combine the mixed salad greens, cherry tomatoes, cucumber, red onion, kalamata olives, and crumbled feta cheese.
- In a small bowl, whisk together the olive oil, lemon juice, dried oregano, salt, and pepper to make the dressing.
- Drizzle the dressing over the salad and toss gently to coat.
- Garnish with fresh herbs if desired.
- Serve the Greek salad immediately.

Shrimp Avocado Salad

INGREDIENTS:

(Calories: 280 / Carbs: 12g / Proteins: 20g / Fats: 18g)

- 4 oz shrimp, peeled and deveined
- 1/2 avocado, sliced
- 1 cup mixed salad greens
- 1/4 cup cherry tomatoes, halved
- 1/4 cup cucumber, sliced
- 1 tablespoon lime juice
- 1 tablespoon olive oil
- 1 tablespoon chopped fresh cilantro
- Salt and pepper to taste

Cooking time: 5 minutes / servings: 1
Preparation time: 15 minutes

INSTRUCTIONS FOR COOKING:

- Preheat the air fryer to 400°F (200°C).
- Place the shrimp in the air fryer basket and cook for 5 minutes, or until they are pink and cooked through.
- In a small bowl, whisk together the lime juice, olive oil, chopped cilantro, salt, and pepper to make the dressing.
- In a serving bowl, combine the mixed salad greens, cherry tomatoes, cucumber, sliced avocado, and cooked shrimp.
- Drizzle the lime-cilantro dressing over the salad and toss gently to coat.
- Serve the shrimp and avocado salad immediately.

Spinach Strawberry Salad

INGREDIENTS:

(Calories: 220 / Carbs: 10g / Proteins: 8g / Fats: 17g)

- 2 cups fresh spinach leaves, 1/2 cup sliced strawberries
- 1/4 cup crumbled goat cheese
- 2 tablespoons chopped walnuts
- 1 tablespoon balsamic vinegar
- 1 tablespoon olive oil, 1/2 teaspoon honey (optional)
- Salt and pepper to taste

Cooking time: 0 minutes / servings: 1
Preparation time: 10 minutes

INSTRUCTIONS FOR COOKING:

- In a large bowl, combine the fresh spinach leaves, sliced strawberries, crumbled goat cheese, and chopped walnuts.
- In a small bowl, whisk together the balsamic vinegar, olive oil, honey (if using), salt, and pepper to make the dressing.
- Drizzle the dressing over the salad and toss gently to coat.
- Serve the spinach and strawberry salad immediately.

Caesar Salad

INGREDIENTS:

(Calories: 280 / Carbs: 10g / Proteins: 40g / Fats: 8g)

- 4 oz boneless, skinless chicken breast
- 2 cups romaine lettuce, torn into bite-sized pieces
- 1/4 cup cherry tomatoes, halved
- 2 tablespoons grated Parmesan cheese
- 2 tablespoons low-fat Greek yogurt
- 1 tablespoon lemon juice, 1 tablespoon Dijon mustard
- 1 clove garlic, minced, Salt and pepper to taste

Cooking time: 10 minutes / servings: 1
Preparation time: 15 minutes

INSTRUCTIONS FOR COOKING:

- Preheat the air fryer to 400°F (200°C).
- Season the chicken breast with salt and pepper. Place it in the air fryer basket and cook for 10 minutes, or until it reaches an internal temperature of 165°F (74°C).
- Remove the chicken from the air fryer and let it rest for a few minutes. Then, slice it into thin strips.
- In a small bowl, whisk together the Greek yogurt, lemon juice, Dijon mustard, minced garlic, salt, and pepper to make the light Caesar dressing.
- In a large bowl, combine the torn romaine lettuce, cherry tomatoes, sliced chicken breast, and grated Parmesan cheese.
- Drizzle the light Caesar dressing over the salad and toss gently to coat.
- Serve the chicken Caesar salad immediately.

Black Bean Salad

INGREDIENTS:

(Calories: 220 / Carbs: 32g / Proteins: 8g / Fats: 8g)

- 1/2 cup canned black beans, rinsed and drained
- 1/4 cup corn kernels (fresh or canned)
- 1/4 cup diced bell peppers (assorted colors)
- 2 tablespoons chopped fresh cilantro
- 1 tablespoon lime juice, 1 tablespoon olive oil
- 1/2 teaspoon cumin powder, Salt and pepper to taste

Cooking time: 0 minutes / servings: 1
Preparation time: 15 minutes

INSTRUCTIONS FOR COOKING:

- In a mixing bowl, combine the black beans, corn kernels, diced bell peppers, and chopped cilantro.
- In a small bowl, whisk together the lime juice, olive oil, cumin powder, salt, and pepper to make the lime dressing.
- Drizzle the lime dressing over the black bean salad and toss gently to coat.
- Serve the Southwest black bean salad immediately.

Tofu Stir-Fry

INGREDIENTS:

(Calories: 220 / Carbs: 18g / Proteins: 18g / Fats: 10g)

- 4 oz firm tofu, drained and cubed
- 1 cup mixed vegetables (such as bell peppers, broccoli, and snap peas), sliced
- 2 tablespoons low-sodium soy sauce
- 1 tablespoon rice vinegar
- 1 tablespoon fresh ginger, grated
- 1 clove garlic, minced, 1/2 teaspoon sesame oil
- 1/2 teaspoon cornstarch (optional, for thickening the sauce)
- Salt and pepper to taste

Cooking time: 15 minutes / servings: 1
Preparation time: 15 minutes

INSTRUCTIONS FOR COOKING:

- Preheat the air fryer to 400°F (200°C).
- In a small bowl, whisk together the soy sauce, rice vinegar, grated ginger, minced garlic, sesame oil, and cornstarch (if using) to make the soy-ginger sauce.
- Place the tofu cubes and sliced vegetables in the air fryer basket. Drizzle half of the soy-ginger sauce over the tofu and vegetables. Toss gently to coat.
- Air fry the tofu and vegetables for 10-12 minutes, shaking the basket halfway through to ensure even cooking.
- Remove the air fryer basket and drizzle the remaining soy-ginger sauce over the cooked tofu and vegetables. Toss gently to coat.
- Season with salt and pepper to taste.
- Serve the air-fried tofu and vegetable stir-fry immediately.

Caprese Salad

INGREDIENTS:

(Calories: 230 / Carbs: 5g / Proteins: 12g / Fats: 18g)

- 2 oz fresh mozzarella cheese, sliced
- 1 medium-sized tomato, sliced
- 1/4 cup fresh basil leaves
- 1 tablespoon extra-virgin olive oil
- 1 tablespoon balsamic vinegar
- Salt and pepper to taste

Cooking time: 0 minutes / servings: 1
Preparation time: 10 minutes

INSTRUCTIONS FOR COOKING:

- Arrange the sliced mozzarella cheese and tomato on a plate.
- Tuck the fresh basil leaves between the cheese and tomato slices.
- Drizzle the extra-virgin olive oil and balsamic vinegar over the salad.
- Season with salt and pepper to taste.
- Serve the Caprese salad immediately.

Tuna Lettuce Wraps

INGREDIENTS:

(Calories: 220 / Carbs: 18g / Proteins: 10g / Fats: 10g)

- 4 oz firm tofu, drained and cubed
- 1 cup mixed vegetables (such as bell peppers, broccoli, and snap peas), sliced
- 2 tablespoons low-sodium soy sauce
- 1 tablespoon rice vinegar
- 1 tablespoon fresh ginger, grated
- 1 clove garlic, minced, 1/2 teaspoon sesame oil
- 1/2 teaspoon cornstarch (optional, for thickening the sauce)
- Salt and pepper to taste

Cooking time: 15 minutes / servings: 1
Preparation time: 15 minutes

INSTRUCTIONS FOR COOKING:

- Preheat the air fryer to 400°F (200°C).
- In a small bowl, whisk together the soy sauce, rice vinegar, grated ginger, minced garlic, sesame oil, and cornstarch (if using) to make the soy-ginger sauce.
- Place the tofu cubes and sliced vegetables in the air fryer basket. Drizzle half of the soy-ginger sauce over the tofu and vegetables. Toss gently to coat.
- Air fry the tofu and vegetables for 10-12 minutes, shaking the basket halfway through to ensure even cooking.
- Remove the air fryer basket and drizzle the remaining soy-ginger sauce over the cooked tofu and vegetables. Toss gently to coat.
- Season with salt and pepper to taste.
- Serve the air-fried tofu and vegetable stir-fry immediately.

Sesame Chicken Salad

INGREDIENTS:

(Calories: 280 / Carbs: 15g / Proteins: 30g / Fats: 10g)

- 4 oz boneless, skinless chicken breast
- 2 cups mixed salad greens, 1/4 cup shredded carrots
- 1/4 cup sliced cucumber, 1 tablespoon sesame seeds
- 1 tablespoon low-sodium soy sauce
- 1 tablespoon rice vinegar, 1 teaspoon sesame oil
- 1/2 teaspoon honey (optional)
- 2-3 crispy wonton strips (store-bought or homemade)

Cooking time: 10 minutes / servings: 1
Preparation time: 20 minutes

INSTRUCTIONS FOR COOKING:

- Preheat the air fryer to 400°F (200°C).
- Season the chicken breast with salt and pepper. Place it in the air fryer basket and cook for 8-10 minutes, or until cooked through. Let it cool slightly, then slice it into thin strips.
- In a small bowl, whisk together the soy sauce, rice vinegar, sesame oil, and honey (if using) to make the dressing.
- In a large bowl, combine the mixed salad greens, shredded carrots, sliced cucumber, sesame seeds, and sliced chicken.
- Drizzle the dressing over the salad and toss gently to coat.
- Top the salad with crispy wonton strips.
- Serve the Asian sesame chicken salad immediately.

Chickpea Salad

INGREDIENTS:

(Calories: 280 / Carbs: 30g / Proteins: 12g / Fats: 13g)

- 1 cup canned chickpeas, rinsed and drained
- 1/2 cup diced cucumber
- 1/2 cup cherry tomatoes, halved
- 1/4 cup crumbled feta cheese
- 2 tablespoons chopped fresh parsley
- 1 tablespoon extra-virgin olive oil
- 1 tablespoon lemon juice, Salt and pepper to taste

Cooking time: 0 minutes / servings: 1
Preparation time: 15 minutes

INSTRUCTIONS FOR COOKING:

- In a bowl, combine the chickpeas, cucumber, cherry tomatoes, feta cheese, and parsley.
- Drizzle with olive oil and lemon juice.
- Season with salt and pepper to taste.
- Toss gently to combine all the ingredients.
- Serve the Mediterranean chickpea salad immediately.

Zucchini Falafel

INGREDIENTS:

(Calories: 150 / Carbs: 20g / Proteins: 8g / Fats: 4g)

- 1 medium zucchini
- 1 cup canned chickpeas, drained and rinsed
- 2 cloves garlic, minced, 1/4 cup finely chopped onion
- 2 tablespoons chopped fresh parsley
- 2 tablespoons chickpea flour (or any other low-carb flour)
- 1/2 teaspoon ground cumin, 1/2 teaspoon ground coriander
- 1/4 teaspoon salt
- Cooking spray (olive oil or canola oil spray)

Cooking time: 15 minutes / servings: 4 falafels
Preparation time: 15 minutes

INSTRUCTIONS FOR COOKING:

- Preheat your air fryer to 400°F (200°C) for 5 minutes.
- Grate the zucchini using a box grater or a food processor with a grating attachment. Squeeze out any excess moisture from the grated zucchini using a clean kitchen towel or paper towels.
- In a mixing bowl, combine the grated zucchini, drained chickpeas, minced garlic, chopped onion, parsley, chickpea flour, ground cumin, ground coriander, and salt. Mix well until all the ingredients are evenly incorporated.
- Shape the mixture into small patties, about 2-3 inches in diameter.
- Lightly coat the air fryer basket with cooking spray to prevent sticking. Place the falafel patties in a single layer in the air fryer basket.
- Air fry the falafels at 400°F (200°C) for 12-15 minutes, flipping them halfway through, until they are golden brown and crispy.
- While the falafels are cooking, prepare the tahini sauce (recipe below).
- Serve the air fried zucchini and chickpea falafels hot with tahini sauce for dipping or as part of a salad or wrap.

Stuffed Peppers

INGREDIENTS:

(Calories: 180 / Carbs: 31g / Proteins: 6g / Fats: 4g)

- 1 bell pepper (any color), 1/4 cup quinoa, cooked
- 1/4 cup zucchini, diced, 1/4 cup red onion, diced
- 1/4 cup cherry tomatoes, halved
- 1 clove garlic, minced, 1 teaspoon olive oil
- 1/2 teaspoon dried basil, Salt and pepper to taste

Cooking time: 35 minutes / servings: 1
Preparation time: + minutes

INSTRUCTIONS FOR COOKING:

- Preheat your air fryer to 375°F (190°C).
- Cut the bell pepper in half lengthwise and remove the seeds and membrane.
- In a bowl, combine the cooked quinoa, diced zucchini, red onion, cherry tomatoes, minced garlic, olive oil, dried basil, salt, and pepper. Mix well.
- Fill each bell pepper half with the quinoa and vegetable mixture.
- Place the stuffed peppers in the air fryer basket and cook for 15-20 minutes or until the peppers are tender and slightly charred.
- Once cooked, remove the stuffed peppers from the air fryer and let them cool for a few minutes before serving.

Cauliflower Rice Bowl

INGREDIENTS:

(Calories: 220 / Carbs: 32g / Proteins: 10g / Fats: 8g)

- 1 cup cauliflower rice
- 1/2 cup black beans, drained and rinsed
- 1/4 cup red bell pepper, diced
- 1/4 cup corn kernels (fresh or frozen)
- 1/4 cup cherry tomatoes, halved
- 1/4 avocado, sliced, 1 tablespoon fresh cilantro, chopped
- 1 tablespoon lime juice, 1/2 teaspoon chili powder
- Salt and pepper to taste

Cooking time: 25 minutes / servings: 1
Preparation time: + minutes

INSTRUCTIONS FOR COOKING:

- Preheat your air fryer to 375°F (190°C).
- Place the cauliflower rice in the air fryer basket and cook for 8-10 minutes or until it becomes tender and slightly golden.
- In a bowl, combine the cooked cauliflower rice, black beans, diced red bell pepper, corn kernels, cherry tomatoes, fresh cilantro, lime juice, chili powder, salt, and pepper. Mix well.
- Transfer the mixture to a serving bowl and top it with sliced avocado.
- Serve the Mexican cauliflower rice bowl immediately.

Kale Quinoa Salad

INGREDIENTS:

(Calories: 250 / Carbs: 45g / Proteins: 8g / Fats: 6g)

- 1 cup kale, chopped
- 1/2 cup cooked quinoa
- 1/2 cup butternut squash, diced
- 2 tablespoons dried cranberries
- 1 tablespoon pumpkin seeds
- 1 tablespoon balsamic vinegar
- 1 teaspoon olive oil, Salt and pepper to taste

Cooking time: 25 minutes / servings: 1
Preparation time: + minutes

INSTRUCTIONS FOR COOKING:

- Preheat your air fryer to 400°F (200°C).
- Place the diced butternut squash in the air fryer basket and cook for 15-20 minutes or until it becomes tender and slightly caramelized.
- In a bowl, combine the chopped kale, cooked quinoa, roasted butternut squash, dried cranberries, pumpkin seeds, balsamic vinegar, olive oil, salt, and pepper. Mix well.
- Allow the salad to sit for a few minutes to let the flavors meld together.
- Serve the kale and quinoa salad immediately.

Teriyaki Salmon Salad

INGREDIENTS:

(Calories: 320 / Carbs: 12g / Proteins: 28g / Fats: 18g)

- 4 ounces salmon fillet, 2 cups mixed greens
- 1/4 cup cucumber, sliced, 1/4 cup cherry tomatoes, halved
- 1/4 cup shredded carrots
- 1 tablespoon low-sodium teriyaki sauce
- 1 tablespoon sesame oil, 1/2 tablespoon rice vinegar
- 1/2 tablespoon low-sodium soy sauce
- 1/2 tablespoon sesame seeds, Salt and pepper to taste

Cooking time: 20 minutes / servings: 1
Preparation time: + minutes

INSTRUCTIONS FOR COOKING:

- Preheat your air fryer to 400°F (200°C).
- Place the salmon fillet in the air fryer basket and brush it with the low-sodium teriyaki sauce.
- Cook the salmon for 10-12 minutes or until it flakes easily with a fork.
- In a small bowl, whisk together the sesame oil, rice vinegar, low-sodium soy sauce, sesame seeds, salt, and pepper to make the dressing.
- In a separate bowl, combine the mixed greens, sliced cucumber, cherry tomatoes, shredded carrots, and teriyaki salmon.
- Drizzle the sesame dressing over the salad and toss gently to coat.
- Serve the teriyaki salmon salad immediately.

Chicken Pita Wraps

INGREDIENTS:

(Calories: 320 / Carbs: 30g / Proteins: 32g / Fats: 7g)

- 4 ounces boneless, skinless chicken breast
- 1 small whole wheat pita bread, 1/4 cup cucumber, diced
- 1/4 cup cherry tomatoes, halved
- 2 tablespoons red onion, sliced, 2 tablespoons Greek yogurt
- 1 tablespoon lemon juice
- 1/2 tablespoon fresh dill, chopped
- Salt and pepper to taste

Cooking time: 20 minutes / servings: 1
Preparation time: + minutes

INSTRUCTIONS FOR COOKING:

- Preheat your air fryer to 375°F (190°C).
- Season the chicken breast with salt and pepper.
- Place the chicken breast in the air fryer basket and cook for 12-15 minutes or until it reaches an internal temperature of 165°F (74°C).
- While the chicken is cooking, prepare the tzatziki sauce by combining Greek yogurt, lemon juice, fresh dill, salt, and pepper in a small bowl. Mix well.
- Once cooked, let the chicken rest for a few minutes before slicing it into thin strips.
- Warm the pita bread in the air fryer for a minute or until it becomes soft and pliable.
- Assemble the Greek chicken pita wraps by spreading a generous amount of tzatziki sauce on the warmed pita bread. Add the sliced chicken, diced cucumber, halved cherry tomatoes, and sliced red onion. Roll the pita bread tightly to form a wrap.
- Serve the Greek chicken pita wraps immediately.

Shrimp Lettuce Cups

INGREDIENTS:

(Calories: 160 / Carbs: 11g / Proteins: 18g / Fats: 6g)

- 4 ounces shrimp, peeled and deveined
- 4 large lettuce leaves (such as butter lettuce or romaine)
- 1/4 cup mango, diced
- 2 tablespoons red bell pepper, diced
- 2 tablespoons red onion, diced, 1 tablespoon lime juice
- 1/2 tablespoon fresh cilantro, chopped
- 1/2 tablespoon olive oil, 1/2 teaspoon chili powder
- Salt and pepper to taste

Cooking time: 15 minutes / servings: 1
Preparation time: + minutes

INSTRUCTIONS FOR COOKING:

- Preheat your air fryer to 400°F (200°C).
- Toss the shrimp with olive oil, chili powder, salt, and pepper in a bowl until evenly coated.
- Place the seasoned shrimp in the air fryer basket and cook for 8-10 minutes or until they turn pink and opaque.
- While the shrimp is cooking, prepare the mango salsa by combining diced mango, red bell pepper, red onion, lime juice, fresh cilantro, salt, and pepper in a bowl. Mix well.
- Once cooked, remove the shrimp from the air fryer and let them cool slightly.
- Take a lettuce leaf and spoon some mango salsa onto it. Top with a few cooked shrimp.
- Repeat with the remaining lettuce leaves and shrimp.
- Serve the air fried shrimp lettuce cups with mango salsa immediately.

Beet Goat Cheese Salad

INGREDIENTS:

(Calories: 220 / Carbs: 10g / Proteins: 7g / Fats: 17g)

- 1 small beet, roasted and diced, 2 cups arugula
- 1 ounce goat cheese, crumbled
- 1 tablespoon walnuts, chopped
- 1 tablespoon balsamic vinegar
- 1 tablespoon olive oil
- Salt and pepper to taste

Cooking time: 45 minutes / servings: 1
Preparation time: + minutes

INSTRUCTIONS FOR COOKING:

- Preheat your air fryer to 400°F (200°C).
- Wrap the beet in aluminum foil and place it in the air fryer basket. Roast for 40-45 minutes or until the beet is tender when pierced with a fork. Let it cool, then peel and dice it.
- In a bowl, combine the diced roasted beet, arugula, crumbled goat cheese, and chopped walnuts.
- In a small jar, combine the balsamic vinegar, olive oil, salt, and pepper. Shake well to emulsify the dressing.
- Drizzle the dressing over the salad and toss gently to coat all the ingredients.
- Serve the roasted beet and goat cheese salad immediately.

BBQ Chicken Salad

INGREDIENTS:

(Calories: 350 / Carbs: 28g / Proteins: 32g / Fats: 10g)

- 4 ounces boneless, skinless chicken breast
- 1/4 cup sugar-free BBQ sauce, 1 ear of corn
- 2 cups mixed salad greens
- 1/4 cup cherry tomatoes, halved
- 1/4 cup cucumber, sliced
- 1 tablespoon red onion, finely chopped
- 2 tablespoons low-fat ranch dressing (sugar-free or reduced-fat)

Cooking time: 25 minutes / servings: 1
Preparation time: 15 minutes

INSTRUCTIONS FOR COOKING:

- Preheat the air fryer to 400°F (200°C).
- Season the chicken breast with salt and pepper. Place it in the air fryer basket and cook for 10 minutes, flipping halfway through.
- Brush the chicken breast with the sugar-free BBQ sauce and continue cooking for another 5 minutes, or until the internal temperature reaches 165°F (74°C).
- While the chicken is cooking, prepare the grilled corn. Remove the husk and silk from the corn and lightly brush it with olive oil. Place it in the air fryer basket and cook for 10 minutes, turning occasionally, until lightly charred. Let it cool slightly, then cut the kernels off the cob.
- In a large salad bowl, combine the mixed salad greens, cherry tomatoes, cucumber, and red onion. Toss to mix well.
- Slice the cooked chicken breast into thin strips.
- Add the sliced chicken and grilled corn kernels to the salad bowl. Drizzle with low-fat ranch dressing and toss gently to coat all the ingredients.

Mushroom Spinach Salad

INGREDIENTS:

(Calories: 90 / Carbs: 12g / Proteins: 5g / Fats: 3g)

- 1 large Portobello mushroom
- 2 cups fresh spinach leaves
- 1 tablespoon balsamic vinegar
- 1 teaspoon olive oil
- 1 clove garlic, minced
- Salt and pepper to taste

Cooking time: 10 minutes / servings: 1
Preparation time: 10 minutes

INSTRUCTIONS FOR COOKING:

- Preheat the air fryer to 400°F (200°C).
- Clean the Portobello mushroom and remove the stem. Slice it into thick strips.
- In a small bowl, whisk together the balsamic vinegar, olive oil, minced garlic, salt, and pepper.
- Place the mushroom slices in the air fryer basket and brush them with the balsamic mixture on both sides.
- Air fry the mushrooms at 400°F (200°C) for 6-7 minutes, flipping them halfway through, until they are tender and slightly browned.
- In a serving bowl, arrange the fresh spinach leaves.
- Once the mushrooms are done, place them on top of the spinach leaves.
- Drizzle any remaining balsamic glaze over the salad.

Thai Beef Salad

INGREDIENTS:

(Calories: 280 / Carbs: 15g / Proteins: 25g / Fats: 14g)

- 4 oz (115g) lean beef steak, thinly sliced
- 2 cups mixed salad greens (such as lettuce, cucumber, and bell peppers), 2 tablespoons unsalted peanuts, crushed
- 1 tablespoon low-sodium soy sauce, 1 tablespoon lime juice
- 1 teaspoon fish sauce, 1 teaspoon honey
- 1 clove garlic, minced, 1/4 teaspoon red pepper flakes (optional)
- Fresh cilantro leaves for garnish

Cooking time: 15 minutes / servings: 1
Preparation time: 15 minutes

INSTRUCTIONS FOR COOKING:

- Preheat the air fryer to 400°F (200°C).
- Season the beef slices with a pinch of salt and pepper.
- Place the beef slices in the air fryer basket and cook at 400°F (200°C) for 6-7 minutes until they are cooked through.
- In a small bowl, whisk together the low-sodium soy sauce, lime juice, fish sauce, honey, minced garlic, and red pepper flakes (if using).
- In a serving bowl, arrange the mixed salad greens.
- Once the beef is cooked, place it on top of the salad greens.
- Drizzle the peanut dressing over the salad.
- Sprinkle the crushed peanuts on top and garnish with fresh cilantro leaves.

Mexican Quinoa Bowl

INGREDIENTS:

(Calories: 400 / Carbs: 35g / Proteins: 35g / Fats: 12g)

- 1/4 cup cooked quinoa
- 4 ounces boneless, skinless chicken breast, grilled and diced
- 1/4 cup black beans, rinsed and drained, 1/4 cup diced tomatoes
- 1/4 cup diced bell peppers (any color)
- 1/4 cup corn kernels, 1/4 cup chopped fresh cilantro
- 1/4 teaspoon chili powder, 1/4 teaspoon cumin
- Salt and pepper to taste, Cooking spray

For the Avocado Lime Dressing:

- 1/4 ripe avocado, 1 tablespoon freshly squeezed lime juice
- 1 tablespoon plain Greek yogurt, 1 tablespoon water
- Salt and pepper to taste

Cooking time: 25 minutes / servings: 1
Preparation time: 15 minutes

INSTRUCTIONS FOR COOKING:

- Preheat the air fryer to 400°F (200°C).
- In a mixing bowl, combine the cooked quinoa, grilled chicken breast, black beans, diced tomatoes, diced bell peppers, corn kernels, chopped cilantro, chili powder, cumin, salt, and pepper. Mix well.
- Lightly coat an air fryer-safe dish or a baking dish with cooking spray.
- Transfer the quinoa mixture to the dish, spreading it out evenly.
- Place the dish in the preheated air fryer and cook for about 15 minutes, stirring halfway through, or until the ingredients are heated through.
- Meanwhile, prepare the Avocado Lime Dressing. In a blender or food processor, combine the ripe avocado, lime juice, Greek yogurt, water, salt, and pepper. Blend until smooth.
- Once the quinoa mixture is cooked, remove it from the air fryer and let it cool slightly.
- Drizzle the Avocado Lime Dressing over the quinoa bowl and serve warm.

Tuna Salad

INGREDIENTS:

(Calories: 250 / Carbs: 9g / Proteins: 25g / Fats: 14g)

- 4 ounces canned tuna, drained
- 1/4 cup diced cucumber, 1/4 cup diced tomatoes
- 1/4 cup sliced Kalamata olives, 1/4 cup thinly sliced red onion
- 2 tablespoons freshly squeezed lemon juice,
- 1 tablespoon extra-virgin olive oil
- 1 tablespoon chopped fresh parsley, Salt and pepper to taste

Cooking time: 0 minutes / servings: 1
Preparation time: 10 minutes

INSTRUCTIONS FOR COOKING:

- In a mixing bowl, combine the drained tuna, diced cucumber, diced tomatoes, sliced Kalamata olives, and thinly sliced red onion.
- In a small separate bowl, whisk together the lemon juice, olive oil, chopped fresh parsley, salt, and pepper to make the dressing.
- Pour the dressing over the tuna mixture and toss gently to coat all the ingredients.
- Serve the Mediterranean Tuna Salad immediately or refrigerate it for later use.

Turkey Kabobs

INGREDIENTS:

(Calories: 220 / Carbs: 10g / Proteins: 32g / Fats: 6g)

For the Kabobs:

- 4 ounces turkey breast, cut into 1-inch cubes
- 1/4 cup diced bell peppers (any color)
- 1/4 cup cherry tomatoes, 1/4 cup diced zucchini
- 1/4 cup diced red onion, Salt and pepper to taste
- Skewers (if using wooden skewers, soak them in water for 30 minutes before using)

For the Yogurt-Dill Sauce:

- 1/4 cup plain Greek yogurt, 1 tablespoon freshly squeezed lemon juice
- 1 tablespoon chopped fresh dill, Salt and pepper to taste

Cooking time: 15 minutes / servings: 1
Preparation time: 15 minutes

INSTRUCTIONS FOR COOKING:

- Preheat the air fryer to 400°F (200°C).
- In a mixing bowl, combine the turkey breast cubes, diced bell peppers, cherry tomatoes, diced zucchini, diced red onion, salt, and pepper. Toss to coat the ingredients evenly.
- Thread the turkey and vegetable cubes onto skewers, alternating between the different ingredients.
- Place the skewers in the preheated air fryer and cook for about 15 minutes, turning halfway through, or until the turkey is cooked through and the vegetables are tender.
- Meanwhile, prepare the Yogurt-Dill Sauce. In a small bowl, mix together the Greek yogurt, lemon juice, chopped fresh dill, salt, and pepper.
- Once the kabobs are cooked, remove them from the air fryer and let them cool for a few minutes.
- Serve the Air-Fried Turkey and Vegetable Kabobs with the Yogurt-Dill Sauce on the side.

Stuffed Bell Peppers

INGREDIENTS:

(Calories: 220 / Carbs: 42g / Proteins: 9g / Fats: 2g)

- 1 medium bell pepper (any color), halved and seeds removed
- 1/4 cup cooked quinoa, 1/4 cup fresh spinach, chopped
- 1/4 cup diced tomatoes, 1/4 cup onion, finely chopped
- 1 clove garlic, minced, 1/2 teaspoon dried oregano
- 1/4 teaspoon dried basil, Salt and pepper to taste
- 1/4 cup low-sodium tomato sauce

Cooking time: 25 minutes / servings: 1
Preparation time: 20 minutes

INSTRUCTIONS FOR COOKING:

- Preheat the air fryer to 375°F (190°C) for 5 minutes.
- In a bowl, combine the cooked quinoa, chopped spinach, diced tomatoes, onion, garlic, dried oregano, dried basil, salt, and pepper. Mix well to combine all the ingredients.
- Spoon the quinoa and spinach mixture into the hollowed-out bell pepper halves.
- Place the stuffed bell pepper halves in the preheated air fryer basket. Cook for 20-25 minutes, until the bell peppers are tender and the filling is heated through.
- Once the stuffed bell peppers are done, remove them from the air fryer and transfer them to a serving plate.
- Drizzle the warm tomato sauce over the stuffed bell peppers.
- Serve hot and enjoy!

Shrimp Caesar Salad

INGREDIENTS:

(Calories: 230 / Carbs: 20g / Proteins: 20g / Fats: 7g)

- 4 ounces of shrimp, peeled and deveined
- 2 cups of romaine lettuce, torn into bite-sized pieces
- 1/4 cup of cherry tomatoes, halved
- 1 tablespoon of grated Parmesan cheese
- 1 tablespoon of low-fat Caesar dressing
- 1 slice of whole wheat bread, cut into cubes for croutons
- 1/2 teaspoon of olive oil
- Salt and pepper to taste

Cooking time: 10 minutes / servings: 1
Preparation time: 15 minutes

INSTRUCTIONS FOR COOKING:

- Preheat the air fryer to 400°F (200°C).
- In a mixing bowl, toss the shrimp with olive oil, salt, and pepper until well-coated.
- Place the shrimp in the air fryer basket and cook for 5-6 minutes, flipping halfway through, until the shrimp are pink and cooked through.
- While the shrimp are cooking, place the bread cubes in the air fryer basket and cook for 3-4 minutes until they become crispy and golden brown, shaking the basket occasionally to ensure even cooking.
- In a salad bowl, combine the romaine lettuce, cherry tomatoes, Parmesan cheese, and grilled shrimp.
- Drizzle the low-fat Caesar dressing over the salad and toss gently to coat all the ingredients.
- Top the salad with the whole wheat croutons.
- Serve immediately and enjoy!

Lentil Salad

INGREDIENTS:

(Calories: ~300 / Carbs: 18g / Proteins: 25g / Fats: 14g)

- 4-6 large shrimp, peeled and deveined
- 2 cups romaine lettuce, washed and chopped
- 1/4 cup cherry tomatoes, halved, 2 tablespoons grated Parmesan cheese
- 1 slice whole wheat bread, cubed for croutons
- 1 tablespoon olive oil, 1 clove garlic, minced
- 1/2 teaspoon lemon zest, 1 tablespoon lemon juice
- 1/2 tablespoon low-fat mayonnaise
- 1/2 teaspoon Dijon mustard, Salt and pepper to taste

Cooking time: 15 minutes / servings: 1
Preparation time: 15 minutes

INSTRUCTIONS FOR COOKING:

- Preheat the air fryer to 400°F (200°C).
- Toss the cubed whole wheat bread with olive oil, minced garlic, salt, and pepper in a bowl.
- Place the seasoned bread cubes in the air fryer basket and cook for 4-5 minutes until they turn golden brown and crispy. Set aside.
- Season the shrimp with salt, pepper, and lemon zest.
- Place the seasoned shrimp in the air fryer basket and cook for 3-4 minutes until they are cooked through and slightly charred. Set aside.
- In a separate bowl, whisk together the lemon juice, low-fat mayonnaise, Dijon mustard, salt, and pepper to make the dressing.
- In a large salad bowl, combine the chopped romaine lettuce, cherry tomatoes, grated Parmesan cheese, grilled shrimp, and whole wheat croutons.
- Drizzle the lemon-tahini dressing over the salad and toss gently to coat all the ingredients.
- Serve immediately.

Noodle Salad

INGREDIENTS:

(Calories: ~350 / Carbs: 32g / Proteins: 30g / Fats: 12g)

- 3 ounces whole wheat noodles, cooked and cooled
- 4-6 ounces boneless, skinless chicken breast
- 1 cup mixed vegetables (such as bell peppers, carrots, and snap peas), thinly sliced
- 1 green onion, sliced, 1 tablespoon sesame seeds
- 1 tablespoon low-sodium soy sauce
- 1 tablespoon rice vinegar, 1 teaspoon sesame oil
- 1/2 teaspoon honey or alternative sweetener
- 1/2 teaspoon grated ginger, Salt and pepper to taste

Cooking time: 20 minutes / servings: 1
Preparation time: 20 minutes

INSTRUCTIONS FOR COOKING:

- Preheat the air fryer to 400°F (200°C).
- Season the chicken breast with salt and pepper.
- Place the chicken breast in the air fryer basket and cook for 10-12 minutes until it reaches an internal temperature of 165°F (74°C). Allow it to rest for a few minutes, then slice it into strips.
- In a small bowl, whisk together the low-sodium soy sauce, rice vinegar, sesame oil, honey, grated ginger, salt, and pepper to make the dressing.
- In a large salad bowl, combine the cooked and cooled whole wheat noodles, mixed vegetables, sliced green onion, and grilled chicken strips.
- Drizzle the sesame dressing over the salad and toss gently to coat all the ingredients.
- Sprinkle sesame seeds on top for garnish.
- Serve immediately.

Watermelon Feta Salad

INGREDIENTS:

(Calories: 120 / Carbs: 12g / Proteins: 5g / Fats: 6g)

- 1 cup diced watermelon, 1/4 cup crumbled feta cheese
- 2-3 fresh mint leaves, chopped, 1 tablespoon balsamic glaze
- 1 tablespoon chopped walnuts (optional)
- Freshly ground black pepper to taste

Cooking time: 10 minutes / servings: 1
Preparation time: 10 minutes

INSTRUCTIONS FOR COOKING:

- In a salad bowl, combine the diced watermelon, crumbled feta cheese, and chopped mint leaves.
- Drizzle the balsamic glaze over the salad.
- Sprinkle the chopped walnuts (if using) and freshly ground black pepper on top.
- Toss gently to combine all the ingredients.
- Serve immediately.

Baked Cod

INGREDIENTS:

(Calories: 300 / Carbs: 22g / Proteins: 30g / Fats: 10g)

- 4-6 ounces cod fillet, 1 tablespoon lemon juice
- 1 teaspoon lemon zest, 1 tablespoon capers, rinsed and drained
- 1 tablespoon low-fat mayonnaise
- 1/2 tablespoon Dijon mustard, Salt and pepper to taste
- 1/4 cup quinoa, cooked
- 1/4 cup mixed vegetables (such as bell peppers, zucchini, and onions), diced, 1/4 cup low-sodium chicken or vegetable broth
- 1/2 teaspoon olive oil, Fresh parsley, chopped for garnish

Cooking time: 25 minutes / servings: 1
Preparation time: 25 minutes

INSTRUCTIONS FOR COOKING:

- Preheat the air fryer to 400°F (200°C).
- Season the cod fillet with salt, pepper, lemon juice, and lemon zest.
- Place the cod fillet in the air fryer basket and cook for 10-12 minutes until it is cooked through and flakes easily with a fork.
- In a small bowl, mix together the capers, low-fat mayonnaise, Dijon mustard, salt, and pepper to make the lemon-caper sauce.
- In a separate pan, heat the olive oil over medium heat.
- Add the mixed vegetables and sauté for 3-4 minutes until they are slightly softened.
- Add the cooked quinoa and chicken or vegetable broth to the pan. Stir well and cook for another 3-4 minutes until the liquid is absorbed.
- Serve the baked cod on top of the quinoa pilaf, drizzle with the lemon-caper sauce, and garnish with chopped fresh parsley.

Chicken Lettuce Wraps

INGREDIENTS:

(Calories: 300 / Carbs: 24g / Proteins: 27g / Fats: 10g)

- 4 oz cod fillet, 1/2 lemon, juiced
- 1 tablespoon olive oil
- 1 tablespoon capers, drained
- 1/4 teaspoon dried dill
- Salt and pepper to taste
- 1/4 cup quinoa
- 1/2 cup low-sodium chicken or vegetable broth
- 1/4 cup diced zucchini, 1/4 cup diced bell pepper
- 1/4 cup diced red onion, 1/4 teaspoon garlic powder

Cooking time: 15 minutes / servings: 1
Preparation time: 10 minutes

INSTRUCTIONS FOR COOKING:

- Preheat the air fryer to 400°F (200°C).
- In a small bowl, mix the lemon juice, olive oil, capers, dried dill, salt, and pepper. Set aside.
- Rinse the quinoa under cold water and drain well.
- In a small saucepan, combine the quinoa and low-sodium broth. Bring to a boil over medium heat, then reduce the heat to low and simmer for 12-15 minutes, or until the quinoa is cooked and the liquid is absorbed. Fluff with a fork and set aside.
- Season the cod fillet with salt, pepper, and garlic powder.
- Place the seasoned cod fillet in the air fryer basket and cook for 10-12 minutes, or until the fish is opaque and flakes easily with a fork.
- While the cod is cooking, heat a non-stick skillet over medium heat. Add the diced zucchini, bell pepper, and red onion. Sauté for 5-7 minutes, or until the vegetables are tender.
- Add the cooked quinoa to the skillet with the sautéed vegetables. Stir well to combine and heat through.
- Serve the baked cod fillet on a plate, drizzle with the lemon-caper sauce, and serve with the quinoa pilaf on the side.

Caprese Skewers

INGREDIENTS:

(Calories: 150 / Carbs: 3g / Proteins: 10g / Fats: 11g)

- 4 cherry tomatoes
- 2 oz mozzarella cheese, cubed
- Fresh basil leaves
- 1 teaspoon balsamic glaze (optional)
- Salt and pepper to taste

Cooking time: 5 minutes / servings: 1
Preparation time: 10 minutes

INSTRUCTIONS FOR COOKING:

- Preheat the air fryer to 400°F (200°C).
- Thread the cherry tomatoes, mozzarella cheese cubes, and fresh basil leaves onto skewers, alternating the ingredients.
- Place the skewers in the air fryer basket and cook for 5 minutes, or until the cheese is melted and the tomatoes are slightly softened.
- Season with salt and pepper to taste.
- Drizzle with balsamic glaze, if desired, for added flavor.
- Serve the Caprese skewers as a light appetizer or snack.

Greek Orzo Salad

INGREDIENTS:

(Calories: 280 / Carbs: 32g / Proteins: 8g / Fats: 14g)

- 1/4 cup orzo pasta, 4 cherry tomatoes, halved
- 1/4 cup diced cucumber, 2 tablespoons diced red onion
- 2 tablespoons crumbled feta cheese
- 1 tablespoon fresh lemon juice
- 1 tablespoon olive oil, 1/2 teaspoon dried oregano
- Salt and pepper to taste
- Fresh parsley for garnish (optional)

Cooking time: 10 minutes (for cooking the orzo)
Servings: 1 / preparation time: 10 minutes

INSTRUCTIONS FOR COOKING:

- Cook the orzo pasta according to the package instructions. Drain and rinse with cold water. Set aside.
- In a medium bowl, combine the cooked orzo, cherry tomatoes, diced cucumber, diced red onion, crumbled feta cheese, lemon juice, olive oil, dried oregano, salt, and pepper. Toss well to combine.
- Let the salad marinate in the refrigerator for at least 30 minutes to allow the flavors to meld together.
- Serve the Greek orzo salad chilled, garnished with fresh parsley if desired.

Falafel Salad

INGREDIENTS:

(Calories: 280 / Carbs: 38g / Proteins: 12g / Fats: 9g)

- 1/4 cup canned chickpeas, drained and rinsed, 1/4 small onion, roughly chopped
- 1 garlic clove, minced, 1 tablespoon fresh parsley, chopped
- 1/2 teaspoon ground cumin, 1/4 teaspoon ground coriander
- 1/4 teaspoon salt, 1/4 teaspoon baking powder
- 1 tablespoon whole wheat flour, Cooking spray
- 2 cups mixed salad greens, 1/4 cup cherry tomatoes, halved
- 1/4 small cucumber, sliced, 2 tablespoons hummus
- 1 tablespoon lemon juice, 1 teaspoon olive oil

Cooking time: 15 minutes / servings: 1
Preparation time: 15 minutes

INSTRUCTIONS FOR COOKING:

- In a food processor, combine the chickpeas, onion, garlic, parsley, cumin, coriander, salt, baking powder, and whole wheat flour. Pulse until well combined and the mixture holds together when pressed.
- Shape the mixture into 4 small patties.
- Preheat the air fryer to 375°F (190°C).
- Lightly coat the falafel patties with cooking spray and place them in the air fryer basket.
- Cook the falafel for 10-12 minutes, flipping halfway through, until golden brown and crispy.
- In a small bowl, whisk together the hummus, lemon juice, and olive oil to make the dressing.
- In a serving bowl, arrange the mixed salad greens, cherry tomatoes, and cucumber slices. Place the cooked falafel on top.
- Drizzle the hummus dressing over the salad and falafel.
- Serve immediately and enjoy!

Zucchini Pad Thai

INGREDIENTS:

(Calories: 270 / Carbs: 18g / Proteins: 26g / Fats: 10g)

- 1 medium zucchini, 4 ounces shrimp, peeled and deveined
- 1/4 cup bean sprouts, 2 tablespoons unsalted peanuts, chopped
- 1 tablespoon chopped green onions
- 1 tablespoon fresh cilantro, chopped
- 1 tablespoon low-sodium soy sauce
- 1 tablespoon fresh lime juice
- 1 teaspoon sesame oil, 1/2 teaspoon minced garlic
- 1/2 teaspoon grated ginger, 1/2 teaspoon honey
- Cooking spray

Cooking time: 10 minutes / servings: 1
Preparation time: 15 minutes

INSTRUCTIONS FOR COOKING:

- Cut the zucchini into thin noodle-like strips using a spiralizer or julienne peeler. Set aside.
- In a small bowl, combine the soy sauce, lime juice, sesame oil, minced garlic, grated ginger, and honey. Stir well to make the peanut sauce.
- Preheat the air fryer to 400°F (200°C).
- Lightly coat the shrimp with cooking spray and place them in the air fryer basket.
- Cook the shrimp for 5-6 minutes, until pink and cooked through.
- In a non-stick skillet, heat a small amount of cooking spray over medium heat. Add the zucchini noodles and bean sprouts, and sauté for 2-3 minutes until the noodles are tender.
- Add the cooked shrimp to the skillet and pour the peanut sauce over the noodles and shrimp. Toss to coat evenly.
- Transfer the zucchini noodle Pad Thai to a serving plate and garnish with chopped peanuts, green onions, and cilantro.
- Serve immediately and enjoy!

Southwest Quinoa Salad

INGREDIENTS:

(Calories: 350 / Carbs: 32g / Proteins: 27g / Fats: 12g)

- 4 ounces boneless, skinless chicken breast
- 1/4 cup cooked quinoa, 1/4 cup black beans, rinsed and drained
- 1/4 cup corn kernels, fresh or frozen
- 1/4 cup cherry tomatoes, halved
- 1/4 small avocado, diced, 2 cups mixed salad greens
- 1 tablespoon fresh cilantro, chopped, 1 tablespoon lime juice
- 1 teaspoon olive oil, 1/2 teaspoon ground cumin
- 1/4 teaspoon chili powder, 1/4 teaspoon garlic powder
- Salt and pepper to taste, Cooking spray

Cooking time: 25 minutes / servings: 1
Preparation time: 15 minutes

INSTRUCTIONS FOR COOKING:

- Preheat the air fryer to 375°F (190°C).
- Season the chicken breast with cumin, chili powder, garlic powder, salt, and pepper.
- Lightly coat the chicken breast with cooking spray and place it in the air fryer basket.
- Cook the chicken for 20-25 minutes, until cooked through and no longer pink in the center. Let it rest for a few minutes, then slice it into thin strips.
- In a large bowl, combine the cooked quinoa, black beans, corn kernels, cherry tomatoes, diced avocado, mixed salad greens, and chopped cilantro.
- In a small bowl, whisk together the lime juice and olive oil to make the chipotle-lime dressing.
- Drizzle the dressing over the salad mixture and toss gently to combine.
- Transfer the salad to a serving plate and top with the sliced chicken breast.
- Serve immediately and enjoy!

Stuffed Chicken Breast

INGREDIENTS:

(Calories: 300 / Carbs: 12g / Proteins: 45g / Fats: 8g)

- 1 boneless, skinless chicken breast
- 1 cup fresh spinach, chopped,
- 1/4 cup mushrooms, sliced
- 1/4 teaspoon garlic powder
- 1/4 teaspoon onion powder
- 1/4 teaspoon dried thyme
- Salt and pepper, to taste, cooking spray
- 1 cup mixed vegetables (such as bell peppers, zucchini, and carrots), cut into bite-sized pieces

Cooking time: 25 minutes / servings: 1
Preparation time: 10 minutes

INSTRUCTIONS FOR COOKING:

- Preheat the air fryer to 375°F (190°C).
- Slice the chicken breast horizontally, but not all the way through, to create a pocket.
- In a small bowl, mix together the chopped spinach, sliced mushrooms, garlic powder, onion powder, dried thyme, salt, and pepper.
- Stuff the spinach and mushroom mixture into the pocket of the chicken breast.
- Lightly coat the air fryer basket with cooking spray. Place the stuffed chicken breast in the basket.
- Arrange the mixed vegetables around the chicken in the air fryer basket.
- Spray the vegetables with cooking spray and season with salt and pepper.
- Place the air fryer basket in the preheated air fryer and cook for 20-25 minutes or until the chicken is cooked through and the vegetables are tender. Flip the chicken halfway through cooking for even browning.

Thai Beef Wraps

INGREDIENTS:

(Calories: 280 / Carbs: 11g / Proteins: 25g / Fats: 16g)

- 4 ounces lean ground beef, 1 tablespoon low-sodium soy sauce
- 1 tablespoon lime juice, 1 teaspoon ginger, minced
- 1 teaspoon garlic, minced, 1/4 teaspoon red pepper flakes (adjust to taste)
- 1 tablespoon natural peanut butter (unsweetened)
- 1 teaspoon low-sodium soy sauce, 1 teaspoon lime juice
- 1 teaspoon honey or a sugar substitute
- 4 large lettuce leaves (such as butter or romaine)
- 2 tablespoons chopped peanuts (optional, for garnish)
- Fresh cilantro, for garnish

Cooking time: 10 minutes / servings: 1
Preparation time: 15 minutes

INSTRUCTIONS FOR COOKING:

- In a bowl, mix together the ground beef, soy sauce, lime juice, minced ginger, minced garlic, and red pepper flakes.
- Preheat the air fryer to 375°F (190°C).
- Cook the beef mixture in the air fryer for 8-10 minutes, or until cooked through, breaking it up with a spoon as it cooks.
- In a separate bowl, whisk together the peanut butter, soy sauce, lime juice, and honey until smooth. Adjust the consistency with a little water if needed.
- Place the cooked ground beef in the lettuce leaves and drizzle with the spicy peanut sauce.
- Garnish with chopped peanuts and fresh cilantro.

Mediterranean Pasta Salad

INGREDIENTS:

(Calories: 350 / Carbs: 38g / Proteins: 12g / Fats: 16g)

- 1/2 cup whole wheat pasta
- 1/2 cup cherry tomatoes, halved
- 2 tablespoons crumbled feta cheese
- 2 tablespoons sliced black olives
- 1 tablespoon extra virgin olive oil
- 1 tablespoon fresh lemon juice
- 1/2 teaspoon dried oregano, salt and pepper to taste
- Fresh basil leaves for garnish (optional)

Cooking time: 10 minutes / servings: 1
Preparation time: 10 minutes

INSTRUCTIONS FOR COOKING:

- Cook the whole wheat pasta according to the package instructions until al dente. Drain and rinse with cold water to stop the cooking process.
- In a medium-sized bowl, combine the cooked pasta, cherry tomatoes, crumbled feta cheese, and sliced black olives.
- In a small bowl, whisk together the extra virgin olive oil, fresh lemon juice, dried oregano, salt, and pepper.
- Pour the dressing over the pasta mixture and toss until everything is well coated.
- Taste and adjust the seasoning if needed.
- Let the pasta salad sit for about 10 minutes to allow the flavors to meld together.
- Garnish with fresh basil leaves, if desired, and serve.

Sesame Tofu Salad

INGREDIENTS:

(Calories: 180 / Carbs: 15g / Proteins: 12g / Fats: 9g)

- 3 ounces firm tofu, drained and cubed
- 1 cup shredded cabbage, 1/2 cup grated carrots
- 2 tablespoons low-sodium soy sauce
- 1 tablespoon rice vinegar, 1 teaspoon sesame oil
- 1 teaspoon honey (or alternative sweetener for diabetics)
- 1/2 teaspoon grated ginger
- 1/2 teaspoon sesame seeds (optional)
- Fresh cilantro leaves for garnish (optional)

Cooking time: 10 minutes / servings: 1
Preparation time: 15 minutes

INSTRUCTIONS FOR COOKING:

- Preheat the air fryer to 400°F (200°C).
- In a medium-sized bowl, combine the tofu cubes, shredded cabbage, and grated carrots.
- In a separate small bowl, whisk together the soy sauce, rice vinegar, sesame oil, honey, and grated ginger.
- Pour the dressing over the tofu and vegetable mixture and toss until well coated.
- Transfer the mixture to the air fryer basket and cook for 8-10 minutes, shaking the basket halfway through, until the tofu is golden brown and crispy.
- Remove from the air fryer and sprinkle with sesame seeds, if desired.
- Garnish with fresh cilantro leaves and serve.

Shrimp Avocado Salad

INGREDIENTS:

(Calories: 240 / Carbs: 9g / Proteins: 20g / Fats: 15g)

- 4 ounces shrimp, peeled and deveined
- 1 cup mixed salad greens, 1/2 avocado, sliced
- 1/4 cup cherry tomatoes, halved, 1 tablespoon lime juice
- 1 tablespoon chopped fresh cilantro
- 1 tablespoon extra virgin olive oil
- 1/2 teaspoon minced garlic, salt and pepper to taste

Cooking time: 5 minutes / servings: 1
Preparation time: 15 minutes

INSTRUCTIONS FOR COOKING:

- Preheat the air fryer to 400°F (200°C).
- In a small bowl, combine the lime juice, chopped cilantro, extra virgin olive oil, minced garlic, salt, and pepper to make the dressing.
- In a separate bowl, toss the shrimp with half of the lime-cilantro dressing.
- Place the shrimp in the air fryer basket and cook for 4-5 minutes until they are pink and cooked through.
- In a serving bowl, arrange the mixed salad greens, sliced avocado, and cherry tomatoes.
- Add the grilled shrimp on top of the salad.
- Drizzle the remaining lime-cilantro dressing over the salad and serve.

Turkey Taco Wraps

INGREDIENTS:

(Calories: 250 / Carbs: 10g / Proteins: 20g / Fats: 15g)

- 4 ounces ground turkey, 1/2 teaspoon chili powder
- 1/4 teaspoon cumin, Salt and pepper to taste
- 4 large lettuce leaves, 1/4 cup diced tomatoes
- 1/4 cup diced onions
- 1 tablespoon chopped fresh cilantro
- 1/4 cup salsa (sugar-free),
- 1/4 avocado, 1/2 lime, juiced

Cooking time: 20 minutes / servings: 1
Preparation time: 20 minutes

INSTRUCTIONS FOR COOKING:

- Preheat the air fryer to 400°F (200°C).
- In a small bowl, mix together the chili powder, cumin, salt, and pepper.
- In a skillet over medium heat, cook the ground turkey until browned. Sprinkle the spice mixture over the turkey and continue cooking for another 2-3 minutes.
- Place the lettuce leaves on a plate. Divide the cooked turkey equally among the lettuce leaves.
- In a separate bowl, combine the diced tomatoes, onions, and chopped cilantro. Toss lightly.
- In another small bowl, mash the avocado and mix in the lime juice to make guacamole.
- Top each lettuce wrap with salsa, the tomato-onion mixture, and a dollop of guacamole.
- Serve and enjoy!

Eggplant Mozzarella Stack

INGREDIENTS:

(Calories: 180 / Carbs: 12g / Proteins: 10g / Fats: 10g)

- 1 small eggplant, sliced into rounds
- Salt to taste, 1/4 cup almond flour
- 1/4 teaspoon garlic powder
- 1/4 teaspoon dried oregano
- 1/4 teaspoon dried basil, 1/4 teaspoon paprika
- 1/4 cup grated Parmesan cheese
- 1 egg, beaten, 1/2 cup sugar-free tomato sauce
- 1/4 cup shredded mozzarella cheese
- Fresh basil leaves for garnish

Cooking time: 25 minutes / servings: 1
Preparation time: 25 minutes

INSTRUCTIONS FOR COOKING:

- Preheat the air fryer to 400°F (200°C).
- Place the eggplant slices on a baking sheet and sprinkle them with salt. Let them sit for about 15 minutes to draw out excess moisture.
- In a shallow dish, mix together the almond flour, garlic powder, dried oregano, dried basil, paprika, and grated Parmesan cheese.
- Dip each eggplant slice into the beaten egg, then coat it in the almond flour mixture.
- Place the coated eggplant slices in a single layer in the air fryer basket. Cook for 10 minutes, flipping them halfway through.
- While the eggplant cooks, heat the sugar-free tomato sauce in a small saucepan over low heat.
- Remove the cooked eggplant slices from the air fryer and assemble the stack: Layer one slice of eggplant, a spoonful of tomato sauce, and a sprinkle of shredded mozzarella. Repeat the layers until you run out of ingredients.
- Return the assembled stacks to the air fryer for another 3-5 minutes or until the cheese is melted and bubbly.
- Garnish with fresh basil leaves. Serve and enjoy!

Quinoa Stuffed Peppers

INGREDIENTS:

(Calories: 250 / Carbs: 40g / Proteins: 10g / Fats: 4g)

- 1 bell pepper, 1/4 cup cooked quinoa
- 1/4 cup canned black beans, rinsed and drained
- 1/4 cup diced tomatoes, 1/4 cup diced onions
- 1/4 teaspoon cumin, Salt and pepper to taste
- 1/4 cup salsa verde (sugar-free)
- Fresh cilantro for garnish

Cooking time: 30 minutes / servings: 1
Preparation time: 30 minutes

INSTRUCTIONS FOR COOKING:

- Preheat the air fryer to 400°F (200°C).
- Cut the bell pepper in half lengthwise and remove the seeds and membrane.
- In a bowl, combine the cooked quinoa, black beans, diced tomatoes, onions, cumin, salt, and pepper.
- Fill each bell pepper half with the quinoa and black bean mixture.
- Place the stuffed bell peppers in the air fryer basket and cook for 20 minutes or until the peppers are tender and lightly browned.
- Remove the stuffed bell peppers from the air fryer and top them with salsa verde.
- Garnish with fresh cilantro.
- Serve and enjoy!

Grilled Chicken Salad

INGREDIENTS:

(Calories: 350 / Carbs: 13g / Proteins: 30g / Fats: 19g)

- 1 small chicken breast, boneless and skinless, 1 tablespoon lemon juice
- 1 teaspoon dried herbs (such as thyme, oregano, or basil)
- Salt and pepper, to taste, 2 cups mixed salad greens
- 1/4 cup cherry tomatoes, halved, 1/4 cup cucumber, sliced
- 1/4 cup red onion, thinly sliced, 1 tablespoon chopped fresh parsley
- 1 tablespoon extra-virgin olive oil, 1 tablespoon Dijon mustard
- 1 tablespoon apple cider vinegar, 1/2 teaspoon honey (optional)

Cooking time: 15 minutes / servings: 1
Preparation time: 15 minutes

INSTRUCTIONS FOR COOKING:

- Preheat the air fryer to 400°F (200°C) for 5 minutes.
- In a bowl, combine the lemon juice, dried herbs, salt, and pepper. Add the chicken breast and marinate for 10 minutes.
- Place the marinated chicken breast in the preheated air fryer basket. Cook for 8-10 minutes, flipping halfway through, until the internal temperature reaches 165°F (74°C). Remove from the air fryer and let it rest for a few minutes before slicing.
- In a large salad bowl, combine the mixed salad greens, cherry tomatoes, cucumber, red onion, and fresh parsley.
- In a small bowl, whisk together the olive oil, Dijon mustard, apple cider vinegar, and honey (if using). Drizzle the dressing over the salad and toss to coat.
- Slice the grilled chicken breast and place it on top of the salad.
- Serve the Lemon Herb Grilled Chicken Salad immediately.

Zucchini Noodle Salad

INGREDIENTS:

(Calories: 150 / Carbs: 8g / Proteins: 5g / Fats: 11g)

- 1 medium zucchini
- 1/2 cup cherry tomatoes, halved
- 2 tablespoons basil pesto (look for a low-sugar or homemade version)
- 1 tablespoon grated Parmesan cheese (optional)
- Salt and pepper, to taste

Cooking time: 10 minutes / servings: 1
Preparation time: 15 minutes

INSTRUCTIONS FOR COOKING:

- Preheat the air fryer to 400°F (200°C) for 5 minutes.
- Using a spiralizer or vegetable peeler, create zucchini noodles from the medium zucchini.
- Place the zucchini noodles in the preheated air fryer basket. Cook for 5-6 minutes, tossing halfway through, until the noodles are tender and slightly crispy.
- In a bowl, combine the air-fried zucchini noodles, cherry tomatoes, basil pesto, and grated Parmesan cheese (if using). Season with salt and pepper to taste. Toss well to coat.
- Serve the Air Fried Zucchini Noodle Salad immediately.

Southwest Quinoa Bowl

INGREDIENTS:

(Calories: 350 / Carbs: 35g / Proteins: 30g / Fats: 10g)

- 1/4 cup quinoa
- 1/2 cup low-sodium black beans, drained and rinsed
- 1 small chicken breast, boneless and skinless
- 1/4 teaspoon chili powder, 1/4 teaspoon cumin
- Salt and pepper, to taste, 1/4 cup diced bell peppers (any color)
- 2 tablespoons diced red onion
- 2 tablespoons chopped fresh cilantro
- 1 tablespoon lime juice
- 1 tablespoon extra virgin olive oil

Cooking time: 20 minutes / servings: 1
Preparation time: 15 minutes

INSTRUCTIONS FOR COOKING:

- In a saucepan, bring 1/2 cup of water to a boil. Add the quinoa, reduce heat to low, cover, and simmer for 15 minutes or until the quinoa is cooked and the water is absorbed. Fluff with a fork and set aside.
- Preheat the air fryer to 400°F (200°C) for 5 minutes.
- Season the chicken breast with chili powder, cumin, salt, and pepper. Place it in the preheated air fryer basket and cook for 12-15 minutes, flipping halfway through, until the internal temperature reaches 165°F (74°C). Remove from the air fryer and let it rest for a few minutes before slicing.
- In a bowl, combine the cooked quinoa, black beans, diced bell peppers, red onion, chopped cilantro, lime juice, and olive oil. Toss well to combine.
- Slice the grilled chicken breast and place it on top of the quinoa and black bean mixture.
- Serve the Southwest Quinoa and Black Bean Bowl with Lime-Cilantro Dressing immediately.

Chapter 5: Dinner

- Grilled Balsamic Chicken
- Lemon-Dill Salmon
- Roasted Veggie Quinoa
- Greek Feta Salad
- Shrimp Avocado Wraps
- Strawberry Spinach Salad
- Light Caesar Chicken
- Black Bean Corn Salad
- Tofu Stir-Fry
- Caprese Skewers
- Tuna Lettuce Wraps
- Sesame Chicken Salad
- Chickpea Cucumber Salad
- Zucchini Chickpea Fritters
- Stuffed Bell Peppers
- Mexican Cauli Bowl
- Kale Butternut Salad
- Teriyaki Salmon Bowl
- Chicken Pita Wraps
- Air-Fried Shrimp Cups
- Beet Goat Cheese Salad
- BBQ Chicken Ranch
- Mushroom Spinach Salad
- Thai Beef Salad
- Mexican Chicken Bowl
- Mediterranean Tuna Salad
- Turkey Veggie Skewers
- Stuffed Bell Peppers
- Grilled Shrimp Caesar
- Lentil Tahini Salad
- Asian Chicken Noodle Salad
- Watermelon Feta Salad
- Lemon-Caper Baked Cod
- Chicken Lettuce Wraps
- Caprese Skewers
- Greek Orzo Salad
- Air-Fried Falafel Salad
- Zucchini Pad Thai
- Southwest Chicken Salad
- Spinach Stuffed Chicken
- Thai Beef Lettuce Wraps
- Mediterranean Pasta Salad
- Asian Tofu Salad
- Grilled Shrimp Salad
- Turkey Taco Lettuce Wraps
- Eggplant Mozzarella Stack
- Quinoa Stuffed Peppers
- Lemon Herb Grilled Chicken
- Zucchini Noodle Salad
- Southwest Quinoa Bowl

Chapter 5: Dinner

Grilled Balsamic Chicken

INGREDIENTS:

(Calories: 180 / Carbs: 3g / Proteins: 30g / Fats: 4g)

- 1 small chicken breast, boneless and skinless
- Salt and pepper, to taste
- 1 tablespoon balsamic vinegar
- 1 teaspoon Dijon mustard
- 1 teaspoon honey (optional)
- 1/2 teaspoon dried herbs (such as thyme, rosemary, or basil)

Cooking time: 10 minutes / servings: 1
Preparation time: 15 minutes

INSTRUCTIONS FOR COOKING:

- Preheat the air fryer to 400°F (200°C) for 5 minutes.
- Season the chicken breast with salt and pepper.
- Place the chicken breast in the preheated air fryer basket. Cook for 12-15 minutes, flipping halfway through, until the internal temperature reaches 165°F (74°C). Remove from the air fryer and let it rest for a few minutes.
- In a small bowl, whisk together the balsamic vinegar, Dijon mustard, honey (if using), and dried herbs.
- Brush the balsamic glaze onto the cooked chicken breast.
- Serve the Grilled Chicken with Balsamic Glaze immediately.

Lemon-Dill Salmon

INGREDIENTS:

(Calories: 280 / Carbs: 0g / Proteins: 22g / Fats: 20g)

- 1 salmon fillet, skin-on
- Salt and pepper, to taste
- 1 tablespoon lemon juice
- 1/2 teaspoon dried dill
- 1 teaspoon extra-virgin olive oil

Cooking time: 10 minutes / servings: 1
Preparation time: 10 minutes

INSTRUCTIONS FOR COOKING:

- Preheat the air fryer to 400°F (200°C) for 5 minutes.
- Season the salmon fillet with salt and pepper.
- Place the salmon fillet in the preheated air fryer basket, skin-side down. Cook for 8-10 minutes, depending on the thickness of the fillet, until it flakes easily with a fork and the internal temperature reaches 145°F (63°C).
- In a small bowl, mix together the lemon juice, dried dill, and olive oil.
- Drizzle the lemon-dill mixture over the cooked salmon fillet.
- Serve the Lemon-Dill Salmon Fillet immediately.

Roasted Veggie Quinoa

INGREDIENTS:

(Calories: 300 / Carbs: 35g / Proteins: 8g / Fats: 14g)

- 1/2 cup cooked quinoa
- 1 cup mixed vegetables (such as bell peppers, zucchini, broccoli, and carrots), chopped
- 1 tablespoon olive oil
- Salt and pepper, to taste
- 1/2 teaspoon dried herbs (such as thyme, oregano, or rosemary)
- 2 tablespoons feta cheese, crumbled

Cooking time: 25 minutes / servings: 1
Preparation time: 10 minutes

INSTRUCTIONS FOR COOKING:

- Preheat the air fryer to 400°F (200°C) for 5 minutes.
- In a bowl, toss the mixed vegetables with olive oil, salt, pepper, and dried herbs.
- Place the vegetables in the preheated air fryer basket. Cook for 20-25 minutes, shaking the basket halfway through, until the vegetables are tender and lightly browned.
- In a serving bowl, combine the cooked quinoa and roasted vegetables.
- Sprinkle the crumbled feta cheese over the quinoa and vegetables.
- Serve the Roasted Vegetable Quinoa Bowl warm.

Greek Feta Salad

INGREDIENTS:

(Calories: 180 / Carbs: 10g / Proteins: 5g / Fats: 14g)

- 2 cups mixed salad greens, 1/4 cup cucumber, diced
- 1/4 cup cherry tomatoes, halved
- 1/4 cup red onion, thinly sliced, 1/4 cup kalamata olives
- 2 tablespoons feta cheese, crumbled
- 1 tablespoon extra-virgin olive oil
- 1 tablespoon lemon juice
- 1/2 teaspoon dried oregano
- Salt and pepper, to taste

Cooking time: 0 minutes / servings: 1
Preparation time: 10 minutes

INSTRUCTIONS FOR COOKING:

- In a large bowl, combine the mixed salad greens, cucumber, cherry tomatoes, red onion, kalamata olives, and feta cheese.
- In a small bowl, whisk together the olive oil, lemon juice, dried oregano, salt, and pepper.
- Drizzle the dressing over the salad and toss to combine.
- Serve the Greek Feta Salad immediately.

Shrimp Avocado Wraps

INGREDIENTS:

(Calories: 250 / Carbs: 19g / Proteins: 19g / Fats: 11g)

- 4 large shrimp, peeled and deveined
- Salt and pepper, to taste, 1/2 teaspoon paprika
- 1/4 teaspoon garlic powder
- 1/4 teaspoon cayenne pepper (optional)
- 1 whole wheat tortilla, 1/4 avocado, sliced
- 1/4 cup mixed salad greens
- 1 tablespoon plain Greek yogurt
- Fresh cilantro, for garnish

Cooking time: 10 minutes / servings: 1
Preparation time: 15 minutes

INSTRUCTIONS FOR COOKING:

- Preheat the air fryer to 400°F (200°C) for 5 minutes.
- Season the shrimp with salt, pepper, paprika, garlic powder, and cayenne pepper (if using).
- Place the seasoned shrimp in the preheated air fryer basket. Cook for 5-7 minutes, until the shrimp are pink and cooked through.
- Warm the whole wheat tortilla in the air fryer for 1-2 minutes.
- Assemble the wrap by placing the sliced avocado, mixed salad greens, and cooked shrimp on the tortilla.
- Drizzle the Greek yogurt over the filling and garnish with fresh cilantro.
- Roll up the wrap tightly and serve the Shrimp and Avocado Wrap immediately.

Strawberry Spinach Salad

INGREDIENTS:

(Calories: 150 / Carbs: 11g / Proteins: 5g / Fats: 10g)

- 2 cups fresh spinach leaves, 1/2 cup strawberries, sliced
- 1 tablespoon sliced almonds, 1 tablespoon crumbled feta cheese
- 1 tablespoon balsamic vinegar
- 1/2 tablespoon extra-virgin olive oil
- 1/2 teaspoon honey (optional)
- Salt and pepper, to taste

Cooking time: 0 minutes / servings: 1
Preparation time: 10 minutes

INSTRUCTIONS FOR COOKING:

- In a large bowl, combine the fresh spinach leaves, sliced strawberries, sliced almonds, and crumbled feta cheese.
- In a small bowl, whisk together the balsamic vinegar, olive oil, honey (if using), salt, and pepper.
- Drizzle the dressing over the salad and toss to combine.
- Serve the Strawberry Spinach Salad immediately.

Light Caesar Chicken

INGREDIENTS:

(Calories: 250 / Carbs: 10g / Proteins: 30g / Fats: 10g)

- 1 small chicken breast, boneless and skinless
- Salt and pepper, to taste
- 1 tablespoon grated Parmesan cheese
- 2 cups romaine lettuce, chopped
- 1 tablespoon low-fat Caesar dressing
- 1 tablespoon whole wheat croutons

Cooking time: 15 minutes / servings: 1
Preparation time: 15 minutes

INSTRUCTIONS FOR COOKING:

- Preheat the air fryer to 400°F (200°C) for 5 minutes.
- Season the chicken breast with salt and pepper.
- Place the chicken breast in the preheated air fryer basket. Cook for 12-15 minutes, flipping halfway through, until the internal temperature reaches 165°F (74°C). Remove from the air fryer and let it rest for a few minutes.
- Slice the cooked chicken breast into thin strips.
- In a large bowl, combine the chopped romaine lettuce, grated Parmesan cheese, and Caesar dressing. Toss well to coat the lettuce.
- Top the salad with the sliced chicken breast and whole wheat croutons.
- Serve the Light Chicken Caesar immediately.

Black Bean Corn Salad

INGREDIENTS:

(Calories: 180 / Carbs: 30g / Proteins: 7g / Fats: 4g)

- 1/2 cup canned black beans, rinsed and drained
- 1/2 cup canned corn, drained, 1/4 cup diced red bell pepper
- 1/4 cup diced red onion
- 1/4 cup cherry tomatoes, halved
- 1 tablespoon chopped fresh cilantro
- 1 tablespoon lime juice
- 1/2 tablespoon extra-virgin olive oil
- 1/2 teaspoon ground cumin
- Salt and pepper, to taste

Cooking time: 0 minutes / servings: 1
Preparation time: 10 minutes

INSTRUCTIONS FOR COOKING:

- In a large bowl, combine the black beans, corn, red bell pepper, red onion, cherry tomatoes, and chopped cilantro.
- In a small bowl, whisk together the lime juice, olive oil, ground cumin, salt, and pepper.
- Pour the dressing over the salad ingredients and toss to combine.
- Serve the Black Bean and Corn Salad immediately.

Tofu Stir-Fry

INGREDIENTS:

(Calories: 200 / Carbs: 12g / Proteins: 16g / Fats: 10g)

- 1/2 cup firm tofu, cubed, 1 tablespoon low-sodium soy sauce
- 1 teaspoon sesame oil, 1/4 teaspoon minced garlic
- 1/4 teaspoon grated ginger, 1/4 cup sliced bell peppers
- 1/4 cup sliced zucchini, 1/4 cup sliced mushrooms
- 1/4 cup broccoli florets, 1/4 cup snap peas
- Salt and pepper, to taste, 1/2 tablespoon chopped green onions (scallions), 1/2 tablespoon sesame seeds (optional)

Cooking time: 10 minutes / servings: 1
Preparation time: 15 minutes

INSTRUCTIONS FOR COOKING:

- Preheat the air fryer to 375°F (190°C) for 5 minutes.
- In a bowl, combine the cubed tofu, soy sauce, sesame oil, minced garlic, and grated ginger. Toss to coat the tofu evenly.
- Place the marinated tofu in the preheated air fryer basket. Cook for 8-10 minutes, shaking the basket occasionally, until the tofu is golden and crispy.
- While the tofu is cooking, prepare the vegetables by slicing the bell peppers, zucchini, mushrooms, and snap peas.
- In a separate bowl, toss the sliced vegetables with a pinch of salt and pepper.
- After the tofu is cooked, transfer it to a plate. Add the seasoned vegetables to the air fryer basket and cook for 5 minutes, shaking occasionally, until they are tender-crisp.
- Serve the tofu and vegetables together, garnished with chopped green onions and sesame seeds (if desired).

Caprese Skewers

INGREDIENTS:

(Calories: 150 / Carbs: 2g / Proteins: 10g / Fats: 11g)

- 4 cherry tomatoes
- 4 small fresh mozzarella balls (bocconcini)
- 4 fresh basil leaves
- 1/2 tablespoon balsamic vinegar
- 1/2 tablespoon extra-virgin olive oil
- Salt and pepper, to taste

Cooking time: 0 minutes / servings: 1
Preparation time: 10 minutes

INSTRUCTIONS FOR COOKING:

- Thread a cherry tomato, a mozzarella ball, and a fresh basil leaf onto a skewer. Repeat with the remaining ingredients.
- In a small bowl, whisk together the balsamic vinegar, olive oil, salt, and pepper.
- Drizzle the dressing over the Caprese skewers.
- Serve the Caprese Skewers immediately.

Tuna Lettuce Wraps

INGREDIENTS:

(Calories: 150 / Carbs: 7g / Proteins: 20g / Fats: 4g)

- 1 small can (85g) tuna in water, drained
- 2 large lettuce leaves, such as romaine or iceberg
- 1/4 cup diced cucumber
- 1/4 cup diced bell pepper
- 1/4 cup diced cherry tomatoes
- 1 tablespoon diced red onion
- 1 tablespoon chopped fresh parsley
- 1 tablespoon lemon juice
- Salt and pepper, to taste

Cooking time: 0 minutes / servings: 1
Preparation time: 10 minutes

INSTRUCTIONS FOR COOKING:

- In a bowl, combine the drained tuna, diced cucumber, diced bell pepper, diced cherry tomatoes, diced red onion, chopped parsley, lemon juice, salt, and pepper. Mix well to combine.
- Place the lettuce leaves on a plate or cutting board.
- Spoon the tuna mixture onto the center of each lettuce leaf.
- Wrap the lettuce around the filling, securing it with toothpicks if needed.
- Serve the Tuna Lettuce Wraps immediately.

Sesame Chicken Salad

INGREDIENTS:

(Calories: 250 / Carbs: 12g / Proteins: 25g / Fats: 10g)

- 1 small chicken breast, boneless and skinless
- Salt and pepper, to taste, 2 cups mixed salad greens
- 1/4 cup shredded carrots, 1/4 cup sliced cucumber
- 1/4 cup sliced bell peppers, 1 tablespoon sesame seeds
- 1 tablespoon low-sodium soy sauce, 1 tablespoon rice vinegar
- 1/2 tablespoon sesame oil
- 1/2 tablespoon honey (optional)

Cooking time: 15 minutes / servings: 1
Preparation time: 15 minutes

INSTRUCTIONS FOR COOKING:

- Preheat the air fryer to 400°F (200°C) for 5 minutes.
- Season the chicken breast with salt and pepper.
- Place the chicken breast in the preheated air fryer basket. Cook for 12-15 minutes, flipping halfway through, until the internal temperature reaches 165°F (74°C). Remove from the air fryer and let it rest for a few minutes.
- Slice the cooked chicken breast into thin strips.
- In a large bowl, combine the mixed salad greens, shredded carrots, sliced cucumber, sliced bell peppers, and sesame seeds.
- In a separate small bowl, whisk together the low-sodium soy sauce, rice vinegar, sesame oil, and honey (if using).
- Drizzle the dressing over the salad and toss to coat the ingredients evenly.
- Top the salad with the sliced chicken breast.
- Serve the Sesame Chicken Salad immediately.

Chickpea Cucumber Salad

INGREDIENTS:

(Calories: 180 / Carbs: 25g / Proteins: 7g / Fats: 7g)

- 1/2 cup canned chickpeas, rinsed and drained
- 1/2 cup diced cucumber
- 1/4 cup diced red bell pepper
- 1/4 cup diced red onion
- 2 tablespoons chopped fresh parsley
- 1 tablespoon lemon juice
- 1 tablespoon extra-virgin olive oil
- Salt and pepper, to taste

Cooking time: 0 minutes / servings: 1
Preparation time: 10 minutes

INSTRUCTIONS FOR COOKING:

- In a bowl, combine the chickpeas, diced cucumber, diced red bell pepper, diced red onion, chopped parsley, lemon juice, olive oil, salt, and pepper. Mix well to combine.
- Adjust the seasoning if needed.
- Serve the Chickpea Cucumber Salad immediately.

Zucchini Chickpea Fritters

INGREDIENTS:

(Calories: 200 / Carbs: 26g / Proteins: 18g / Fats: 6g)

- 1 small zucchini, grated
- 1/2 cup canned chickpeas, rinsed and drained
- 2 tablespoons almond flour
- 1 tablespoon chopped fresh parsley
- 1/4 teaspoon garlic powder
- 1/4 teaspoon cumin powder
- Salt and pepper, to taste
- Cooking spray

Cooking time: 10 minutes / servings: 1
Preparation time: 15 minutes

INSTRUCTIONS FOR COOKING:

- Preheat the air fryer to 375°F (190°C) for 5 minutes.
- Place the grated zucchini in a clean kitchen towel and squeeze out the excess moisture.
- In a mixing bowl, combine the grated zucchini, chickpeas, almond flour, chopped parsley, garlic powder, cumin powder, salt, and pepper. Mix well to combine and form a thick batter.
- Form the mixture into small patties or fritters.
- Lightly spray the air fryer basket with cooking spray.
- Place the fritters in the preheated air fryer basket, making sure they are not touching each other.
- Cook for 8-10 minutes, flipping halfway through, until the fritters are golden brown and crispy.
- Remove the fritters from the air fryer and let them cool slightly before serving.

Stuffed Bell Peppers

INGREDIENTS:

(Calories: 200 / Carbs: 38g / Proteins: 9g / Fats: 2g)

- 1 large bell pepper, 1/4 cup cooked quinoa
- 1/4 cup canned black beans, rinsed and drained
- 2 tablespoons diced tomatoes, 2 tablespoons diced onion
- 1 tablespoon chopped fresh parsley
- 1/2 teaspoon cumin powder, Salt and pepper, to taste
- Cooking spray

Cooking time: 20 minutes / servings: 1
Preparation time: 15 minutes

INSTRUCTIONS FOR COOKING:

- Preheat the air fryer to 375°F (190°C) for 5 minutes.
- Slice off the top of the bell pepper and remove the seeds and membrane.
- In a mixing bowl, combine the cooked quinoa, black beans, diced tomatoes, diced onion, chopped parsley, cumin powder, salt, and pepper. Mix well to combine.
- Stuff the bell pepper with the quinoa mixture, pressing it down lightly.
- Lightly spray the air fryer basket with cooking spray.
- Place the stuffed bell pepper in the preheated air fryer basket.
- Cook for 18-20 minutes, until the bell pepper is tender and the filling is heated through.
- Remove the stuffed bell pepper from the air fryer and let it cool slightly before serving.

Mexican Cauli Bowl

INGREDIENTS:

(Calories: 150 / Carbs: 28g / Proteins: 8g / Fats: 1g)

- 1 cup cauliflower florets
- 1/4 cup canned black beans, rinsed and drained
- 1/4 cup diced tomatoes, 2 tablespoons diced red onion
- 2 tablespoons chopped fresh cilantro
- 1 tablespoon lime juice, 1/2 teaspoon chili powder
- 1/4 teaspoon cumin powder
- Salt and pepper, to taste
- Cooking spray

Cooking time: 20 minutes / servings: 1
Preparation time: 10 minutes

INSTRUCTIONS FOR COOKING:

- Preheat the air fryer to 375°F (190°C) for 5 minutes.
- In a mixing bowl, combine the cauliflower florets, black beans, diced tomatoes, diced red onion, chopped cilantro, lime juice, chili powder, cumin powder, salt, and pepper. Mix well to combine.
- Lightly spray the air fryer basket with cooking spray.
- Place the cauliflower mixture in the preheated air fryer basket.
- Cook for 18-20 minutes, tossing halfway through, until the cauliflower is tender and lightly browned.
- Remove the Mexican cauliflower mixture from the air fryer and let it cool slightly before serving.

Kale Butternut Salad

INGREDIENTS:

(Calories: 300 / Carbs: 25g / Proteins: 8g / Fats: 20g)

- 2 cups kale, stems removed and torn into bite-sized pieces
- 1/2 cup cubed butternut squash
- 2 tablespoons chopped walnuts
- 2 tablespoons crumbled feta cheese
- 1 tablespoon dried cranberries
- 1 tablespoon extra-virgin olive oil
- 1 tablespoon balsamic vinegar
- Salt and pepper, to taste

Cooking time: 15 minutes / servings: 1
Preparation time: 15 minutes

INSTRUCTIONS FOR COOKING:

- Preheat the air fryer to 375°F (190°C) for 5 minutes.
- Place the cubed butternut squash in the air fryer basket and cook for 12-15 minutes, until tender and lightly browned.
- In a mixing bowl, combine the kale, roasted butternut squash, chopped walnuts, crumbled feta cheese, and dried cranberries.
- Drizzle the olive oil and balsamic vinegar over the salad. Season with salt and pepper.
- Toss the salad gently until the ingredients are well coated with the dressing.
- Serve immediately.

Teriyaki Salmon Bowl

INGREDIENTS:

(Calories: 400 / Carbs: 45g / Proteins: 25g / Fats: 12g)

- 4 oz salmon fillet, 1 cup cooked brown rice
- 1/2 cup steamed broccoli florets
- 1/4 cup sliced carrots
- 2 tablespoons low-sodium teriyaki sauce
- 1 tablespoon sesame seeds
- 1 green onion, sliced

Cooking time: 15 minutes / servings: 1
Preparation time: 10 minutes

INSTRUCTIONS FOR COOKING:

- Preheat the air fryer to 400°F (200°C) for 5 minutes.
- Season the salmon fillet with salt and pepper.
- Place the salmon fillet in the air fryer basket and cook for 12-15 minutes, until cooked through.
- In a serving bowl, arrange the cooked brown rice, steamed broccoli florets, and sliced carrots.
- Place the cooked salmon fillet on top of the rice and vegetables.
- Drizzle the teriyaki sauce over the salmon and sprinkle with sesame seeds.
- Garnish with sliced green onions.
- Serve immediately.

Chicken Pita Wraps

INGREDIENTS:

(Calories: 350 / Carbs: 32g / Proteins: 35g / Fats: 9g)

- 4 oz boneless, skinless chicken breast
- 1 whole wheat pita bread, 1/4 cup diced tomatoes
- 1/4 cup sliced cucumber
- 2 tablespoons diced red onion
- 2 tablespoons plain Greek yogurt
- 1 tablespoon fresh lemon juice
- 1 teaspoon dried dill
- Salt and pepper, to taste

Cooking time: 15 minutes / servings: 1
Preparation time: 15 minutes

INSTRUCTIONS FOR COOKING:

- Preheat the air fryer to 375°F (190°C) for 5 minutes.
- Season the chicken breast with salt and pepper.
- Place the chicken breast in the air fryer basket and cook for 12-15 minutes, until cooked through and internal temperature reaches 165°F (74°C).
- Remove the chicken from the air fryer and let it rest for a few minutes. Then, slice it into thin strips.
- In a small bowl, combine the Greek yogurt, lemon juice, dried dill, salt, and pepper to make the sauce.
- Warm the whole wheat pita bread in the air fryer for a minute or two.
- Open the pita bread and fill it with the sliced chicken, diced tomatoes, sliced cucumber, and diced red onion.
- Drizzle the Greek yogurt sauce over the fillings.
- Fold the pita bread to form a wrap.
- Serve immediately.

Air-Fried Shrimp Cups

INGREDIENTS:

(Calories: 225 / Carbs: 20g / Proteins: 20g / Fats: 6g)

- 4 ounces raw shrimp, peeled and deveined
- 2 small low-carb tortillas, 1/4 cup diced bell peppers
- 1/4 cup diced onions, 1/4 cup diced tomatoes
- 1/2 teaspoon paprika
- 1/2 teaspoon garlic powder
- 1/2 teaspoon dried parsley
- Salt and pepper to taste
- Cooking spray

Cooking time: 10 minutes / servings: 1
Preparation time: 10 minutes

INSTRUCTIONS FOR COOKING:

- Preheat the air fryer to 400°F (200°C).
- In a bowl, combine the shrimp, diced bell peppers, onions, tomatoes, paprika, garlic powder, dried parsley, salt, and pepper. Mix well to coat the shrimp and vegetables.
- Cut each tortilla into four equal-sized circles using a round cookie cutter or a sharp knife.
- Lightly spray the air fryer basket with cooking spray.
- Place the tortilla circles in the air fryer basket and lightly spray the tops with cooking spray.
- Cook the tortillas in the air fryer for 2-3 minutes, or until they turn crispy and golden brown. Remove them from the air fryer and set aside.
- Place the shrimp and vegetable mixture in the air fryer basket and cook for 6-8 minutes, or until the shrimp is cooked through.
- Once cooked, assemble the shrimp cups by placing the cooked shrimp and vegetables inside the crispy tortilla cups.
- Serve the air fried shrimp cups immediately.

Beet Goat Cheese Salad

INGREDIENTS:

(Calories: 250 / Carbs: 15g / Proteins: 8g / Fats: 18g)

- 1 medium beet, cooked and sliced, 2 cups mixed salad greens
- 2 tablespoons crumbled goat cheese
- 1 tablespoon chopped walnuts
- 1 tablespoon balsamic vinegar
- 1 tablespoon extra-virgin olive oil
- Salt and pepper to taste

Cooking time: 0 minutes / servings: 1
Preparation time: 15 minutes

INSTRUCTIONS FOR COOKING:

- In a salad bowl, combine the mixed salad greens, sliced beets, crumbled goat cheese, and chopped walnuts.
- In a separate small bowl, whisk together the balsamic vinegar, extra-virgin olive oil, salt, and pepper to make the dressing.
- Drizzle the dressing over the salad ingredients.
- Toss the salad gently to coat all the ingredients evenly.
- Serve the beet and goat cheese salad immediately.

BBQ Chicken Ranch

INGREDIENTS:

(Calories: 200 / Carbs: 5g / Proteins: 35g / Fats: 3g)

- 4 ounces boneless, skinless chicken breast
- 1 tablespoon sugar-free BBQ sauce
- 1 tablespoon low-fat ranch dressing
- 1/2 teaspoon garlic powder
- 1/2 teaspoon paprika
- Salt and pepper to taste

Cooking time: 15 minutes / servings: 1
Preparation time: 10 minutes

INSTRUCTIONS FOR COOKING:

- Preheat the air fryer to 400°F (200°C).
- Season the chicken breast with garlic powder, paprika, salt, and pepper.
- Place the seasoned chicken breast in the air fryer basket.
- Cook the chicken breast in the air fryer for 12-15 minutes, or until the internal temperature reaches 165°F (74°C) and the chicken is cooked through.
- Remove the chicken breast from the air fryer and let it rest for a few minutes.
- Slice the cooked chicken breast into thin strips.
- Drizzle the sugar-free BBQ sauce and low-fat ranch dressing over the sliced chicken.
- Serve the BBQ chicken ranch immediately.

Mushroom Spinach Salad

INGREDIENTS:

(Calories: 80 / Carbs: 7g / Proteins: 3g / Fats: 5g)

- 2 cups fresh spinach leaves
- 4-5 medium-sized mushrooms, sliced
- 1/4 cup cherry tomatoes, halved
- 1/4 cup sliced cucumbers
- 1 tablespoon sliced red onions
- 1 tablespoon lemon juice
- 1 tablespoon extra-virgin olive oil
- Salt and pepper to taste

Cooking time: 0 minutes / servings: 1
Preparation time: 10 minutes

INSTRUCTIONS FOR COOKING:

- In a salad bowl, combine the fresh spinach leaves, sliced mushrooms, cherry tomatoes, sliced cucumbers, and red onions.
- In a small bowl, whisk together the lemon juice, extra-virgin olive oil, salt, and pepper to make the dressing.
- Drizzle the dressing over the salad ingredients.
- Toss the salad gently to coat all the ingredients evenly.
- Serve the mushroom spinach salad immediately.

Thai Beef Salad

INGREDIENTS:

(Calories: 230 / Carbs: 8g / Proteins: 25g / Fats: 10g)

- 4 ounces beef sirloin, thinly sliced, 2 cups mixed salad greens
- 1/4 cup sliced red bell peppers, 1/4 cup sliced cucumbers
- 2 tablespoons chopped fresh cilantro, 1 tablespoon lime juice
- 1 tablespoon low-sodium soy sauce, 1/2 teaspoon minced garlic
- 1/2 teaspoon minced ginger, 1/2 teaspoon honey (optional)
- Salt and pepper to taste

Cooking time: 10 minutes / servings: 1
Preparation time: 15 minutes

INSTRUCTIONS FOR COOKING:

- Preheat the air fryer to 400°F (200°C).
- Season the beef sirloin slices with salt and pepper.
- Place the seasoned beef slices in the air fryer basket and cook for 8-10 minutes, or until the beef is cooked to your desired level of doneness.
- Remove the beef slices from the air fryer and let them rest for a few minutes.
- In a salad bowl, combine the mixed salad greens, sliced red bell peppers, sliced cucumbers, and chopped fresh cilantro.
- In a separate small bowl, whisk together the lime juice, low-sodium soy sauce, minced garlic, minced ginger, honey (if using), salt, and pepper to make the dressing.
- Drizzle the dressing over the salad ingredients.
- Slice the cooked beef slices into thin strips and add them to the salad.
- Toss the salad gently to coat all the ingredients evenly.
- Serve the Thai beef salad immediately.

Mexican Chicken Bowl

INGREDIENTS:

(Calories: 330 / Carbs: 26g / Proteins: 37g / Fats: 9g)

- 4 ounces boneless, skinless chicken breast
- 1/4 cup cooked quinoa
- 1/4 cup black beans, rinsed and drained
- 1/4 cup diced tomatoes, 1/4 cup diced avocado
- 1 tablespoon chopped fresh cilantro
- 1 tablespoon lime juice, 1/2 teaspoon chili powder
- 1/2 teaspoon cumin
- Salt and pepper to taste

Cooking time: 15 minutes / servings: 1
Preparation time: 10 minutes

INSTRUCTIONS FOR COOKING:

- Preheat the air fryer to 375°F (190°C).
- Season the chicken breast with chili powder, cumin, salt, and pepper.
- Place the seasoned chicken breast in the air fryer basket and cook for 12-15 minutes, or until the internal temperature reaches 165°F (74°C) and the chicken is cooked through.
- Remove the chicken breast from the air fryer and let it rest for a few minutes. Then, slice it into thin strips.
- In a bowl, combine the cooked quinoa, black beans, diced tomatoes, diced avocado, chopped fresh cilantro, lime juice, salt, and pepper.
- Add the sliced chicken to the bowl and toss everything together to mix well.
- Serve the Mexican chicken bowl immediately.

Mediterranean Tuna Salad

INGREDIENTS:

(Calories: 230 / Carbs: 8g / Proteins: 27g / Fats: 10g)

- 1 can (5 ounces) tuna in water, drained
- 2 cups mixed salad greens, 1/4 cup sliced cucumbers
- 1/4 cup cherry tomatoes, halved
- 2 tablespoons sliced Kalamata olives
- 1 tablespoon crumbled feta cheese
- 1 tablespoon lemon juice,
- 1 tablespoon extra-virgin olive oil
- 1/2 teaspoon dried oregano, salt and pepper to taste

Cooking time: 0 minutes / servings: 1
Preparation time: 10 minutes

INSTRUCTIONS FOR COOKING:

- In a salad bowl, combine the mixed salad greens, sliced cucumbers, cherry tomatoes, Kalamata olives, and crumbled feta cheese.
- In a separate small bowl, whisk together the lemon juice, extra-virgin olive oil, dried oregano, salt, and pepper to make the dressing.
- Add the drained tuna to the salad bowl.
- Drizzle the dressing over the salad ingredients.
- Toss the salad gently to coat all the ingredients evenly.
- Serve the Mediterranean tuna salad immediately.

Turkey Veggie Skewers

INGREDIENTS:

(Calories: 150 / Carbs: 14g / Proteins: 3g / Fats: 10g)

- 1 small zucchini, sliced into rounds
- 1 small bell pepper, cut into chunks
- 1 small red onion, cut into chunks
- 4 cherry tomatoes, 2 tablespoons olive oil
- 1 teaspoon dried oregano
- 1/2 teaspoon ground cumin
- Salt and pepper to taste

Cooking time: 12 minutes / servings: 1
Preparation time: 15 minutes

INSTRUCTIONS FOR COOKING:

- Preheat the air fryer to 400°F (200°C).
- In a bowl, combine the zucchini, bell pepper, red onion, cherry tomatoes, olive oil, dried oregano, ground cumin, salt, and pepper.
- Toss the vegetables to coat them evenly with the seasonings and oil.
- Thread the vegetable pieces onto skewers, alternating between different vegetables.
- Place the vegetable skewers in the air fryer basket and cook for 10-12 minutes, or until the vegetables are tender and slightly charred.
- Remove the skewers from the air fryer and serve them hot.

Stuffed Bell Peppers

INGREDIENTS:

(Calories: 220 / Carbs: 25g / Proteins: 9g / Fats: 10g)

- 1 medium-sized bell pepper, 1/4 cup cooked quinoa
- 1/4 cup black beans, rinsed and drained
- 1/4 cup diced tomatoes, 2 tablespoons chopped fresh parsley
- 2 tablespoons shredded low-fat cheese
- 1 tablespoon olive oil, 1/2 teaspoon minced garlic
- 1/2 teaspoon dried basil, salt and pepper to taste
- 1 tablespoon red onion, finely chopped
- 2 tablespoons low-fat ranch dressing (sugar-free or reduced-fat)

Cooking time: 20 minutes / servings: 1
Preparation time: 20 minutes

INSTRUCTIONS FOR COOKING:

- Preheat the air fryer to 375°F (190°C).
- Cut the top off the bell pepper and remove the seeds and membranes from the inside.
- In a bowl, combine the cooked quinoa, black beans, diced tomatoes, chopped fresh parsley, shredded low-fat cheese, olive oil, minced garlic, dried basil, salt, and pepper.
- Stuff the bell pepper with the quinoa mixture.
- Place the stuffed bell pepper in the air fryer basket and cook for 18-20 minutes, or until the bell pepper is tender and the filling is heated through.
- Remove the stuffed bell pepper from the air fryer and let it cool slightly before serving.

Grilled Shrimp Caesar

INGREDIENTS:

(Calories: 220 / Carbs: 6g / Proteins: 25g / Fats: 11g)

- 4 ounces shrimp, peeled and deveined
- 2 cups romaine lettuce, chopped
- 2 tablespoons grated Parmesan cheese
- 1 tablespoon lemon juice
- 1 tablespoon extra-virgin olive oil
- 1/2 teaspoon minced garlic
- Salt and pepper to taste

Cooking time: 8 minutes / servings: 1
Preparation time: 10 minutes

INSTRUCTIONS FOR COOKING:

- Preheat the air fryer to 400°F (200°C).
- In a bowl, toss the shrimp with lemon juice, olive oil, minced garlic, salt, and pepper.
- Place the marinated shrimp in the air fryer basket and cook for 6-8 minutes, or until the shrimp are pink and cooked through.
- Remove the shrimp from the air fryer and let them cool slightly.
- In a salad bowl, combine the romaine lettuce, grated Parmesan cheese, and grilled shrimp.
- Drizzle with additional lemon juice and olive oil if desired.
- Toss the salad gently to coat all the ingredients evenly.
- Serve the grilled shrimp Caesar immediately.

Lentil Tahini Salad

INGREDIENTS:

(Calories: 280 / Carbs: 31g / Proteins: 14g / Fats: 12g)

- 1/2 cup cooked lentils, 2 cups mixed salad greens
- 1/4 cup diced cucumbers, 1/4 cup diced tomatoes
- 2 tablespoons chopped fresh parsley
- 2 tablespoons tahini, 1 tablespoon lemon juice
- 1/2 teaspoon minced garlic
- Salt and pepper to taste

Cooking time: 20 minutes / servings: 1
Preparation time: 15 minutes

INSTRUCTIONS FOR COOKING:

- In a salad bowl, combine the cooked lentils, mixed salad greens, diced cucumbers, diced tomatoes, and chopped fresh parsley.
- In a separate small bowl, whisk together the tahini, lemon juice, minced garlic, salt, and pepper to make the dressing.
- Drizzle the dressing over the salad ingredients.
- Toss the salad gently to coat all the ingredients evenly.
- Serve the lentil salad with tahini immediately.

Asian Chicken Noodle Salad

INGREDIENTS:

(Calories: 310 / Carbs: 35g / Proteins: 29g / Fats: 5g)

- 4 ounces boneless, skinless chicken breast
- 1 cup cooked rice noodles, 1 cup mixed salad greens
- 1/4 cup shredded carrots, 1/4 cup sliced cucumber
- 2 tablespoons chopped fresh cilantro
- 2 tablespoons low-sodium soy sauce
- 1 tablespoon rice vinegar, 1/2 teaspoon grated ginger
- 1/2 teaspoon minced garlic, 1/2 teaspoon sesame oil
- Salt and pepper to taste

Cooking time: 8 minutes / servings: 1
Preparation time: 15 minutes

INSTRUCTIONS FOR COOKING:

- Preheat the air fryer to 375°F (190°C).
- Season the chicken breast with salt and pepper.
- Place the seasoned chicken breast in the air fryer basket and cook for 6-8 minutes, or until the internal temperature reaches 165°F (74°C) and the chicken is cooked through.
- Remove the chicken breast from the air fryer and let it rest for a few minutes. Then, slice it into thin strips.
- In a bowl, combine the cooked rice noodles, mixed salad greens, shredded carrots, sliced cucumber, chopped fresh cilantro, low-sodium soy sauce, rice vinegar, grated ginger, minced garlic, sesame oil, salt, and pepper.
- Add the sliced chicken to the bowl and toss everything together to mix well.
- Serve the Asian chicken noodle salad immediately.

Watermelon Feta Salad

INGREDIENTS:

(Calories: 180 / Carbs: 15g / Proteins: 5g / Fats: 12g)

- 2 cups cubed watermelon
- 2 cups mixed salad greens
- 1/4 cup crumbled feta cheese
- 2 tablespoons sliced red onions
- 1 tablespoon balsamic vinegar
- 1 tablespoon extra-virgin olive oil
- 1/2 teaspoon honey
- Salt and pepper to taste

Cooking time: 0 minutes / servings: 1
Preparation time: 10 minutes

INSTRUCTIONS FOR COOKING:

- In a salad bowl, combine the cubed watermelon, mixed salad greens, crumbled feta cheese, and sliced red onions.
- In a separate small bowl, whisk together the balsamic vinegar, extra-virgin olive oil, honey, salt, and pepper to make the dressing.
- Drizzle the dressing over the salad ingredients.
- Toss the salad gently to coat all the ingredients evenly.
- Serve the watermelon feta salad immediately.

Lemon-Caper Baked Cod

INGREDIENTS:

(Calories: 170 / Carbs: 1g / Proteins: 25g / Fats: 8g)

- 4 ounces cod fillet
- 1 tablespoon lemon juice
- 1 tablespoon olive oil
- 1 tablespoon capers
- 1/2 teaspoon minced garlic
- Salt and pepper to taste
- Fresh parsley for garnish (optional)

Cooking time: 12 minutes / servings: 1
Preparation time: 10 minutes

INSTRUCTIONS FOR COOKING:

- Preheat the air fryer to 375°F (190°C).
- Season the cod fillet with lemon juice, olive oil, minced garlic, salt, and pepper. Let it marinate for a few minutes.
- Place the cod fillet in the air fryer basket and sprinkle capers on top.
- Cook the cod in the air fryer for 10-12 minutes, or until it flakes easily with a fork and is cooked through.
- Remove the cod from the air fryer and garnish with fresh parsley, if desired.
- Serve the lemon caper baked cod immediately.

Chicken Lettuce Wraps

INGREDIENTS:

(Calories: 220 / Carbs: 9g / Proteins: 25g / Fats: 9g)

- 4 ounces ground chicken
- 4 large lettuce leaves (such as iceberg or butter lettuce)
- 1/4 cup diced bell peppers, 1/4 cup diced onions
- 2 tablespoons low-sodium soy sauce
- 1 tablespoon rice vinegar, 1/2 teaspoon minced garlic
- 1/2 teaspoon grated ginger
- 1/4 teaspoon red pepper flakes (optional)
- Salt and pepper to taste

Cooking time: 10 minutes / servings: 1
Preparation time: 15 minutes

INSTRUCTIONS FOR COOKING:

- Preheat the air fryer to 375°F (190°C).
- In a skillet, cook the ground chicken until it is browned and cooked through. Drain any excess fat if necessary.
- Add the diced bell peppers and onions to the skillet and cook for a few minutes until they are slightly softened.
- In a small bowl, mix together the low-sodium soy sauce, rice vinegar, minced garlic, grated ginger, red pepper flakes (if using), salt, and pepper.
- Pour the sauce mixture over the chicken and vegetables in the skillet. Cook for another minute to heat through and let the flavors meld together.
- Place the lettuce leaves on a plate and spoon the chicken mixture onto each lettuce leaf.
- Roll up the lettuce leaves to form wraps.
- Serve the chicken lettuce wraps immediately.

Caprese Skewers

INGREDIENTS:

(Calories: 180 / Carbs: 4g / Proteins: 12g / Fats: 13g)

- 4 cherry tomatoes
- 4 small fresh mozzarella balls (bocconcini)
- 4 fresh basil leaves
- 1 tablespoon balsamic glaze
- 1/2 tablespoon extra-virgin olive oil
- Salt and pepper to taste

Cooking time: 0 minutes / servings: 1
Preparation time: 10 minutes

INSTRUCTIONS FOR COOKING:

- Thread a cherry tomato, a mozzarella ball, and a basil leaf onto each skewer.
- Arrange the skewers on a plate.
- Drizzle the balsamic glaze and extra-virgin olive oil over the skewers.
- Season with salt and pepper to taste.
- Serve the Caprese skewers immediately.

Greek Orzo Salad

INGREDIENTS:

(Calories: 250 / Carbs: 32g / Proteins: 8g / Fats: 10g)

- 1/2 cup cooked orzo pasta, 1/4 cup diced cucumber
- 1/4 cup diced cherry tomatoes
- 2 tablespoons crumbled feta cheese
- 1 tablespoon sliced Kalamata olives
- 1 tablespoon diced red onions
- 1 tablespoon chopped fresh parsley, 1 tablespoon lemon juice
- 1/2 tablespoon extra-virgin olive oil
- Salt and pepper to taste

Cooking time: 10 minutes / servings: 1
Preparation time: 15 minutes

INSTRUCTIONS FOR COOKING:

- In a bowl, combine the cooked orzo pasta, diced cucumber, diced cherry tomatoes, crumbled feta cheese, sliced Kalamata olives, diced red onions, and chopped fresh parsley.
- In a small separate bowl, whisk together the lemon juice, extra-virgin olive oil, salt, and pepper to make the dressing.
- Pour the dressing over the salad ingredients and toss to coat evenly.
- Adjust the seasoning with salt and pepper if needed.
- Serve the Greek orzo salad immediately.

Air-Fried Falafel Salad

INGREDIENTS:

(Calories: 350 / Carbs: 35g / Proteins: 15g / Fats: 15g)

- 4 falafel balls (store-bought or homemade)
- 2 cups mixed salad greens, 1/4 cup diced cucumbers
- 1/4 cup diced tomatoes, 2 tablespoons diced red onions
- 2 tablespoons crumbled feta cheese
- 1 tablespoon chopped fresh parsley
- 1 tablespoon lemon juice
- 1/2 tablespoon extra-virgin olive oil
- Salt and pepper to taste

Cooking time: 15 minutes / servings: 1
Preparation time: 15 minutes

INSTRUCTIONS FOR COOKING:

- Preheat the air fryer to 375°F (190°C).
- Place the falafel balls in the air fryer basket and cook for 12-15 minutes, or until they are crispy and cooked through.
- In a bowl, combine the mixed salad greens, diced cucumbers, diced tomatoes, diced red onions, crumbled feta cheese, and chopped fresh parsley.
- In a small separate bowl, whisk together the lemon juice, extra-virgin olive oil, salt, and pepper to make the dressing.
- Pour the dressing over the salad ingredients and toss to coat evenly.
- Once the falafel balls are cooked, remove them from the air fryer and let them cool for a minute. Then, slice each falafel ball into quarters.
- Arrange the sliced falafel on top of the salad.
- Serve the air fried falafel salad immediately.

Zucchini Pad Thai

INGREDIENTS:

(Calories: 250 / Carbs: 15g / Proteins: 8g / Fats: 18g)

- 1 medium zucchini, spiralized or julienned
- 2 tablespoons low-sodium soy sauce
- 1 tablespoon rice vinegar, 1 tablespoon lime juice
- 1 tablespoon natural peanut butter
- 1/2 tablespoon honey or a sugar substitute (optional)
- 1/2 tablespoon vegetable oil, 2 tablespoons chopped peanuts
- 2 tablespoons chopped fresh cilantro
- Lime wedges for serving (optional)

Cooking time: 10 minutes / servings: 1
Preparation time: 15 minutes

INSTRUCTIONS FOR COOKING:

- Preheat the air fryer to 375°F (190°C).
- In a small bowl, whisk together the low-sodium soy sauce, rice vinegar, lime juice, peanut butter, and honey (if using) to make the sauce.
- Heat the vegetable oil in a skillet over medium heat. Add the spiralized or julienned zucchini and cook for about 2-3 minutes until it becomes slightly softened.
- Pour the sauce over the zucchini in the skillet and cook for another 2-3 minutes, stirring occasionally, until the zucchini is coated and the sauce is heated through.
- Transfer the zucchini Pad Thai to a plate and sprinkle with chopped peanuts and fresh cilantro.
- Serve the zucchini Pad Thai with lime wedges on the side, if desired.

Southwest Chicken Salad

INGREDIENTS:

(Calories: 300 / Carbs: 25g / Proteins: 30g / Fats: 10g)

- 4 ounces boneless, skinless chicken breast
- 1 teaspoon olive oil, 1/2 teaspoon chili powder
- 1/4 teaspoon cumin, Salt and pepper to taste
- 2 cups mixed salad greens
- 1/4 cup canned black beans, rinsed and drained
- 1/4 cup diced tomatoes, 1/4 cup diced red onions
- 1/4 cup diced avocado, 2 tablespoons chopped fresh cilantro
- 1 tablespoon lime juice, 1 tablespoon low-fat Greek yogurt (optional)

Cooking time: 15 minutes / servings: 1
Preparation time: 10 minutes

INSTRUCTIONS FOR COOKING:

- Preheat the air fryer to 375°F (190°C).
- Season the chicken breast with chili powder, cumin, salt, and pepper.
- Rub the chicken breast with olive oil and place it in the air fryer basket.
- Cook the chicken in the air fryer for 12-15 minutes or until it reaches an internal temperature of 165°F (74°C).
- Once cooked, remove the chicken from the air fryer and let it rest for a few minutes. Then, slice it into thin strips.
- In a bowl, combine the mixed salad greens, black beans, diced tomatoes, diced red onions, diced avocado, and chopped cilantro.
- Drizzle the lime juice over the salad ingredients and toss to coat evenly.
- Top the salad with the sliced chicken breast.
- Optionally, garnish with a dollop of low-fat Greek yogurt.

Spinach Stuffed Chicken

INGREDIENTS:

(Calories: 250 / Carbs: 2g / Proteins: 40g / Fats: 8g)

- 1 boneless, skinless chicken breast
- 1/4 cup frozen chopped spinach, thawed and drained
- 2 tablespoons crumbled feta cheese
- 1/2 teaspoon dried oregano
- Salt and pepper to taste
- 1 teaspoon olive oil

Cooking time: 20 minutes / servings: 1
Preparation time: 15 minutes

INSTRUCTIONS FOR COOKING:

- Preheat the air fryer to 375°F (190°C).
- Slice the chicken breast horizontally, creating a pocket for the filling.
- In a small bowl, mix together the chopped spinach, crumbled feta cheese, dried oregano, salt, and pepper.
- Stuff the spinach and cheese mixture into the pocket of the chicken breast.
- Use toothpicks to secure the opening of the chicken breast.
- Rub the chicken breast with olive oil to coat it evenly.
- Place the chicken breast in the air fryer basket and cook for 18-20 minutes or until the chicken is cooked through and reaches an internal temperature of 165°F (74°C).
- Remove the chicken from the air fryer and let it rest for a few minutes before removing the toothpicks.
- Serve the spinach stuffed chicken as a main dish with a side of vegetables or a salad.

Thai Beef Lettuce Wraps

INGREDIENTS:

(Calories: 250 / Carbs: 8g / Proteins: 25g / Fats: 12g)

- 4 ounces lean beef, thinly sliced
- 1 tablespoon low-sodium soy sauce
- 1 teaspoon fish sauce, 1 teaspoon lime juice
- 1/2 teaspoon minced garlic, 1/2 teaspoon grated ginger
- 1/4 teaspoon red pepper flakes (optional)
- 4 large lettuce leaves, 1/4 cup shredded carrots
- 1/4 cup thinly sliced cucumbers
- 2 tablespoons chopped fresh cilantro
- 1 tablespoon chopped peanuts (optional)

Cooking time: 10 minutes / servings: 1
Preparation time: 15 minutes

INSTRUCTIONS FOR COOKING:

- In a small bowl, whisk together the soy sauce, fish sauce, lime juice, minced garlic, grated ginger, and red pepper flakes (if using).
- Place the thinly sliced beef in a shallow dish and pour the marinade over it. Let it marinate for 10 minutes.
- Preheat the air fryer to 400°F (200°C).
- Place the marinated beef in the air fryer basket and cook for 6-8 minutes, or until the beef is cooked to your desired doneness.
- Remove the beef from the air fryer and let it rest for a few minutes.
- Assemble the lettuce wraps by placing a scoop of cooked beef on each lettuce leaf.
- Top with shredded carrots, sliced cucumbers, chopped cilantro, and chopped peanuts (if using).
- Roll up the lettuce leaves to enclose the filling.
- Serve the Thai beef lettuce wraps as a flavorful and low-carb meal option.

Mediterranean Pasta Salad

INGREDIENTS:

(Calories: 200 / Carbs: 26g / Proteins: 7g / Fats: 8g)

- 1 ounce whole wheat pasta (e.g., penne or rotini)
- 1/4 cup diced cucumbers, 1/4 cup diced tomatoes
- 1/4 cup diced red onions, 2 tablespoons sliced black olives
- 2 tablespoons crumbled feta cheese
- 1 tablespoon chopped fresh parsley
- 1 tablespoon lemon juice, 1 tablespoon extra virgin olive oil
- Salt and pepper to taste

Cooking time: 10 minutes / servings: 1
Preparation time: 15 minutes

INSTRUCTIONS FOR COOKING:

- Cook the whole wheat pasta according to the package instructions until al dente. Drain and let it cool.
- In a bowl, combine the cooked pasta, diced cucumbers, diced tomatoes, diced red onions, sliced black olives, crumbled feta cheese, and chopped parsley.
- In a separate small bowl, whisk together the lemon juice, extra virgin olive oil, salt, and pepper.
- Pour the dressing over the pasta salad and toss to coat all the ingredients evenly.
- Adjust the seasoning if needed.
- Let the Mediterranean pasta salad sit for a few minutes to allow the flavors to meld together.
- Serve the pasta salad as a refreshing and satisfying side dish or light meal.

Asian Tofu Salad

INGREDIENTS:

(Calories: 250 / Carbs: 16g / Proteins: 18g / Fats: 14g)

- 4 ounces firm tofu, drained and cubed
- 1 cup mixed salad greens, 1/4 cup shredded carrots
- 1/4 cup sliced cucumbers, 1/4 cup edamame beans, cooked
- 2 tablespoons sliced almonds
- 1 tablespoon low-sodium soy sauce
- 1 tablespoon rice vinegar, 1 teaspoon sesame oil
- 1/2 teaspoon grated ginger, 1/2 teaspoon honey (optional)
- Sesame seeds for garnish

Cooking time: 10 minutes / servings: 1
Preparation time: 15 minutes

INSTRUCTIONS FOR COOKING:

- Preheat the air fryer to 400°F (200°C) for 5 minutes.
- In a mixing bowl, toss the tofu cubes with 1/2 tablespoon of soy sauce until well coated.
- Place the tofu cubes in the air fryer basket and cook for 10 minutes, shaking halfway through, until golden and crispy.
- In a separate bowl, whisk together the remaining soy sauce, rice vinegar, sesame oil, grated ginger, and honey (if using).
- In a serving bowl, arrange the mixed salad greens, shredded carrots, sliced cucumbers, and edamame beans.
- Add the air-fried tofu cubes on top and drizzle the dressing over the salad.
- Sprinkle with sliced almonds and sesame seeds for garnish.

Grilled Shrimp Salad

INGREDIENTS:

(Calories: 180 / Carbs: 10g / Proteins: 20g / Fats: 7g)

- 4 ounces shrimp, peeled and deveined
- 2 cups mixed salad greens, 1/4 cup cherry tomatoes, halved
- 1/4 cup sliced cucumbers, 1/4 cup sliced red bell peppers
- 2 tablespoons chopped fresh cilantro
- 1 tablespoon lemon juice
- 1 tablespoon olive oil
- 1/2 teaspoon minced garlic
- Salt and pepper to taste

Cooking time: 10 minutes / servings: 1
Preparation time: 15 minutes

INSTRUCTIONS FOR COOKING:

- Preheat the grill or air fryer to medium-high heat.
- In a bowl, toss the shrimp with olive oil, minced garlic, salt, and pepper.
- Grill the shrimp for 2-3 minutes on each side until pink and cooked through.
- In a large salad bowl, combine the mixed salad greens, cherry tomatoes, sliced cucumbers, sliced red bell peppers, and chopped cilantro.
- In a small bowl, whisk together the lemon juice, olive oil, salt, and pepper to make the dressing.
- Add the grilled shrimp to the salad and drizzle the dressing over the top.
- Toss gently to coat all the ingredients.

Turkey Taco Lettuce Wraps

INGREDIENTS:

(Calories: 180 / Carbs: 8g / Proteins: 20g / Fats: 7g)

- 4 ounces ground turkey, 1/4 cup diced onions
- 1/4 cup diced bell peppers, 1/2 teaspoon chili powder
- 1/4 teaspoon cumin, 1/4 teaspoon garlic powder, salt and pepper to taste
- 4 large lettuce leaves (such as romaine or iceberg)
- 2 tablespoons salsa, 2 tablespoons diced tomatoes
- 1 tablespoon chopped fresh cilantro
- Optional toppings: shredded cheese, diced avocado, sour cream

Cooking time: 10 minutes / servings: 1
Preparation time: 15 minutes

INSTRUCTIONS FOR COOKING:

- Preheat the air fryer to 400°F (200°C) for 5 minutes.
- In a non-stick skillet, cook the ground turkey over medium heat until browned and cooked through.
- Add the diced onions and bell peppers to the skillet and cook for an additional 2-3 minutes until softened.
- Stir in the chili powder, cumin, garlic powder, salt, and pepper. Cook for another minute to combine the flavors.
- Place the lettuce leaves on a serving plate. Spoon the turkey mixture onto each lettuce leaf.
- Top with salsa, diced tomatoes, and chopped cilantro.
- Optional: Add your choice of toppings such as shredded cheese, diced avocado, or sour cream.

Eggplant Mozzarella Stack

INGREDIENTS:

(Calories: 220 / Carbs: 10g / Proteins: 8g / Fats: 17g)

- 1 small eggplant, sliced into rounds,
- 2 tablespoons olive oil
- 1/4 teaspoon dried oregano
- Salt and pepper to taste
- 1 small tomato, sliced
- 2 ounces fresh mozzarella, sliced
- 1 tablespoon balsamic vinegar
- Fresh basil leaves for garnish

Cooking time: 20 minutes / servings: 1
Preparation time: 10 minutes

INSTRUCTIONS FOR COOKING:

- Preheat the air fryer to 400°F (200°C) for 5 minutes.
- Brush both sides of the eggplant slices with olive oil and season with dried oregano, salt, and pepper.
- Place the eggplant slices in the air fryer basket and cook for 10 minutes, flipping halfway through, until tender and slightly browned.
- Remove the eggplant slices from the air fryer and let them cool slightly.
- Assemble the eggplant stacks by layering one eggplant slice, a tomato slice, and a mozzarella slice. Repeat to make a stack with 3 layers.
- Drizzle the balsamic vinegar over the stacks.
- Garnish with fresh basil leaves.

Quinoa Stuffed Peppers

INGREDIENTS:

(Calories: 150 / Carbs: 27g / Proteins: 5g / Fats: 2g)

- 1 bell pepper (any color), 1/4 cup cooked quinoa
- 2 tablespoons diced onions, 2 tablespoons diced zucchini
- 2 tablespoons diced tomatoes
- 2 tablespoons diced mushrooms
- 1/4 teaspoon garlic powder, 1/4 teaspoon dried oregano
- Salt and pepper to taste
- Optional toppings: grated Parmesan cheese, chopped fresh parsley

Cooking time: 30 minutes / servings: 1
Preparation time: 15 minutes

INSTRUCTIONS FOR COOKING:

- Preheat the air fryer to 375°F (190°C) for 5 minutes.
- Cut the top off the bell pepper and remove the seeds and membrane.
- In a bowl, mix together the cooked quinoa, diced onions, zucchini, tomatoes, mushrooms, garlic powder, dried oregano, salt, and pepper.
- Stuff the quinoa mixture into the bell pepper.
- Place the stuffed pepper in the air fryer basket and cook for 25-30 minutes, or until the pepper is tender.
- Optional: Sprinkle grated Parmesan cheese and chopped fresh parsley on top before serving.

Lemon Herb Grilled Chicken

INGREDIENTS:

(Calories: 170 / Carbs: 2g / Proteins: 26g / Fats: 6g)

- 4 ounces boneless, skinless chicken breast
- Juice of 1/2 lemon, 1 teaspoon olive oil
- 1/2 teaspoon dried oregano, 1/2 teaspoon dried basil
- 1/4 teaspoon garlic powder
- Salt and pepper to taste
- Optional garnish: fresh lemon slices, chopped fresh parsley

Cooking time: 15 minutes / servings: 1
Preparation time: 10 minutes (plus marinating time)

INSTRUCTIONS FOR COOKING:

- In a bowl, whisk together the lemon juice, olive oil, dried oregano, dried basil, garlic powder, salt, and pepper.
- Place the chicken breast in a resealable plastic bag and pour the marinade over it. Seal the bag and let it marinate in the refrigerator for at least 30 minutes, or up to 4 hours.
- Preheat the air fryer to 400°F (200°C) for 5 minutes.
- Remove the chicken breast from the marinade, allowing any excess marinade to drip off.
- Place the chicken breast in the air fryer basket and cook for 12-15 minutes, flipping halfway through, until the internal temperature reaches 165°F (74°C).
- Optional: Garnish with fresh lemon slices and chopped fresh parsley before serving.

Zucchini Noodle Salad

INGREDIENTS:

(Calories: 120 / Carbs: 8g / Proteins: 2g / Fats: 10g)

- 1 medium zucchini
- 1/4 cup cherry tomatoes, halved
- 2 tablespoons diced red onion
- 2 tablespoons diced cucumber
- 1 tablespoon chopped fresh basil
- 1 tablespoon extra-virgin olive oil
- 1 tablespoon lemon juice
- Salt and pepper to taste
- Optional toppings: crumbled feta cheese, sliced almonds

Cooking time: 0 minutes / servings: 1
Preparation time: 15 minutes

INSTRUCTIONS FOR COOKING:

- Using a spiralizer or a vegetable peeler, make zucchini noodles from the zucchini.
- In a bowl, combine the zucchini noodles, cherry tomatoes, red onion, cucumber, and fresh basil.
- In a separate small bowl, whisk together the olive oil, lemon juice, salt, and pepper.
- Pour the dressing over the salad and toss to combine.
- Optional: Top with crumbled feta cheese and sliced almonds before serving.

Southwest Quinoa Bowl

INGREDIENTS:

(Calories: 180 / Carbs: 27g / Proteins: 7g / Fats: 6g)

- 1/4 cup cooked quinoa
- 1/4 cup black beans, rinsed and drained
- 1/4 cup diced bell peppers (any color)
- 2 tablespoons diced red onion
- 2 tablespoons diced avocado
- 2 tablespoons diced tomatoes
- 1 tablespoon chopped fresh cilantro
- 1 tablespoon lime juice
- 1/2 teaspoon ground cumin
- 1/4 teaspoon chili powder
- Salt and pepper to taste
- Optional toppings: plain Greek yogurt, sliced jalapeños

Cooking time: 15 minutes / servings: 1
Preparation time: 15 minutes

INSTRUCTIONS FOR COOKING:

- In a bowl, combine the cooked quinoa, black beans, diced bell peppers, red onion, avocado, tomatoes, and fresh cilantro.
- In a separate small bowl, whisk together the lime juice, ground cumin, chili powder, salt, and pepper.
- Pour the dressing over the quinoa mixture and toss to combine.
- Optional: Top with a dollop of plain Greek yogurt and sliced jalapeños before serving.

Chapter 6: Poultry and meat

Grilled Lemon Chicken
Roasted Turkey Breast
Balsamic Glazed Salmon
Grilled Shrimp
Mediterranean Chicken
Teriyaki Beef Skewers
Roasted Chicken Thighs
Cajun Grilled Chicken
Air-Fried Chicken Wings
Honey Mustard Pork Tenderloin
Grilled Lamb Chops
Spicy Shrimp Skewers
Parmesan Chicken Tenders
Honey Sriracha Salmon
Grilled Chicken Breast
Sesame Beef Stir-Fry
Balsamic Pork Chops
Teriyaki Turkey Meatballs
Grilled Pork Tenderloin
Greek Grilled Chicken

Grilled Chicken Drumsticks
Lime Grilled Shrimp
Roasted Turkey Legs
Glazed Pork Belly Slices
Grilled Sirloin Steak
Honey Mustard Chicken
Bacon-Wrapped Chicken
Orange Ginger Salmon
Teriyaki Chicken Thighs
Grilled Shrimp Skewers
Glazed Pork Belly Bites
Grilled Lamb Skewers
Tandoori Chicken
Cajun Shrimp Skewers
Air-Fried Chicken Drumsticks
Honey Garlic Salmon
Grilled Pork Chops
Ginger Soy Turkey Breast
Garlic Grilled Steak
Honey Mustard Chicken Thighs

Chapter 6: Poultry and meat

Grilled Lemon Chicken

INGREDIENTS:

(Calories: 180 / Carbs: 2g / Proteins: 30g / Fats: 5g)

- 4 oz boneless, skinless chicken breast
- 1 tablespoon fresh lemon juice
- 1 teaspoon olive oil
- 1 clove garlic, minced
- 1/2 teaspoon dried oregano
- Salt and pepper to taste

Cooking time: 20 minutes / servings: 1
Preparation time: 10 minutes

INSTRUCTIONS FOR COOKING:

- Preheat the air fryer to 375°F (190°C) for 5 minutes.
- In a small bowl, mix together the lemon juice, olive oil, minced garlic, dried oregano, salt, and pepper.
- Place the chicken breast in a resealable plastic bag and pour the marinade over it. Seal the bag and massage the marinade into the chicken, ensuring it is well coated. Let it marinate for 10 minutes.
- Remove the chicken from the marinade and place it in the air fryer basket.
- Cook the chicken in the air fryer for 10 minutes, then flip it over and cook for an additional 10 minutes, or until the internal temperature reaches 165°F (74°C) and the chicken is cooked through.
- Once cooked, remove the chicken from the air fryer and let it rest for a few minutes before serving.
- Serve the grilled lemon chicken with a side of steamed vegetables or a fresh salad.

Roasted Turkey Breast

INGREDIENTS:

(Calories: 160 / Carbs: 0g / Proteins: 34g / Fats: 2g)

- 4 oz turkey breast
- 1 teaspoon olive oil
- 1/2 teaspoon dried thyme
- 1/2 teaspoon dried rosemary
- 1/2 teaspoon dried sage
- Salt and pepper to taste

Cooking time: 25 minutes / servings: 1
Preparation time: 15 minutes

INSTRUCTIONS FOR COOKING:

- Preheat the air fryer to 375°F (190°C) for 5 minutes.
- Rub the turkey breast with olive oil, ensuring it is evenly coated.
- In a small bowl, mix together the dried thyme, dried rosemary, dried sage, salt, and pepper.
- Sprinkle the herb mixture over the turkey breast, pressing it gently to adhere.
- Place the turkey breast in the air fryer basket.
- Cook the turkey in the air fryer for 15 minutes, then flip it over and cook for an additional 10 minutes, or until the internal temperature reaches 165°F (74°C) and the turkey is cooked through.
- Once cooked, remove the turkey breast from the air fryer and let it rest for a few minutes before slicing and serving.
- Serve the herb-roasted turkey breast with a side of roasted vegetables or a mixed green salad.

Balsamic Glazed Salmon

INGREDIENTS:

(Calories: 240 / Carbs: 4g / Proteins: 26g / Fats: 13g)

- 4 oz salmon fillet
- 1 tablespoon balsamic vinegar
- 1 teaspoon olive oil
- 1/2 teaspoon Dijon mustard
- 1/2 teaspoon honey (optional, omit for a sugar-free version)
- Salt and pepper to taste

Cooking time: 12 minutes / servings: 1
Preparation time: 10 minutes

INSTRUCTIONS FOR COOKING:

- Preheat the air fryer to 400°F (200°C) for 5 minutes.
- In a small bowl, whisk together the balsamic vinegar, olive oil, Dijon mustard, honey (if using), salt, and pepper.
- Place the salmon fillet in a shallow dish and pour the balsamic glaze over it. Let it marinate for 5 minutes.
- Remove the salmon from the marinade and place it in the air fryer basket.
- Cook the salmon in the air fryer for 8 minutes. Open the air fryer, brush the salmon with the remaining glaze, and cook for an additional 4 minutes or until the salmon flakes easily with a fork and reaches an internal temperature of 145°F (63°C).
- Once cooked, remove the salmon from the air fryer and let it rest for a few minutes before serving.
- Serve the balsamic glazed salmon with a side of steamed vegetables or a leafy green salad.

Grilled Shrimp

INGREDIENTS:

(Calories: 140 / Carbs: 2g / Proteins: 24g / Fats: 3g)

- 4 oz shrimp, peeled and deveined
- 1 tablespoon fresh lemon juice
- 1 tablespoon fresh lime juice
- 1 teaspoon olive oil
- 1 clove garlic, minced
- 1/2 teaspoon paprika
- Salt and pepper to taste

Cooking time: 8 minutes / servings: 1
Preparation time: 10 minutes

INSTRUCTIONS FOR COOKING:

- Preheat the air fryer to 400°F (200°C) for 5 minutes.
- In a bowl, combine the lemon juice, lime juice, olive oil, minced garlic, paprika, salt, and pepper.
- Add the shrimp to the bowl and toss to coat them evenly in the marinade. Let them marinate for 10 minutes.
- Remove the shrimp from the marinade and place them in the air fryer basket.
- Cook the shrimp in the air fryer for 4 minutes. Open the air fryer, flip the shrimp over, and cook for an additional 4 minutes or until they are pink, opaque, and cooked through.
- Once cooked, remove the shrimp from the air fryer and let them rest for a few minutes before serving.
- Serve the citrus-marinated grilled shrimp with a side of quinoa or a cucumber salad.

Mediterranean Chicken

INGREDIENTS:

(Calories: 220 / Carbs: 1g / Proteins: 32g / Fats: 9g)

- 4 oz boneless, skinless chicken breast
- 1 tablespoon olive oil
- 1 teaspoon lemon juice
- 1 clove garlic, minced
- 1/2 teaspoon dried oregano
- 1/4 teaspoon dried thyme
- Salt and pepper to taste

Cooking time: 15 minutes / servings: 1
Preparation time: 10 minutes

INSTRUCTIONS FOR COOKING:

- Preheat the air fryer to 375°F (190°C) for 5 minutes.
- In a small bowl, combine the olive oil, lemon juice, minced garlic, dried oregano, dried thyme, salt, and pepper.
- Place the chicken breast in a shallow dish and pour the marinade over it. Let it marinate for 10 minutes.
- Remove the chicken from the marinade and place it in the air fryer basket.
- Cook the chicken in the air fryer for 8 minutes. Open the air fryer, flip the chicken over, and cook for an additional 7 minutes or until the internal temperature reaches 165°F (74°C) and the chicken is cooked through.
- Once cooked, remove the chicken from the air fryer and let it rest for a few minutes before serving.
- Serve the Mediterranean grilled chicken with a side of Greek salad or roasted vegetables.

Teriyaki Beef Skewers

INGREDIENTS:

(Calories: 250 / Carbs: 4g / Proteins: 26g / Fats: 14g)

- 4 oz beef sirloin, cut into cubes
- 2 tablespoons low-sodium teriyaki sauce
- 1 teaspoon low-sodium soy sauce
- 1 teaspoon honey (optional, omit for a sugar-free version)
- 1/2 teaspoon sesame oil
- 1/4 teaspoon garlic powder
- Bamboo skewers, soaked in water for 30 minutes

Cooking time: 10 minutes / servings: 1
Preparation time: 15 minutes

INSTRUCTIONS FOR COOKING:

- Preheat the air fryer to 400°F (200°C) for 5 minutes.
- In a bowl, mix together the teriyaki sauce, soy sauce, honey (if using), sesame oil, and garlic powder.
- Add the beef cubes to the bowl and toss to coat them in the marinade. Let them marinate for 10 minutes.
- Thread the marinated beef cubes onto the soaked bamboo skewers.
- Place the skewers in the air fryer basket.
- Cook the beef skewers in the air fryer for 5 minutes. Open the air fryer, flip the skewers over, and cook for an additional 5 minutes or until the beef reaches the desired level of doneness.
- Once cooked, remove the skewers from the air fryer and let them rest for a few minutes before serving.
- Serve the teriyaki beef skewers with a side of steamed broccoli or cauliflower rice.

Roasted Chicken Thighs

INGREDIENTS:

(Calories: 230 / Carbs: 1g / Proteins: 24g / Fats: 15g)

- 1 chicken thigh, bone-in and skin-on
- 1 teaspoon olive oil
- 1 clove garlic, minced
- 1/2 teaspoon dried rosemary
- Salt and pepper to taste

Cooking time: 25 minutes / servings: 1
Preparation time: 10 minutes

INSTRUCTIONS FOR COOKING:

- Preheat the air fryer to 400°F (200°C) for 5 minutes.
- In a small bowl, mix together the olive oil, minced garlic, dried rosemary, salt, and pepper.
- Rub the chicken thigh with the garlic and rosemary mixture, making sure to coat it evenly.
- Place the chicken thigh in the air fryer basket, skin-side down.
- Cook the chicken in the air fryer for 15 minutes. Open the air fryer, flip the chicken over, and cook for an additional 10 minutes or until the chicken reaches an internal temperature of 165°F (74°C) and the skin is crispy.
- Once cooked, remove the chicken from the air fryer and let it rest for a few minutes before serving.
- Serve the garlic and rosemary roasted chicken thigh with a side of roasted vegetables or a mixed green salad.

Cajun Grilled Chicken

INGREDIENTS:

(Calories: 180 / Carbs: 1g / Proteins: 31g / Fats: 5g)

- 1 chicken breast, boneless and skinless
- 1 teaspoon olive oil
- 1/2 teaspoon Cajun seasoning
- 1/4 teaspoon paprika
- 1/4 teaspoon garlic powder
- Salt and pepper to taste

Cooking time: 12 minutes / servings: 1
Preparation time: 10 minutes

INSTRUCTIONS FOR COOKING:

- Preheat the air fryer to 400°F (200°C) for 5 minutes.
- In a small bowl, combine the olive oil, Cajun seasoning, paprika, garlic powder, salt, and pepper.
- Rub the chicken breast with the Cajun spice mixture, ensuring it is evenly coated.
- Place the chicken breast in the air fryer basket.
- Cook the chicken in the air fryer for 6 minutes. Open the air fryer, flip the chicken over, and cook for an additional 6 minutes or until the chicken reaches an internal temperature of 165°F (74°C).
- Once cooked, remove the chicken from the air fryer and let it rest for a few minutes before serving.
- Serve the Cajun spiced grilled chicken with a side of steamed vegetables or a quinoa salad.

Air-Fried Chicken Wings

INGREDIENTS:

(Calories: 210 / Carbs: 0g / Proteins: 23g / Fats: 13g)

- 4 chicken wings
- 1 teaspoon olive oil
- 1/2 teaspoon lemon zest
- 1/2 teaspoon ground black pepper
- 1/4 teaspoon garlic powder
- Salt to taste

Cooking time: 20 minutes / servings: 1
Preparation time: 10 minutes

INSTRUCTIONS FOR COOKING:

- Preheat the air fryer to 400°F (200°C) for 5 minutes.
- In a bowl, combine the olive oil, lemon zest, ground black pepper, garlic powder, and salt.
- Add the chicken wings to the bowl and toss them in the seasoning mixture until evenly coated.
- Place the chicken wings in the air fryer basket, making sure they are not overcrowded.
- Cook the chicken wings in the air fryer for 10 minutes. Open the air fryer, flip the wings over, and cook for an additional 10 minutes or until the chicken is cooked through and golden brown.
- Once cooked, remove the chicken wings from the air fryer and let them rest for a few minutes before serving.
- Serve the lemon pepper air fried chicken wings with a side of celery sticks or a fresh salad.

Honey Mustard Pork Tenderloin

INGREDIENTS:

(Calories: 250 / Carbs: 11g / Proteins: 26g / Fats: 9g)

- 4 oz pork tenderloin
- 1 tablespoon Dijon mustard
- 1 tablespoon honey
- 1 teaspoon low-sodium soy sauce
- 1/2 teaspoon garlic powder
- Salt and pepper to taste

Cooking time: 20 minutes / servings: 1
Preparation time: 10 minutes

INSTRUCTIONS FOR COOKING:

- Preheat the air fryer to 400°F (200°C) for 5 minutes.
- In a small bowl, mix together the Dijon mustard, honey, soy sauce, garlic powder, salt, and pepper.
- Coat the pork tenderloin with the honey mustard glaze, making sure it is evenly coated.
- Place the pork tenderloin in the air fryer basket.
- Cook the pork tenderloin in the air fryer for 10 minutes. Open the air fryer, flip the tenderloin over, and cook for an additional 10 minutes or until the pork reaches an internal temperature of 145°F (63°C).
- Once cooked, remove the pork tenderloin from the air fryer and let it rest for a few minutes before slicing.
- Serve the honey mustard glazed pork tenderloin with a side of roasted vegetables or steamed brown rice.

Grilled Lamb Chops

INGREDIENTS:

(Calories: 320 / Carbs: 2g / Proteins: 32g / Fats: 21g)

- 2 lamb chops
- 1 teaspoon olive oil
- 2 cloves garlic, minced
- 1/2 teaspoon dried rosemary
- 1/2 teaspoon dried thyme
- Salt and pepper to taste

Cooking time: 10 minutes / servings: 1
Preparation time: 10 minutes

INSTRUCTIONS FOR COOKING:

- Preheat the air fryer to 400°F (200°C) for 5 minutes.
- In a small bowl, mix together the olive oil, minced garlic, dried rosemary, dried thyme, salt, and pepper.
- Rub the lamb chops with the garlic and herb mixture, making sure to coat them evenly.
- Place the lamb chops in the air fryer basket.
- Cook the lamb chops in the air fryer for 5 minutes. Open the air fryer, flip the chops over, and cook for an additional 5 minutes or until the lamb reaches the desired level of doneness.
- Once cooked, remove the lamb chops from the air fryer and let them rest for a few minutes before serving.
- Serve the garlic and herb grilled lamb chops with a side of roasted vegetables or a green salad.

Spicy Shrimp Skewers

INGREDIENTS:

(Calories: 120 / Carbs: 2g / Proteins: 18g / Fats: 5g)

- 6 large shrimp, peeled and deveined
- 1 teaspoon olive oil
- 1/2 teaspoon paprika
- 1/4 teaspoon cayenne pepper
- 1/4 teaspoon garlic powder
- Salt and pepper to taste

Cooking time: 8 minutes / servings: 1
Preparation time: 15 minutes

INSTRUCTIONS FOR COOKING:

- Preheat the air fryer to 400°F (200°C) for 5 minutes.
- In a bowl, combine the olive oil, paprika, cayenne pepper, garlic powder, salt, and pepper.
- Add the shrimp to the bowl and toss them in the spicy seasoning mixture until coated.
- Thread the shrimp onto skewers.
- Place the shrimp skewers in the air fryer basket.
- Cook the shrimp in the air fryer for 4 minutes. Open the air fryer, flip the skewers over, and cook for an additional 4 minutes or until the shrimp are pink and cooked through.
- Once cooked, remove the shrimp skewers from the air fryer and let them cool for a minute before serving.
- Serve the spicy grilled shrimp skewers with a side of cauliflower rice or a cucumber and tomato salad.

Parmesan Chicken Tenders

INGREDIENTS:

(Calories: 250 / Carbs: 4g / Proteins: 36g / Fats: 9g)

- 1 boneless, skinless chicken breast (4-5 ounces)
- 1/4 cup grated Parmesan cheese
- 1/4 cup almond flour
- 1/2 teaspoon garlic powder
- 1/2 teaspoon paprika
- Salt and pepper to taste
- Cooking spray

Cooking time: 15 minutes / servings: 1
Preparation time: 10 minutes

INSTRUCTIONS FOR COOKING:

- Preheat your air fryer to 400°F (200°C) for about 5 minutes.
- In a shallow bowl, mix together the grated Parmesan cheese, almond flour, garlic powder, paprika, salt, and pepper.
- Cut the chicken breast into strips or tenders.
- Dip each chicken tender into the Parmesan mixture, pressing gently to coat all sides.
- Place the coated chicken tenders in the air fryer basket, making sure they are not overlapping.
- Lightly spray the chicken tenders with cooking spray to help them turn crispy.
- Cook the chicken tenders in the air fryer for 10-12 minutes, flipping them halfway through, until they are golden brown and cooked through.
- Remove the chicken tenders from the air fryer and let them rest for a couple of minutes before serving.

Honey Sriracha Salmon

INGREDIENTS:

(Calories: 300 / Carbs: 14g / Proteins: 28g / Fats: 15g)

- 1 salmon fillet (4-5 ounces)
- 1 tablespoon honey
- 1 tablespoon reduced-sodium soy sauce
- 1/2 tablespoon Sriracha sauce
- 1/2 teaspoon grated fresh ginger
- 1/2 teaspoon minced garlic, cooking spray
- Optional garnish: chopped green onions or sesame seeds

Cooking time: 12 minutes / servings: 1
Preparation time: 5 minutes

INSTRUCTIONS FOR COOKING:

- Preheat your air fryer to 400°F (200°C) for about 5 minutes.
- In a small bowl, whisk together the honey, soy sauce, Sriracha sauce, grated ginger, and minced garlic to make the glaze.
- Pat dry the salmon fillet with a paper towel and place it on a greased air fryer basket or tray.
- Brush the glaze generously over the salmon, ensuring it is evenly coated.
- Lightly spray the air fryer basket or tray with cooking spray to prevent sticking.
- Place the salmon fillet in the air fryer and cook for 10-12 minutes or until the salmon is cooked through and flakes easily with a fork.
- If desired, sprinkle chopped green onions or sesame seeds on top of the cooked salmon for garnish.

Grilled Chicken Breast

INGREDIENTS:

(Calories: 150 / Carbs: 0g / Proteins: 31g / Fats: 2g)

- 1 boneless, skinless chicken breast (4-5 ounces)
- 1 teaspoon dried Italian herb seasoning
- 1/2 teaspoon garlic powder
- Salt and pepper to taste
- Cooking spray

Cooking time: 15 minutes / servings: 1
Preparation time: 10 minutes

INSTRUCTIONS FOR COOKING:

- Preheat your air fryer to 400°F (200°C) for about 5 minutes.
- Season the chicken breast with dried Italian herb seasoning, garlic powder, salt, and pepper. Rub the seasoning evenly on both sides of the chicken breast.
- Lightly spray the air fryer basket or tray with cooking spray to prevent sticking.
- Place the seasoned chicken breast in the air fryer basket or tray.
- Cook the chicken breast in the air fryer for 12-15 minutes or until it reaches an internal temperature of 165°F (74°C) and is no longer pink in the center. Flip the chicken breast halfway through cooking.
- Once cooked, remove the chicken breast from the air fryer and let it rest for a couple of minutes before serving.

Sesame Beef Stir-Fry

INGREDIENTS:

(Calories: 250 / Carbs: 12g / Proteins: 25g / Fats: 11g)

- 4 ounces beef sirloin, thinly sliced
- 1 tablespoon reduced-sodium soy sauce
- 1 tablespoon rice vinegar, 1/2 tablespoon sesame oil
- 1/2 tablespoon grated fresh ginger
- 1 clove garlic, minced
- 1 cup mixed vegetables (broccoli florets, bell peppers, carrots, etc.)
- Salt and pepper to taste, cooking spray

Cooking time: 10 minutes / servings: 1
Preparation time: 15 minutes

INSTRUCTIONS FOR COOKING:

- Preheat your air fryer to 400°F (200°C) for about 5 minutes.
- In a small bowl, whisk together the soy sauce, rice vinegar, sesame oil, grated ginger, and minced garlic to make the marinade.
- Place the thinly sliced beef in a shallow dish and pour the marinade over it. Let it marinate for 10 minutes.
- Lightly spray the air fryer basket or tray with cooking spray to prevent sticking.
- Place the marinated beef and mixed vegetables in the air fryer.
- Cook the beef stir-fry in the air fryer for 8-10 minutes, stirring halfway through, until the beef is cooked to your desired doneness and the vegetables are tender-crisp.
- Season with salt and pe pper to taste.
- Serve the sesame ginger beef stir-fry hot.

Balsamic Pork Chops

INGREDIENTS:

(Calories: 200 / Carbs: 3g / Proteins: 28g / Fats: 9g)

- 1 boneless pork chop (4-5 ounces)
- 1 tablespoon balsamic vinegar, 1 teaspoon olive oil
- 1/2 teaspoon Dijon mustard
- 1/2 teaspoon dried rosemary
- Salt and pepper to taste
- Cooking spray

Cooking time: 15 minutes / servings: 1
Preparation time: 10 minutes

INSTRUCTIONS FOR COOKING:

- Preheat your air fryer to 400°F (200°C) for about 5 minutes.
- In a small bowl, whisk together the balsamic vinegar, olive oil, Dijon mustard, dried rosemary, salt, and pepper to make the glaze.
- Pat dry the pork chop with a paper towel and place it on a greased air fryer basket or tray.
- Brush the glaze generously over the pork chop, coating both sides.
- Lightly spray the air fryer basket or tray with cooking spray to prevent sticking.
- Place the pork chop in the air fryer and cook for 12-15 minutes, flipping it halfway through, until the pork chop reaches an internal temperature of 145°F (63°C) and is slightly pink in the center.
- Once cooked, remove the pork chop from the air fryer and let it rest for a couple of minutes before serving.

Teriyaki Turkey Meatballs

INGREDIENTS:

(Calories: 180 / Carbs: 8g / Proteins: 22g / Fats: 6g)

- 4 ounces ground turkey
- 1 tablespoon reduced-sodium soy sauce
- 1 tablespoon water, 1/2 tablespoon honey
- 1/2 tablespoon rice vinegar
- 1/2 teaspoon grated fresh ginger
- 1 clove garlic, minced
- 1/4 teaspoon cornstarch (optional, for thickening sauce)
- Cooking spray

Cooking time: 15 minutes / servings: 1
Preparation time: 15 minutes

INSTRUCTIONS FOR COOKING:

- Preheat your air fryer to 400°F (200°C) for about 5 minutes.
- In a bowl, mix together the ground turkey, soy sauce, water, honey, rice vinegar, grated ginger, and minced garlic until well combined.
- Shape the turkey mixture into small meatballs, about 1-inch in diameter.
- Lightly spray the air fryer basket or tray with cooking spray to prevent sticking.
- Place the turkey meatballs in the air fryer, making sure they are not touching.
- Cook the meatballs in the air fryer for 12-15 minutes, shaking the basket or flipping the meatballs halfway through, until they are cooked through and browned.
- If desired, in a small saucepan, whisk together the cornstarch with a little water to make a slurry. Add the slurry to the remaining teriyaki glaze and cook over low heat until thickened. Drizzle the thickened sauce over the cooked meatballs.
- Serve the teriyaki glazed turkey meatballs hot.

Grilled Pork Tenderloin

INGREDIENTS:

(Calories: 180 / Carbs: 1g / Proteins: 25g / Fats: 8g)

- 4-ounce pork tenderloin
- 1 tablespoon lemon juice
- 1 teaspoon olive oil
- 1/2 teaspoon dried thyme
- 1/2 teaspoon dried rosemary
- Salt and pepper to taste
- Cooking spray

Cooking time: 15 minutes / servings: 1
Preparation time: 10 minutes

INSTRUCTIONS FOR COOKING:

- Preheat your air fryer to 400°F (200°C) for about 5 minutes.
- In a small bowl, mix together the lemon juice, olive oil, dried thyme, dried rosemary, salt, and pepper to make the marinade.
- Place the pork tenderloin in a shallow dish and pour the marinade over it. Make sure the pork is coated evenly.
- Lightly spray the air fryer basket or tray with cooking spray to prevent sticking.
- Place the marinated pork tenderloin in the air fryer.
- Cook the pork tenderloin in the air fryer for 12-15 minutes, flipping it halfway through, until it reaches an internal temperature of 145°F (63°C) and is slightly pink in the center.
- Once cooked, remove the pork tenderloin from the air fryer and let it rest for a couple of minutes before slicing and serving.

Greek Grilled Chicken

INGREDIENTS:

(Calories: 180 / Carbs: 2g / Proteins: 28g / Fats: 6g)

- 4 ounces boneless, skinless chicken breast, cut into cubes
- 1 tablespoon lemon juice
- 1 tablespoon olive oil
- 1 clove garlic, minced
- 1/2 teaspoon dried oregano
- Salt and pepper to taste
- Cooking spray

Cooking time: 15 minutes / servings: 1
Preparation time: 15 minutes

INSTRUCTIONS FOR COOKING:

- Preheat your air fryer to 400°F (200°C) for about 5 minutes.
- In a bowl, combine the lemon juice, olive oil, minced garlic, dried oregano, salt, and pepper to make the marinade.
- Add the chicken breast cubes to the marinade and toss to coat them evenly. Let it marinate for 10 minutes.
- Lightly spray the air fryer basket or tray with cooking spray to prevent sticking.
- Skewer the marinated chicken cubes onto skewers.
- Place the chicken skewers in the air fryer.
- Cook the chicken souvlaki in the air fryer for 12-15 minutes, turning them halfway through, until the chicken is cooked through and slightly browned.
- Once cooked, remove the chicken souvlaki from the air fryer and let them rest for a couple of minutes before serving.

Grilled Chicken Drumsticks

INGREDIENTS:

(Calories: 220 / Carbs: 2g / Proteins: 26g / Fats: 12g)

- 2 chicken drumsticks
- 1 teaspoon paprika
- 1/2 teaspoon garlic powder
- 1/2 teaspoon onion powder
- 1/4 teaspoon cayenne pepper
- Salt and pepper to taste
- Cooking spray

Cooking time: 25 minutes / servings: 1
Preparation time: 10 minutes

INSTRUCTIONS FOR COOKING:

- Preheat your air fryer to 400°F (200°C) for about 5 minutes.
- In a small bowl, mix together the paprika, garlic powder, onion powder, cayenne pepper, salt, and pepper to make the spice rub.
- Pat dry the chicken drumsticks with a paper towel.
- Sprinkle the spice rub over the drumsticks, coating them evenly.
- Lightly spray the air fryer basket or tray with cooking spray to prevent sticking.
- Place the seasoned drumsticks in the air fryer.
- Cook the drumsticks in the air fryer for 20-25 minutes, flipping them halfway through, until they reach an internal temperature of 165°F (74°C) and the skin is crispy and golden brown.
- Once cooked, remove the drumsticks from the air fryer and let them rest for a couple of minutes before serving.

Lime Grilled Shrimp

INGREDIENTS:

(Calories: 80 / Carbs: 1g / Proteins: 15g / Fats: 2g)

- 6 large shrimp, peeled and deveined
- 1 tablespoon lime juice
- 1 teaspoon olive oil
- 1/2 teaspoon chili powder
- 1/4 teaspoon cumin
- Salt and pepper to taste
- Cooking spray

Cooking time: 5 minutes / servings: 1
Preparation time: 10 minutes

INSTRUCTIONS FOR COOKING:

- Preheat your air fryer to 400°F (200°C) for about 5 minutes.
- In a bowl, mix together the lime juice, olive oil, chili powder, cumin, salt, and pepper to make the marinade.
- Add the shrimp to the marinade and toss to coat them evenly. Let them marinate for 5 minutes.
- Lightly spray the air fryer basket or tray with cooking spray to prevent sticking.
- Place the marinated shrimp in the air fryer, making sure they are not touching.
- Cook the shrimp in the air fryer for 4-5 minutes, flipping them halfway through, until they are pink and opaque.
- Once cooked, remove the shrimp from the air fryer and let them rest for a couple of minutes before serving.

Roasted Turkey Legs

INGREDIENTS:

(Calories: 300 / Carbs: 1g / Proteins: 28g / Fats: 20g)

- 1 turkey leg
- 1 tablespoon olive oil
- 2 cloves garlic, minced
- 1/2 teaspoon dried thyme
- 1/2 teaspoon dried rosemary
- Salt and pepper to taste
- Cooking spray

Cooking time: 45 minutes / servings: 1
Preparation time: 10 minutes

INSTRUCTIONS FOR COOKING:

- Preheat your air fryer to 375°F (190°C) for about 5 minutes.
- In a small bowl, mix together the olive oil, minced garlic, dried thyme, dried rosemary, salt, and pepper to make the herb marinade.
- Pat dry the turkey leg with a paper towel.
- Rub the herb marinade all over the turkey leg, ensuring it is coated evenly.
- Lightly spray the air fryer basket or tray with cooking spray to prevent sticking.
- Place the marinated turkey leg in the air fryer.
- Cook the turkey leg in the air fryer for 40-45 minutes, flipping it halfway through, until it reaches an internal temperature of 165°F (74°C) and the skin is crispy and golden brown.
- Once cooked, remove the turkey leg from the air fryer and let it rest for a couple of minutes before serving.

Glazed Pork Belly Slices

INGREDIENTS:

(Calories: 350 / Carbs: 10g / Proteins: 20g / Fats: 25g)

- 2 slices of pork belly
- 1 tablespoon reduced-sodium soy sauce
- 1 tablespoon rice vinegar
- 1 tablespoon honey
- 1 clove garlic, minced
- 1/2 teaspoon grated fresh ginger
- 1/4 teaspoon red pepper flakes (optional, for heat)
- Cooking spray

Cooking time: 20 minutes / servings: 1
Preparation time: 10 minutes

INSTRUCTIONS FOR COOKING:

- Preheat your air fryer to 400°F (200°C) for about 5 minutes.
- In a bowl, whisk together the soy sauce, rice vinegar, honey, minced garlic, grated ginger, and red pepper flakes (if using) to make the glaze.
- Lightly spray the air fryer basket or tray with cooking spray to prevent sticking.
- Place the pork belly slices in the air fryer.
- Cook the pork belly slices in the air fryer for 15-20 minutes, flipping them halfway through, until they are cooked through and the edges are crispy.
- Once cooked, brush the glaze over the pork belly slices and cook for an additional 1-2 minutes to caramelize the glaze.
- Remove the pork belly slices from the air fryer and let them rest for a couple of minutes before serving.

Grilled Sirloin Steak

INGREDIENTS:

(Calories: 200 / Carbs: 1g / Proteins: 25g / Fats: 10g)

- 4-ounce sirloin steak
- 1 tablespoon lemon juice
- 1 clove garlic, minced
- 1/2 teaspoon dried oregano
- Salt and pepper to taste
- Cooking spray

Cooking time: 15 minutes / servings: 1
Preparation time: 10 minutes

INSTRUCTIONS FOR COOKING:

- Preheat your air fryer to 400°F (200°C) for about 5 minutes.
- In a small bowl, mix together the lemon juice, minced garlic, dried oregano, salt, and pepper to make the marinade.
- Pat dry the sirloin steak with a paper towel.
- Rub the marinade all over the steak, ensuring it is coated evenly.
- Lightly spray the air fryer basket or tray with cooking spray to prevent sticking.
- Place the marinated steak in the air fryer.
- Cook the steak in the air fryer for 12-15 minutes, flipping it halfway through, until it reaches your desired level of doneness.
- Once cooked, remove the steak from the air fryer and let it rest for a couple of minutes before slicing and serving.

Chapter 7: Snacks and appetiserz

- Air-Fried Zucchini Fries
- Buffalo Cauliflower Bites
- Baked Parmesan Wings
- Mediterranean Stuffed Mushrooms
- Roasted Chickpeas
- Caprese Skewers
- Spicy Tofu Wraps
- Spinach Artichoke Dip
- Zucchini Pizza Bites
- Teriyaki Turkey Meatballs
- Smoky Eggplant Dip
- Lemon Pepper Shrimp
- Quinoa Sushi Rolls
- Roasted Red Pepper Hummus
- Turkey Lettuce Wraps
- Baked Sweet Potato Fries
- Cilantro Lime Shrimp Skewers
- Spinach Feta Mushrooms
- Greek Chicken Meatballs
- Avocado Egg Salad Wraps
- Buffalo Cauliflower Poppers
- Quinoa Stuffed Zucchini
- Asian Beef Skewers with Sesame Seeds
- Chicken Bites with Garlic and Parmesan
- Mediterranean Cucumber Roll-Ups
- Spicy Edamame
- Greek Yogurt Veggie Dip
- Air Fried Mozzarella Sticks
- Teriyaki Tofu Skewers
- Caprese Salad Skewers
- Zucchini Nachos
- Roasted Red Pepper Dip
- Turkey Bacon Asparagus
- Baked Buffalo Cauliflower
- Quinoa Stuffed Mushrooms
- Greek Lamb Kebabs
- Avocado Shrimp Ceviche
- Baked Sweet Potato Chips
- Asian Sesame Tofu Skewers
- Spinach Feta Phyllo Cups

Chapter 7: Snacks and appetiserz

Air-Fried Zucchini Fries

INGREDIENTS:

(Calories: 150 / Carbs: 19g / Proteins: 9g / Fats: 4g)

- 1 medium zucchini
- 1/4 cup whole wheat breadcrumbs
- 1 tablespoon grated Parmesan cheese
- 1/2 teaspoon dried oregano, 1/4 teaspoon garlic powder
- Salt and pepper to taste
- Cooking spray, 2 tablespoons Greek yogurt
- 1/2 teaspoon lemon juice, 1/4 teaspoon dried dill
- 1/4 teaspoon garlic powder

Cooking time: 10-12 minutes / servings: 1
Preparation time: 10 minutes

INSTRUCTIONS FOR COOKING:

- Preheat your air fryer to 400°F (200°C) for about 5 minutes.
- Cut the zucchini into fries-like shapes, about 1/2 inch thick.
- In a shallow bowl, combine the breadcrumbs, grated Parmesan cheese, dried oregano, garlic powder, salt, and pepper.
- Dip each zucchini fry into the breadcrumb mixture, pressing lightly to adhere the breadcrumbs.
- Lightly spray the air fryer basket or tray with cooking spray.
- Place the coated zucchini fries in a single layer in the air fryer.
- Cook the zucchini fries in the air fryer for 10-12 minutes, flipping them halfway through, until they are golden brown and crispy.
- In a separate small bowl, mix together the Greek yogurt, lemon juice, dried dill, garlic powder, salt, and pepper to make the dipping sauce.
- Serve the air-fried zucchini fries with the Greek yogurt dipping sauce.

Buffalo Cauliflower Bites

INGREDIENTS:

(Calories: 130 / Carbs: 10g / Proteins: 5g / Fats: 9g)

- 1 cup cauliflower florets, 1 tablespoon olive oil
- 2 tablespoons hot sauce (sugar-free)
- 1/2 teaspoon garlic powder, 1/4 teaspoon smoked paprika
- Salt and pepper to taste, Cooking spray
- 2 tablespoons Greek yogurt
- 1 tablespoon crumbled blue cheese
- 1/2 teaspoon lemon juice, 1/4 teaspoon dried dill
- Salt and pepper to taste

Cooking time: 15-20 minutes / servings: 1
Preparation time: 15 minutes

INSTRUCTIONS FOR COOKING:

- Preheat your air fryer to 400°F (200°C) for about 5 minutes.
- In a bowl, toss the cauliflower florets with olive oil, hot sauce, garlic powder, smoked paprika, salt, and pepper until well coated.
- Lightly spray the air fryer basket or tray with cooking spray.
- Place the coated cauliflower florets in a single layer in the air fryer.
- Cook the cauliflower in the air fryer for 15-20 minutes, shaking the basket or flipping the florets halfway through, until they are tender and crispy.
- In a separate small bowl, mix together the Greek yogurt, crumbled blue cheese, lemon juice, dried dill, salt, and pepper to make the dipping sauce.
- Serve the buffalo cauliflower bites with the blue cheese yogurt dip.

Baked Parmesan Wings

INGREDIENTS:

(Calories: 260 / Carbs: 1g / Proteins: 23g / Fats: 18g)

- 4 chicken wings, 1 tablespoon olive oil
- 2 tablespoons grated Parmesan cheese
- 1/2 teaspoon garlic powder
- 1/4 teaspoon dried thyme
- Salt and pepper to taste
- Cooking spray

Cooking time: 30-35 minutes / servings: 1
Preparation time: 10 minutes

INSTRUCTIONS FOR COOKING:

- Preheat your air fryer to 400°F (200°C) for about 5 minutes.
- In a bowl, toss the chicken wings with olive oil, grated Parmesan cheese, garlic powder, dried thyme, salt, and pepper until well coated.
- Lightly spray the air fryer basket or tray with cooking spray.
- Place the coated chicken wings in a single layer in the air fryer.
- Cook the chicken wings in the air fryer for 30-35 minutes, flipping them halfway through, until they are golden brown and crispy.
- Serve the baked Parmesan chicken wings as a delicious appetizer or main dish.

Mediterranean Stuffed Mushrooms

INGREDIENTS:

(Calories: 80 / Carbs: 4g / Proteins: 5g / Fats: 4g)

- 2 large mushrooms
- 2 tablespoons diced tomatoes (canned, no added sugar)
- 1 tablespoon crumbled feta cheese
- 1 tablespoon chopped black olives
- 1/2 teaspoon dried oregano
- Salt and pepper to taste
- Cooking spray

Cooking time: 15-20 minutes / servings: 1
Preparation time: 15 minutes

INSTRUCTIONS FOR COOKING:

- Preheat your air fryer to 375°F (190°C) for about 5 minutes.
- Remove the stems from the mushrooms and hollow out the caps slightly to create space for the stuffing.
- In a bowl, mix together the diced tomatoes, crumbled feta cheese, chopped black olives, dried oregano, salt, and pepper.
- Stuff the mushroom caps with the mixture, dividing it evenly between the two mushrooms.
- Lightly spray the air fryer basket or tray with cooking spray.
- Place the stuffed mushrooms in the air fryer, stuffed side up.
- Cook the mushrooms in the air fryer for 15-20 minutes until the mushrooms are tender and the filling is heated through.
- Serve the Mediterranean stuffed mushrooms as a tasty appetizer or side dish.

Roasted Chickpeas

INGREDIENTS:

(Calories: 160 / Carbs: 19g / Proteins: 6g / Fats: 7g)

- 1/2 cup canned chickpeas (garbanzo beans), drained and rinsed
- 1 tablespoon olive oil
- 1/2 teaspoon garlic powder
- 1/4 teaspoon dried thyme
- 1/4 teaspoon dried rosemary
- Salt and pepper to taste

Cooking time: 20-25 minutes / servings: 1
Preparation time: 5 minutes

INSTRUCTIONS FOR COOKING:

- Preheat your air fryer to 400°F (200°C) for about 5 minutes.
- In a bowl, toss the chickpeas with olive oil, garlic powder, dried thyme, dried rosemary, salt, and pepper until well coated.
- Lightly spray the air fryer basket or tray with cooking spray.
- Place the seasoned chickpeas in a single layer in the air fryer.
- Cook the chickpeas in the air fryer for 20-25 minutes, shaking the basket or flipping them halfway through, until they are golden brown and crispy.
- Remove the roasted chickpeas from the air fryer and let them cool slightly before serving as a healthy and crunchy snack.

Caprese Skewers

INGREDIENTS:

(Calories: 120 / Carbs: 4g / Proteins: 8g / Fats: 8g)

- 3 cherry tomatoes
- 3 small fresh mozzarella balls
- 3 fresh basil leaves
- Balsamic glaze (store-bought or homemade)
- Salt and pepper to taste

Cooking time: 0 minutes / servings: 1
Preparation time: 10 minutes

INSTRUCTIONS FOR COOKING:

- Wash the cherry tomatoes and fresh basil leaves. Pat them dry with a paper towel.
- Thread one cherry tomato, one mozzarella ball, and one basil leaf onto a skewer. Repeat this process to create two more skewers.
- Arrange the Caprese skewers on a serving plate.
- Drizzle the skewers with balsamic glaze.
- Season with salt and pepper to taste.
- Serve the Caprese skewers as a refreshing and flavorful appetizer or snack.

Spicy Tofu Wraps

INGREDIENTS:

(Calories: 170 / Carbs: 10g / Proteins: 14g / Fats: 8g)

- 4 ounces firm tofu, drained and crumbled
- 1/4 cup diced bell peppers (any color)
- 1/4 cup diced onions, 1/4 cup shredded carrots
- 1 tablespoon low-sodium soy sauce
- 1/2 teaspoon chili garlic sauce (adjust to taste)
- 1/2 teaspoon sesame oil
- Lettuce leaves (such as butter lettuce or iceberg lettuce) for wrapping
- Optional toppings: chopped green onions, chopped peanuts

Cooking time: 10 minutes / servings: 1
Preparation time: 15 minutes

INSTRUCTIONS FOR COOKING:

- Preheat your air fryer to 375°F (190°C) for about 5 minutes.
- In a bowl, mix together crumbled tofu, diced bell peppers, diced onions, shredded carrots, low-sodium soy sauce, chili garlic sauce, and sesame oil.
- Lightly spray the air fryer basket or tray with cooking spray.
- Place the tofu mixture in the air fryer and cook for 8-10 minutes, stirring occasionally, until the tofu is heated through and slightly crispy.
- Remove the tofu mixture from the air fryer and let it cool slightly.
- Spoon the tofu mixture onto lettuce leaves, top with optional toppings if desired, and wrap the lettuce around the filling to create lettuce wraps.
- Serve the spicy tofu lettuce wraps as a light and flavorful meal.

Spinach Artichoke Dip

INGREDIENTS:

(Calories: 90 / Carbs: 8g / Proteins: 10g / Fats: 3g)

- 1/4 cup Greek yogurt
- 1/4 cup chopped cooked spinach (drained well)
- 1/4 cup chopped canned artichoke hearts (drained well)
- 1 tablespoon grated Parmesan cheese
- 1/2 teaspoon garlic powder
- Salt and pepper to taste

Cooking time: 0 minutes / servings: 1
Preparation time: 10 minutes

INSTRUCTIONS FOR COOKING:

- In a bowl, mix together Greek yogurt, chopped cooked spinach, chopped artichoke hearts, grated Parmesan cheese, garlic powder, salt, and pepper until well combined.
- Adjust the seasoning to taste.
- Serve the Greek yogurt spinach and artichoke dip with vegetable sticks, such as cucumber slices or carrot sticks, as a healthy and flavorful dip.

Zucchini Pizza Bites

INGREDIENTS:

(Calories: 80 / Carbs: 7g / Proteins: 5g / Fats: 4g)

- 1 medium-sized zucchini
- 2 tablespoons low-sodium tomato sauce
- 2 tablespoons shredded mozzarella cheese
- 2 tablespoons diced bell peppers (any color)
- 2 tablespoons sliced black olives
- 1/2 teaspoon dried oregano
- Salt and pepper to taste

Cooking time: 12 minutes / servings: 1
Preparation time: 10 minutes

INSTRUCTIONS FOR COOKING:

- Preheat your air fryer to 400°F (200°C) for about 5 minutes.
- Slice the zucchini into rounds, about 1/4 inch thick.
- Lightly spray the air fryer basket or tray with cooking spray.
- Arrange the zucchini slices in a single layer in the air fryer.
- Spread a small amount of tomato sauce on each zucchini slice.
- Top each slice with shredded mozzarella cheese, diced bell peppers, sliced black olives, dried oregano, salt, and pepper.
- Air fry for 10-12 minutes until the cheese is melted and the zucchini is tender.
- Remove the zucchini pizza bites from the air fryer and let them cool slightly before serving.

Teriyaki Turkey Meatballs

INGREDIENTS:

(Calories: 170 / Carbs: 6g / Proteins: 20g / Fats: 7g)

- 4 ounces ground turkey
- 2 tablespoons low-sodium soy sauce
- 1 tablespoon minced green onions
- 1 tablespoon whole wheat bread crumbs
- 1/2 teaspoon minced garlic, 1/2 teaspoon grated ginger
- 1/2 teaspoon honey or a sugar substitute
- 1/2 teaspoon sesame oil
- Sesame seeds and sliced green onions for garnish (optional)

Cooking time: 15 minutes / servings: 1
Preparation time: 15 minutes

INSTRUCTIONS FOR COOKING:

- Preheat your air fryer to 375°F (190°C) for about 5 minutes.
- In a bowl, combine ground turkey, low-sodium soy sauce, minced green onions, whole wheat bread crumbs, minced garlic, grated ginger, honey or sugar substitute, and sesame oil. Mix well.
- Shape the mixture into small meatballs, about 1 inch in diameter.
- Lightly spray the air fryer basket or tray with cooking spray.
- Place the meatballs in a single layer in the air fryer.
- Air fry for 12-15 minutes, shaking the basket or flipping the meatballs halfway through, until they are cooked through and browned.
- Remove the teriyaki turkey meatballs from the air fryer and let them cool slightly before serving.
- Garnish with sesame seeds and sliced green onions, if desired.

Smoky Eggplant Dip

INGREDIENTS:

(Calories: 120 / Carbs: 20g / Proteins: 5g / Fats: 2g)

- 1 small eggplant
- 1 tablespoon lemon juice
- 1 tablespoon tahini (sesame paste)
- 1 clove garlic, minced
- 1/2 teaspoon smoked paprika
- Salt and pepper to taste
- Whole wheat pita bread for serving

Cooking time: 20 minutes / servings: 1
Preparation time: 10 minutes

INSTRUCTIONS FOR COOKING:

- Preheat your air fryer to 400°F (200°C) for about 5 minutes.
- Prick the eggplant with a fork in a few places.
- Place the eggplant in the air fryer basket.
- Air fry the eggplant for 20 minutes until the skin is charred and the flesh is soft.
- Remove the eggplant from the air fryer and let it cool for a few minutes.
- Cut the eggplant in half and scoop out the flesh into a bowl.
- Add lemon juice, tahini, minced garlic, smoked paprika, salt, and pepper to the bowl.
- Mash and mix everything together until well combined and smooth.
- Serve the smoky eggplant dip with whole wheat pita bread.

Lemon Pepper Shrimp

INGREDIENTS:

(Calories: 100 / Carbs: 1g / Proteins: 18g / Fats: 2g)

- 6 large shrimp, peeled and deveined
- 1 teaspoon olive oil
- 1 teaspoon lemon zest
- 1/2 teaspoon ground black pepper
- Salt to taste
- Lemon wedges for serving

Cooking time: 8 minutes / servings: 1
Preparation time: 10 minutes

INSTRUCTIONS FOR COOKING:

- Preheat your air fryer to 400°F (200°C) for about 5 minutes.
- In a bowl, toss the shrimp with olive oil, lemon zest, ground black pepper, and salt.
- Lightly spray the air fryer basket or tray with cooking spray.
- Arrange the shrimp in a single layer in the air fryer.
- Air fry the shrimp for 6-8 minutes, flipping them halfway through, until they are cooked through and golden brown.
- Remove the shrimp from the air fryer and let them cool for a minute.
- Serve the lemon pepper air fried shrimp with lemon wedges on the side.

Quinoa Sushi Rolls

INGREDIENTS:

(Calories: 250 / Carbs: 32g / Proteins: 7g / Fats: 10g)

- 2 nori seaweed sheets
- 1/2 cup cooked quinoa
- 1/4 cup cucumber, julienned
- 1/4 cup carrot, julienned
- 1/4 avocado, sliced
- 1 tablespoon low-sodium soy sauce
- 1/2 tablespoon rice vinegar
- 1/2 teaspoon sesame seeds

Cooking time: 15 minutes / servings: 1
Preparation time: 30 minutes

INSTRUCTIONS FOR COOKING:

- Cook the quinoa according to the package instructions and let it cool.
- Lay a bamboo sushi rolling mat on a flat surface and place a nori seaweed sheet on top.
- Wet your hands and spread half of the quinoa evenly over the nori, leaving a 1-inch border at the top.
- Arrange half of the cucumber, carrot, and avocado slices in a line on top of the quinoa.
- Moisten the top border of the nori with water to help seal the roll.
- Using the bamboo mat, roll the sushi tightly, applying gentle pressure to shape it.
- Repeat the process with the second nori sheet and the remaining ingredients.
- Slice each sushi roll into bite-sized pieces.
- Serve the quinoa and vegetable sushi rolls with low-sodium soy sauce for dipping, sprinkled with rice vinegar and sesame seeds.

Roasted Red Pepper Hummus

INGREDIENTS:

(Calories: 180 / Carbs: 28g / Proteins: 8g / Fats: 5g)

- 1 large red bell pepper
- 1 cup canned chickpeas, rinsed and drained
- 1 tablespoon lemon juice
- 1 clove garlic, minced
- 1 tablespoon tahini (sesame paste)
- 1/2 teaspoon cumin
- Salt and pepper to taste
- Assorted vegetable sticks (carrots, celery, bell pepper) for serving

Cooking time: 25 minutes / servings: 1
Preparation time: 10 minutes

INSTRUCTIONS FOR COOKING:

- Preheat your air fryer to 400°F (200°C) for about 5 minutes.
- Cut the red bell pepper in half and remove the seeds and stem.
- Place the red bell pepper halves in the air fryer basket, cut side down.
- Air fry the red bell pepper for 20-25 minutes until the skin is charred and the flesh is tender.
- Remove the red bell pepper from the air fryer and let it cool.
- Peel off the charred skin from the red bell pepper.
- In a food processor, combine the roasted red pepper, chickpeas, lemon juice, minced garlic, tahini, cumin, salt, and pepper
- Process until smooth and creamy, adding a little water if needed to reach the desired consistency.
- Serve the roasted red pepper hummus with assorted vegetable sticks for dipping.

Turkey Lettuce Wraps

INGREDIENTS:

(Calories: 200 / Carbs: 10g / Proteins: 20g / Fats: 8g)

- 4 large lettuce leaves (such as butter lettuce or romaine)
- 4 ounces ground turkey, 1/2 cup cucumber, julienned
- 1/2 cup carrot, julienned
- 2 tablespoons low-sodium soy sauce
- 1 tablespoon rice vinegar, 1/2 teaspoon sesame oil
- 1/2 teaspoon grated ginger, 1 clove garlic, minced
- Fresh cilantro leaves, for garnish

Cooking time: 15 minutes / servings: 1
Preparation time: 20 minutes

INSTRUCTIONS FOR COOKING:

- In a skillet, cook the ground turkey over medium heat until it is browned and cooked through. Set aside.
- In a bowl, combine the julienned cucumber and carrot.
- In a separate small bowl, whisk together the soy sauce, rice vinegar, sesame oil, grated ginger, and minced garlic.
- Pour the dressing over the cucumber and carrot mixture and toss to coat.
- Lay the lettuce leaves on a plate.
- Divide the cooked ground turkey evenly among the lettuce leaves.
- Top with the cucumber and carrot slaw.
- Garnish with fresh cilantro leaves.
- Roll up the lettuce leaves to form wraps and serve.

Baked Sweet Potato Fries

INGREDIENTS:

(Calories: 220 / Carbs: 30g / Proteins: 8g / Fats: 7g)

- 1 medium sweet potato, cut into fries
- 1 tablespoon olive oil
- 1/2 teaspoon paprika
- 1/4 teaspoon garlic powder
- Salt and pepper to taste
- 1/4 cup plain Greek yogurt
- 1/2 teaspoon chipotle powder
- Fresh cilantro, chopped, for garnish

Cooking time: 20 minutes / servings: 1
Preparation time: 10 minutes

INSTRUCTIONS FOR COOKING:

- Preheat your air fryer to 400°F (200°C) for about 5 minutes.
- In a bowl, toss the sweet potato fries with olive oil, paprika, garlic powder, salt, and pepper.
- Place the seasoned sweet potato fries in the air fryer basket.
- Air fry the sweet potato fries for 15-20 minutes, shaking the basket halfway through, until they are golden and crispy.
- While the sweet potato fries are cooking, prepare the chipotle yogurt dip by mixing together the plain Greek yogurt and chipotle powder in a small bowl.
- Once the sweet potato fries are done, remove them from the air fryer and let them cool slightly.
- Garnish the sweet potato fries with fresh cilantro.
- Serve the baked sweet potato fries with the chipotle yogurt dip on the side.

Cilantro Lime Shrimp Skewers

INGREDIENTS:

(Calories: 70 / Carbs: 1g / Proteins: 14g / Fats: 1g)

- 4-6 large shrimp, peeled and deveined
- 1 tablespoon fresh cilantro, chopped
- 1 tablespoon lime juice
- 1 clove garlic, minced
- 1/2 teaspoon chili powder
- Salt and pepper to taste
- Wooden skewers, soaked in water for 30 minutes

Cooking time: 6-8 minutes / servings: 1
Preparation time: 15 minutes

INSTRUCTIONS FOR COOKING:

- Preheat your air fryer to 400°F (200°C) for about 5 minutes.
- In a bowl, combine the chopped cilantro, lime juice, minced garlic, chili powder, salt, and pepper.
- Add the shrimp to the bowl and toss to coat them evenly with the marinade.
- Thread the marinated shrimp onto the soaked wooden skewers.
- Place the shrimp skewers in the air fryer basket.
- Air fry the shrimp skewers for 6-8 minutes, flipping them halfway through, until they are cooked through and slightly charred.
- Remove the shrimp skewers from the air fryer and let them cool for a minute before serving.

Spinach Feta Mushrooms

INGREDIENTS:

(Calories: 80 / Carbs: 5g / Proteins: 6g / Fats: 4g)

- 3-4 medium-sized mushrooms
- 1/4 cup fresh spinach, chopped
- 1 tablespoon feta cheese, crumbled
- 1 tablespoon grated Parmesan cheese
- 1/2 teaspoon garlic powder
- Salt and pepper to taste

Cooking time: 15 minutes / servings: 1
Preparation time: 15 minutes

INSTRUCTIONS FOR COOKING:

- Preheat your air fryer to 375°F (190°C) for about 5 minutes.
- Remove the stems from the mushrooms and set them aside.
- In a bowl, mix together the chopped spinach, feta cheese, grated Parmesan cheese, garlic powder, salt, and pepper.
- Fill each mushroom cap with the spinach and feta mixture.
- Place the stuffed mushroom caps and the mushroom stems in the air fryer basket.
- Air fry the stuffed mushrooms for 15 minutes, or until the mushrooms are tender and the filling is heated through and lightly browned.
- Remove the stuffed mushrooms from the air fryer and let them cool for a minute before serving.

Greek Chicken Meatballs

INGREDIENTS:

(Calories: 220 / Carbs: 15g / Proteins: 20g / Fats: 8g)

For the meatballs:
- 4 ounces ground chicken, 1/4 cup breadcrumbs (preferably whole wheat)
- 1/4 cup finely chopped onion, 1 clove garlic, minced
- 1/2 teaspoon dried oregano, 1/2 teaspoon dried basil
- Salt and pepper to taste

For the tzatziki sauce:
- 1/4 cup Greek yogurt (plain, low-fat)
- 1/4 cup grated cucumber, squeezed to remove excess moisture
- 1 teaspoon lemon juice, 1/2 teaspoon minced garlic
- 1/2 teaspoon dried dill, salt to taste

Cooking time: 12-15 minutes / servings: 1
Preparation time: 15 minutes

INSTRUCTIONS FOR COOKING:

- Preheat your air fryer to 375°F (190°C) for about 5 minutes.
- In a bowl, combine the ground chicken, breadcrumbs, chopped onion, minced garlic, dried oregano, dried basil, salt, and pepper. Mix well to incorporate all the ingredients.
- Shape the mixture into small meatballs, about 1 inch in diameter.
- Place the meatballs in the air fryer basket, making sure they are not overcrowded.
- Air fry the meatballs for 12-15 minutes, or until they are cooked through and browned on the outside.
- While the meatballs are cooking, prepare the tzatziki sauce by combining the Greek yogurt, grated cucumber, lemon juice, minced garlic, dried dill, and salt in a separate bowl. Mix well.
- Serve the Greek chicken meatballs with the tzatziki sauce on the side.

Avocado Egg Salad Wraps

INGREDIENTS:

(Calories: 250 / Carbs: 10g / Proteins: 12g / Fats: 18g)

- 2 hard-boiled eggs, peeled and chopped
- 1/2 ripe avocado, mashed
- 1 tablespoon diced red onion
- 1 tablespoon diced celery
- 1 teaspoon lemon juice
- Salt and pepper to taste
- Lettuce leaves for wrapping (e.g., butter lettuce, romaine lettuce)

Cooking time: 0 minutes / servings: 1
Preparation time: 10 minutes

INSTRUCTIONS FOR COOKING:

- In a bowl, combine the chopped hard-boiled eggs, mashed avocado, diced red onion, diced celery, lemon juice, salt, and pepper. Mix well to combine all the ingredients.
- Place a spoonful of the avocado egg salad onto each lettuce leaf.
- Wrap the lettuce leaf around the filling, creating a lettuce wrap.
- Repeat with the remaining filling and lettuce leaves.
- Serve the avocado egg salad lettuce wraps as a healthy and refreshing meal or snack.

Buffalo Cauliflower Poppers

INGREDIENTS:

(Calories: 120 / Carbs: 9g / Proteins: 5g / Fats: 8g)

For the cauliflower poppers:
- 1 cup cauliflower florets, 2 tablespoons hot sauce
- 1 tablespoon olive oil, 1/2 teaspoon garlic powder
- Salt and pepper to taste

For the ranch dip:
- 2 tablespoons Greek yogurt (plain, low-fat)
- 1/2 teaspoon dried dill, 1/2 teaspoon dried parsley
- 1/4 teaspoon garlic powder, salt and pepper to taste

Cooking time: 15-20 minutes / servings: 1
Preparation time: 10 minutes

INSTRUCTIONS FOR COOKING:

- Preheat your air fryer to 375°F (190°C) for about 5 minutes.
- In a bowl, combine the cauliflower florets, hot sauce, olive oil, garlic powder, salt, and pepper. Toss until the cauliflower is coated evenly.
- Place the cauliflower florets in the air fryer basket, making sure they are not overcrowded.
- Air fry the cauliflower for 15-20 minutes, or until they are tender and crispy, tossing halfway through the cooking time.
- While the cauliflower is cooking, prepare the ranch dip by combining the Greek yogurt, dried dill, dried parsley, garlic powder, salt, and pepper in a separate bowl. Mix well.
- Serve the buffalo cauliflower poppers with the ranch dip on the side.

Quinoa Stuffed Zucchini

INGREDIENTS:

(Calories: 200 / Carbs: 31g / Proteins: 10g / Fats: 3g)

- 1 medium-sized zucchini, 1/4 cup cooked quinoa
- 1/4 cup canned black beans, rinsed and drained
- 2 tablespoons diced red bell pepper
- 2 tablespoons diced onion, 1/2 teaspoon cumin
- 1/4 teaspoon chili powder,
- Salt and pepper to taste
- 1 tablespoon shredded low-fat cheese (optional)

Cooking time: 25-30 minutes / servings: 1
Preparation time: 15 minutes

INSTRUCTIONS FOR COOKING:

- Preheat your air fryer to 375°F (190°C) for about 5 minutes.
- Cut the zucchini in half lengthwise and scoop out the seeds and some of the flesh, creating a hollow space for the filling.
- In a bowl, combine the cooked quinoa, black beans, diced red bell pepper, diced onion, cumin, chili powder, salt, and pepper. Mix well.
- Stuff the quinoa and black bean mixture into the hollowed-out zucchini halves.
- Place the stuffed zucchini boats in the air fryer basket.
- Air fry the zucchini boats for 25-30 minutes, or until the zucchini is tender and the filling is heated through.
- If desired, sprinkle the shredded low-fat cheese over the zucchini boats and air fry for an additional 2-3 minutes, or until the cheese is melted and bubbly.
- Serve the quinoa and black bean stuffed zucchini boats as a satisfying and nutritious meal.

Asian Beef Skewers with Sesame Seeds

INGREDIENTS:

(Calories: ~180 / Carbs: 2g / Proteins: 23g / Fats: 9g)

- 1 pound lean beef (such as sirloin or flank steak), cut into thin strips
- 2 tablespoons low-sodium soy sauce
- 1 tablespoon sesame oil
- 1 tablespoon rice vinegar
- 1 tablespoon fresh ginger, minced
- 2 cloves garlic, minced
- 1 tablespoon sesame seeds
- Bamboo skewers, soaked in water for 30 minutes

Cooking time: 12 minutes / servings: 4
Preparation time: 15 minutes (+marinating time)

INSTRUCTIONS FOR COOKING:

- In a bowl, mix together soy sauce, sesame oil, rice vinegar, minced ginger, and minced garlic. Add the beef strips to the marinade and let them marinate for at least 30 minutes (or up to 2 hours) in the refrigerator.
- Preheat your air fryer to 375°F (190°C) for about 5 minutes.
- Assemble the Skewers: Thread the marinated beef strips onto the soaked bamboo skewers, weaving them back and forth.
- Place the beef skewers in a single layer in the air fryer basket. Cook for about 10-12 minutes, flipping halfway through, until the beef is cooked to your desired level of doneness.
- While the skewers are cooking, toast the sesame seeds in a dry skillet over medium heat until they are lightly golden. Keep an eye on them as they can burn quickly.
- Once the beef skewers are done, sprinkle them with toasted sesame seeds before serving.

Chicken Bites with Garlic and Parmesan

INGREDIENTS:

(Calories: 170 / Carbs: 1g / Proteins: 25g / Fats: 7g)

- 1 pound boneless, skinless chicken breast, cut into bite-sized pieces
- 2 tablespoons olive oil
- 2 cloves garlic, minced
- 1/4 cup grated Parmesan cheese
- 1/4 teaspoon black pepper
- Chopped fresh parsley, for garnish

Cooking time: 15 minutes / servings: 4
Preparation time: 10 minutes

INSTRUCTIONS FOR COOKING:

- Preheat your air fryer to 375°F (190°C) for about 5 minutes.
- In a bowl, toss the chicken pieces with olive oil, minced garlic, grated Parmesan cheese, and black pepper, ensuring even coating.
- Place the seasoned chicken pieces in a single layer in the air fryer basket. Cook for about 12-15 minutes, shaking the basket halfway through, until the chicken is cooked through and golden brown.
- Once cooked, transfer the chicken bites to a serving dish and garnish with chopped fresh parsley.

Mediterranean Cucumber Roll-Ups

INGREDIENTS:

(Calories: ~80 / Carbs: 7g / Proteins: 3g / Fats: 5g)

- 2 large cucumbers
- 1/2 cup hummus (choose a low-fat, low-sugar option)
- 1/4 cup roasted red pepper, thinly sliced
- 1/4 cup Kalamata olives, pitted and chopped
- 1/4 cup crumbled feta cheese
- Fresh parsley, chopped, for garnish

Cooking time: 0 minutes / servings: 4
Preparation time: 15 minutes

INSTRUCTIONS FOR COOKING:

- Wash the cucumbers and slice them lengthwise into thin strips using a vegetable peeler or mandoline. Pat the cucumber strips dry with a paper towel.
- Lay a cucumber strip flat and spread a thin layer of hummus over it. Place a few slices of roasted red pepper, chopped Kalamata olives, and crumbled feta cheese along one end of the cucumber strip.
- Roll Up: Carefully roll up the cucumber strip, starting from the end with the toppings. Continue rolling until you reach the other end. Secure the roll with a toothpick if needed.
- Repeat the process with the remaining cucumber strips and filling ingredients.
- Arrange the cucumber roll-ups on a serving platter and sprinkle chopped fresh parsley over the top.

Spicy Edamame

INGREDIENTS:

(Calories: 100 / Carbs: 6g / Proteins: 8g / Fats: 5g)

- 2 cups frozen edamame, thawed
- 1 tablespoon olive oil
- 1/2 teaspoon chili powder
- 1/4 teaspoon garlic powder
- 1/4 teaspoon paprika
- Salt to taste

Cooking time: 5 minutes / servings: 4
Preparation time: 10 minutes

INSTRUCTIONS FOR COOKING:

- Preheat your air fryer to 375°F (190°C) for about 5 minutes.
- In a bowl, toss the thawed edamame with olive oil, chili powder, garlic powder, paprika, and a pinch of salt until evenly coated.
- Place the seasoned edamame in the air fryer basket in a single layer. Cook for about 8-10 minutes, shaking the basket halfway through, until the edamame is heated through and slightly crispy.
- Once cooked, transfer the spicy edamame to a serving dish and serve immediately.

Greek Yogurt Veggie Dip

INGREDIENTS:

(Calories: 60 / Carbs: 5g / Proteins: 7g / Fats: 1g)

- 1 cup Greek yogurt (choose a low-fat, plain option)
- 1/2 cup cucumber, finely grated and drained
- 1/4 cup red bell pepper, finely chopped
- 2 tablespoons fresh dill, chopped
- 1 clove garlic, minced
- 1 tablespoon lemon juice
- Salt and pepper to taste

Cooking time: 0 minutes / servings: 4
Preparation time: 10 minutes

INSTRUCTIONS FOR COOKING:

- In a bowl, combine Greek yogurt, grated cucumber (make sure to squeeze out excess moisture), chopped red bell pepper, fresh dill, minced garlic, lemon juice, salt, and pepper. Mix well until all ingredients are incorporated.
- Cover the bowl with plastic wrap and refrigerate the dip for at least 30 minutes to allow the flavors to meld.
- Before serving, give the dip a final stir and transfer it to a serving bowl. Serve with your favorite sliced vegetables as dippers.

Air Fried Mozzarella Sticks

INGREDIENTS:

(Calories: ~180 / Carbs: 14g / Proteins: 12g / Fats: 8g)

- 8 mozzarella string cheese sticks, cut in half
- 1/2 cup whole wheat or almond flour
- 2 large eggs, beaten
- 1 cup whole grain breadcrumbs
- 1 teaspoon dried Italian herbs (such as oregano and basil)
- Cooking spray

Cooking time: 10 minutes / servings: 4
Preparation time: 15 minutes (+freezing time)

INSTRUCTIONS FOR COOKING:

- Place the halved mozzarella sticks in the freezer for about 15 minutes to firm them up.
- Preheat your air fryer to 375°F (190°aC) for about 5 minutes.
- Set up a breading station with three separate bowls. Place flour in the first bowl, beaten eggs in the second bowl, and breadcrumbs mixed with dried Italian herbs in the third bowl.
- Dip each frozen mozzarella stick into the flour, then into the beaten eggs, and finally into the breadcrumb mixture, pressing gently to adhere the breadcrumbs.
- Lightly grease the air fryer basket with cooking spray. Place the breaded mozzarella sticks in a single layer in the basket, making sure they are not touching. Cook for about 5-6 minutes, until they are golden and crispy.
- Once cooked, carefully remove the mozzarella sticks from the air fryer and serve them immediately with a side of low-sugar marinara sauce.

Teriyaki Tofu Skewers

INGREDIENTS:

(Calories: ~140 / Carbs: 6g / Proteins: 12g / Fats: 8g)

- 14 oz (400g) firm tofu, pressed and cut into cubes
- 1/4 cup low-sodium soy sauce
- 2 tablespoons low-sugar teriyaki sauce
- 1 tablespoon rice vinegar, 1 tablespoon sesame oil
- 1 tablespoon honey or a sugar substitute (such as stevia or erythritol)
- 1 teaspoon fresh ginger, minced
- Bamboo skewers, soaked in water for 30 minutes
- Sliced green onions, for garnish

Cooking time: 15 minutes / servings: 4
Preparation time: 20 minutes (+marinating time)

INSTRUCTIONS FOR COOKING:

- In a bowl, whisk together soy sauce, teriyaki sauce, rice vinegar, sesame oil, honey or sugar substitute, and minced ginger. Add the tofu cubes to the marinade and let them marinate for at least 30 minutes (or up to 2 hours) in the refrigerator.
- Preheat your air fryer to 375°F (190°C) for about 5 minutes.
- Assemble the Skewers: Thread the marinated tofu cubes onto the soaked bamboo skewers.
- Place the tofu skewers in a single layer in the air fryer basket. Cook for about 12-15 minutes, turning them occasionally, until the tofu is heated through and slightly crispy on the edges.
- Once cooked, remove the skewers from the air fryer and place them on a serving plate. Garnish with sliced green onions before serving.

Caprese Salad Skewers

INGREDIENTS:

(Calories: ~80 / Carbs: 2g / Proteins: 6g / Fats: 5g)

- 1 pound boneless, skinless chicken breast, cut into bite-sized pieces
- 2 tablespoons olive oil
- 2 cloves garlic, minced
- 1/4 cup grated Parmesan cheese
- 1/4 teaspoon black pepper
- Chopped fresh parsley, for garnish

Cooking time: 0 minutes / servings: 4
Preparation time: 15 minutes

INSTRUCTIONS FOR COOKING:

- Thread a cherry tomato onto a toothpick, followed by a mozzarella ball, and a folded basil leaf. Repeat for the desired number of skewers.
- Arrange the Caprese skewers on a serving platter and drizzle them with balsamic glaze.
- Serve the skewers immediately as a fresh and light appetizer or snack.

Zucchini Nachos

INGREDIENTS:

(Calories: ~90 / Carbs: 6g / Proteins: 5g / Fats: 5g)

- 2 large zucchinis, sliced into thin rounds
- 1 tablespoon olive oil, 1 teaspoon chili powder
- 1/2 teaspoon ground cumin, 1/2 teaspoon garlic powder
- Salt and pepper to taste
- 1/2 cup shredded low-fat cheddar cheese
- 1/4 cup diced tomatoes, 1/4 cup diced red onion
- 1/4 cup sliced black olives
- 2 tablespoons chopped fresh cilantro
- Sliced jalapenos (optional)

Cooking time: 15 minutes / servings: 4
Preparation time: 15 minutes

INSTRUCTIONS FOR COOKING:

- Preheat your air fryer to 375°F (190°C) for about 5 minutes.
- In a bowl, toss the zucchini slices with olive oil, chili powder, ground cumin, garlic powder, salt, and pepper until they are coated.
- Place the seasoned zucchini slices in a single layer in the air fryer basket. Cook for about 8-10 minutes, shaking the basket halfway through, until the zucchini is crisp-tender.
- Once the zucchini slices are cooked, arrange them on a serving platter. Sprinkle shredded cheddar cheese over the zucchini, and then add diced tomatoes, diced red onion, sliced black olives, and chopped cilantro. If desired, add sliced jalapenos for extra heat.
- Serve the zucchini nachos immediately as a delicious and low-carb alternative to traditional nachos.

Roasted Red Pepper Dip

INGREDIENTS:

(Calories: ~70 / Carbs: 4g / Proteins: 4g / Fats: 5g)

- 2 large red bell peppers
- 1/2 cup plain Greek yogurt (choose a low-fat option)
- 1/4 cup light cream cheese, 2 cloves garlic, minced
- 1 tablespoon lemon juice, 1 tablespoon olive oil
- 1/2 teaspoon smoked paprika
- Salt and pepper to taste
- Chopped fresh parsley, for garnish

Cooking time: 15 minutes / servings: 4
Preparation time: 10 minutes

INSTRUCTIONS FOR COOKING:

- Preheat your oven's broiler. Place the red bell peppers on a baking sheet and broil, turning occasionally, until the skin is charred and blistered. Transfer the peppers to a bowl, cover with plastic wrap, and let them steam for about 10 minutes. Peel off the skin, remove the seeds and stems, and dice the roasted peppers.
- In a food processor, combine the diced roasted red peppers, Greek yogurt, light cream cheese, minced garlic, lemon juice, olive oil, smoked paprika, salt, and pepper. Blend until the mixture is smooth and well combined.
- Transfer the dip to a serving bowl, cover, and refrigerate for at least 30 minutes to allow the flavors to meld. Before serving, garnish with chopped fresh parsley.

Turkey Bacon Asparagus

INGREDIENTS:

(Calories: ~90 / Carbs: 5g / Proteins: 8g / Fats: 4g)

- 1 pound asparagus spears, tough ends trimmed
- 8 slices turkey bacon
- 1 tablespoon olive oil
- Salt and pepper to taste
- Lemon wedges, for serving

Cooking time: 12 minutes / servings: 4
Preparation time: 10 minutes

INSTRUCTIONS FOR COOKING:

- Preheat your air fryer to 375°F (190°C) for about 5 minutes.
- Toss the asparagus spears with olive oil, salt, and pepper. Wrap each asparagus spear with a slice of turkey bacon, spiraling it around the spear from top to bottom.
- Place the wrapped asparagus spears in a single layer in the air fryer basket. Cook for about 10-12 minutes, turning them occasionally, until the turkey bacon is crispy and the asparagus is tender.
- Once cooked, remove the turkey bacon-wrapped asparagus from the air fryer and serve with lemon wedges on the side.

Baked Buffalo Cauliflower

INGREDIENTS:

(Calories: ~100 / Carbs: 8g / Proteins: 4g / Fats: 6g)

- 1 medium head cauliflower, cut into bite-sized florets
- 1/4 cup buffalo hot sauce (choose a low-sugar option)
- 2 tablespoons olive oil, 1/4 cup whole wheat or almond flour
- 1/2 teaspoon garlic powder, 1/2 teaspoon onion powder
- Salt and pepper to taste
- Ranch or blue cheese dressing for dipping (choose a low-fat option)
- Chopped fresh parsley, for garnish

Cooking time: 20 minutes / servings: 4
Preparation time: 15 minutes

INSTRUCTIONS FOR COOKING:

- Preheat your air fryer to 375°F (190°C) for about 5 minutes.
- In a bowl, whisk together buffalo hot sauce and olive oil. Add cauliflower florets and toss to coat.
- In another bowl, combine flour, garlic powder, onion powder, salt, and pepper. Toss the buffalo-coated cauliflower in the flour mixture to coat evenly.
- Place the breaded cauliflower florets in a single layer in the air fryer basket. Cook for about 15-20 minutes, shaking the basket occasionally, until the cauliflower is crispy and golden.
- Once cooked, transfer the buffalo cauliflower to a serving dish. Garnish with chopped fresh parsley and serve with a side of ranch or blue cheese dressing for dipping.

Quinoa Stuffed Mushrooms

INGREDIENTS:

(Calories: ~140 / Carbs: 18g / Proteins: 7g / Fats: 4g)

- 16 large button mushrooms, stems removed and reserved
- 1/2 cup quinoa, rinsed and drained
- 1 cup low-sodium vegetable broth
- 1/4 cup onion, finely chopped
- 1/4 cup red bell pepper, finely chopped
- 1/4 cup zucchini, finely chopped, 2 cloves garlic, minced
- 1/4 teaspoon dried oregano, 1/4 teaspoon dried thyme
- Salt and pepper to taste
- 1/4 cup grated low-fat mozzarella cheese
- Chopped fresh parsley, for garnish

Cooking time: 20 minutes / servings: 4
Preparation time: 20 minutes

INSTRUCTIONS FOR COOKING:

- Preheat your air fryer to 375°F (190°C) for about 5 minutes.
- Lightly brush or spray the mushroom caps with a bit of olive oil to prevent sticking.
- In a saucepan, combine quinoa and vegetable broth. Bring to a boil, then reduce the heat to low, cover, and simmer for about 15 minutes, or until the quinoa is cooked and the liquid is absorbed.
- In a skillet, heat a teaspoon of olive oil over medium heat. Add the chopped mushroom stems, onion, red bell pepper, zucchini, garlic, dried oregano, dried thyme, salt, and pepper. Sauté for 5-6 minutes, until the vegetables are tender.
- In a bowl, combine the cooked quinoa with the sautéed vegetable mixture. Stir in the grated mozzarella cheese.
- Spoon the quinoa mixture into the mushroom caps, pressing gently to pack the filling.
- Place the stuffed mushrooms in the air fryer basket in a single layer. Cook for about 10-12 minutes, until the mushrooms are tender and the filling is heated through.
- Once cooked, remove the stuffed mushrooms from the air fryer and garnish with chopped fresh parsley before serving

Greek Lamb Kebabs

INGREDIENTS:

(Calories: ~220 / Carbs: 4g / Proteins: 22g / Fats: 12g)

- 1 pound lean lamb meat, cut into bite-sized pieces
- 1/4 cup plain Greek yogurt (choose a low-fat option)
- 2 tablespoons lemon juice, 2 cloves garlic, minced
- 1 teaspoon dried oregano
- 1/2 teaspoon dried rosemary
- Salt and pepper to taste
- Cherry tomatoes and red onion wedges, for skewering

Cooking time: 15 minutes / servings: 4
Preparation time: 25 minutes (+marinating time)

INSTRUCTIONS FOR COOKING:

- In a bowl, whisk together Greek yogurt, lemon juice, minced garlic, dried oregano, dried rosemary, salt, and pepper. Add the lamb pieces to the marinade and let them marinate for at least 30 minutes (or up to 2 hours) in the refrigerator.
- Preheat your air fryer to 375°F (190°C) for about 5 minutes.
- Thread marinated lamb pieces, cherry tomatoes, and red onion wedges onto skewers, alternating them.
- Place the assembled kebabs in the air fryer basket. Cook for about 12-15 minutes, turning the kebabs occasionally, until the lamb is cooked to your desired level of doneness.
- Once cooked, remove the kebabs from the air fryer and serve with a side of Greek yogurt sauce or tzatziki.

Avocado Shrimp Ceviche

INGREDIENTS:

(Calories: ~220 / Carbs: 10g / Proteins: 15g / Fats: 14g)

- 1/2 pound cooked shrimp, peeled, deveined, and chopped
- 2 ripe avocados, diced, 1 cup diced cucumber
- 1/2 cup diced red onion, 1/4 cup chopped fresh cilantro
- 1 jalapeno, seeds removed and finely chopped
- 1/4 cup freshly squeezed lime juice, salt and pepper to taste

Cooking time: 0 minutes / servings: 4
Preparation time: 15 minutes (+chilling time)

INSTRUCTIONS FOR COOKING:

- In a bowl, combine the chopped shrimp, diced avocados, diced cucumber, diced red onion, chopped cilantro, and finely chopped jalapeno.
- Pour the freshly squeezed lime juice over the mixture. Gently toss to combine all ingredients. Season with salt and pepper to taste.
- Cover the bowl with plastic wrap and refrigerate the ceviche for at least 30 minutes to allow the flavors to meld and the shrimp to marinate in the lime juice.
- Once chilled, give the ceviche a gentle stir and transfer it to serving dishes. Serve with baked sweet potato chips for a refreshing and light appetizer.

Baked Sweet Potato Chips

INGREDIENTS:

(Calories: ~120 / Carbs: 20g / Proteins: 2g / Fats: 4g)

- 2 medium sweet potatoes, peeled and thinly sliced
- 1 tablespoon olive oil, 1/2 teaspoon paprika
- 1/4 teaspoon garlic powder, salt to taste

Cooking time: 20 minutes / servings: 4
Preparation time: 10 minutes

INSTRUCTIONS FOR COOKING:

- Preheat your air fryer to 375°F (190°C) for about 5 minutes.
- In a bowl, toss the sweet potato slices with olive oil, paprika, garlic powder, and a pinch of salt, ensuring even coating.
- Place the seasoned sweet potato slices in a single layer in the air fryer basket. You may need to do this in batches depending on the size of your air fryer. Cook for about 10-12 minutes, shaking the basket occasionally, until the sweet potato chips are crispy and golden.
- Once cooked, transfer the sweet potato chips to a serving dish and sprinkle with a bit more salt if desired.

Asian Sesame Tofu Skewers

INGREDIENTS:

(Calories: ~140 / Carbs: 7g / Proteins: 10g / Fats: 8g)

- 14 oz (400g) firm tofu, pressed and cut into cubes
- 2 tablespoons low-sodium soy sauce
- 1 tablespoon rice vinegar, 1 tablespoon sesame oil
- 1 tablespoon low-sugar hoisin sauce
- 1 teaspoon fresh ginger, minced, 1 clove garlic, minced
- Bamboo skewers, soaked in water for 30 minutes
- Sesame seeds and sliced green onions, for garnish

Cooking time: 15 minutes / servings: 4
Preparation time: 30 minutes (+marinating time)

INSTRUCTIONS FOR COOKING:

- In a bowl, whisk together soy sauce, rice vinegar, sesame oil, hoisin sauce, minced ginger, and minced garlic. Add the tofu cubes to the marinade and let them marinate for at least 30 minutes (or up to 2 hours) in the refrigerator.
- Preheat your air fryer to 375°F (190°C) for about 5 minutes.
- Thread the marinated tofu cubes onto the soaked bamboo skewers.
- Place the tofu skewers in a single layer in the air fryer basket. Cook for about 12-15 minutes, turning them occasionally, until the tofu is heated through and slightly crispy on the edges.
- Once cooked, remove the skewers from the air fryer and sprinkle sesame seeds and sliced green onions over the top before serving.

Spinach Feta Phyllo Cups

INGREDIENTS:

(Calories: ~180 / Carbs: 15g / Proteins: 6g / Fats: 10g)

- 8 sheets phyllo dough, thawed, cooking spray
- 2 cups fresh spinach, chopped
- 1/2 cup crumbled feta cheese
- 1/4 cup chopped sun-dried tomatoes (packed in oil, drained)
- 1/4 teaspoon dried oregano, salt and pepper to taste

Cooking time: 10 minutes / servings: 4
Preparation time: 15 minutes

INSTRUCTIONS FOR COOKING:

- Preheat your air fryer to 375°F (190°C) for about 5 minutes.
- Lay out one sheet of phyllo dough and lightly coat it with cooking spray. Place another sheet on top and repeat until you have a stack of 4 phyllo sheets. Cut the stack into 4 equal squares. Repeat with the remaining phyllo sheets to make a total of 8 squares.
- Gently press each phyllo square into a muffin tin, creating a cup shape. Layer chopped spinach, crumbled feta cheese, chopped sun-dried tomatoes, dried oregano, salt, and pepper inside each phyllo cup.
- Place the filled phyllo cups in the air fryer basket. Cook for about 8-10 minutes, until the phyllo cups are golden and crispy.
- Once cooked, carefully remove the phyllo cups from the air fryer and serve them as a delightful and savory appetizer.

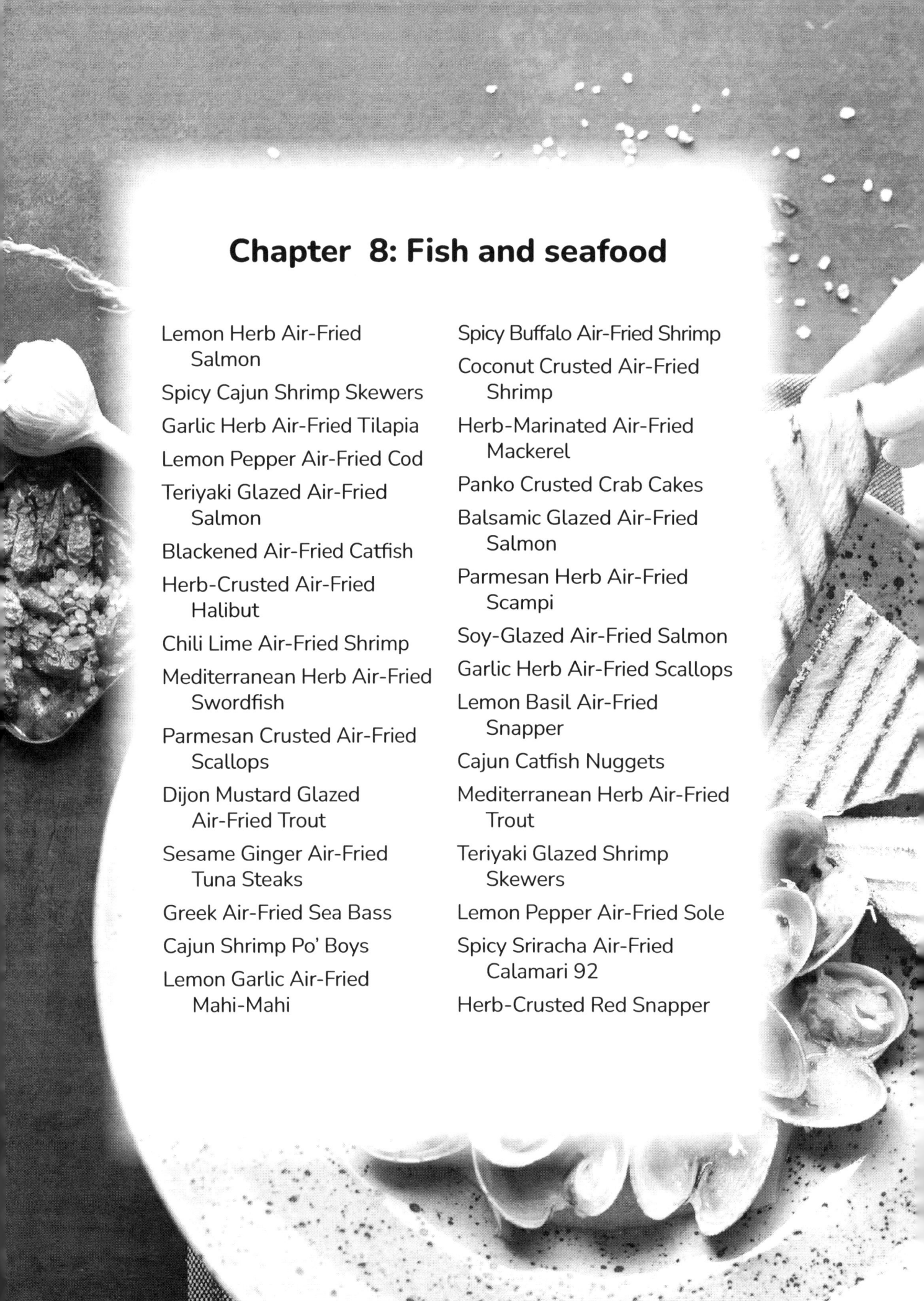

Chapter 8: Fish and seafood

- Lemon Herb Air-Fried Salmon
- Spicy Cajun Shrimp Skewers
- Garlic Herb Air-Fried Tilapia
- Lemon Pepper Air-Fried Cod
- Teriyaki Glazed Air-Fried Salmon
- Blackened Air-Fried Catfish
- Herb-Crusted Air-Fried Halibut
- Chili Lime Air-Fried Shrimp
- Mediterranean Herb Air-Fried Swordfish
- Parmesan Crusted Air-Fried Scallops
- Dijon Mustard Glazed Air-Fried Trout
- Sesame Ginger Air-Fried Tuna Steaks
- Greek Air-Fried Sea Bass
- Cajun Shrimp Po' Boys
- Lemon Garlic Air-Fried Mahi-Mahi
- Spicy Buffalo Air-Fried Shrimp
- Coconut Crusted Air-Fried Shrimp
- Herb-Marinated Air-Fried Mackerel
- Panko Crusted Crab Cakes
- Balsamic Glazed Air-Fried Salmon
- Parmesan Herb Air-Fried Scampi
- Soy-Glazed Air-Fried Salmon
- Garlic Herb Air-Fried Scallops
- Lemon Basil Air-Fried Snapper
- Cajun Catfish Nuggets
- Mediterranean Herb Air-Fried Trout
- Teriyaki Glazed Shrimp Skewers
- Lemon Pepper Air-Fried Sole
- Spicy Sriracha Air-Fried Calamari 92
- Herb-Crusted Red Snapper

Chapter 8: Fish and seafood

Lemon Herb Air-Fried Salmon

INGREDIENTS:

(Calories: 220 / Carbs: 1g / Proteins: 27g / Fats: 12g)

- 4 ounces salmon fillet,
- 1 tablespoon fresh lemon juice
- 1 teaspoon olive oil
- 1/2 teaspoon dried dill
- 1/2 teaspoon dried parsley
- 1/4 teaspoon garlic powder
- Salt and pepper to taste
- Lemon wedges for serving (optional)

Cooking time: 10 minutes / servings: 1
Preparation time: 5 minutes

INSTRUCTIONS FOR COOKING:

- Preheat your air fryer to 400°F (200°C) for about 5 minutes.
- In a small bowl, combine the lemon juice, olive oil, dried dill, dried parsley, garlic powder, salt, and pepper. Mix well to create a marinade.
- Place the salmon fillet in a shallow dish and pour the marinade over it. Make sure the salmon is evenly coated with the marinade. Let it marinate for 5 minutes.
- Lightly coat the air fryer basket with cooking spray to prevent sticking.
- Place the marinated salmon fillet in the air fryer basket, skin-side down.
- Air fry the salmon for 8-10 minutes, depending on the thickness of the fillet, until it flakes easily with a fork and reaches the desired level of doneness.
- Remove the salmon from the air fryer and let it rest for a few minutes before serving.
- Squeeze fresh lemon juice over the salmon fillet and serve it as a nutritious and flavorful meal.

Spicy Cajun Shrimp Skewers

INGREDIENTS:

(Calories: 110 / Carbs: 1g / Proteins: 23g / Fats: 1g)

- 4 ounces shrimp, peeled and deveined
- 1 teaspoon olive oil
- 1 teaspoon Cajun seasoning
- 1/4 teaspoon garlic powder
- 1/4 teaspoon paprika
- Pinch of cayenne pepper (optional)
- Lemon wedges for serving (optional)

Cooking time: 8 minutes / servings: 1
Preparation time: 10 minutes

INSTRUCTIONS FOR COOKING:

- Preheat your air fryer to 400°F (200°C) for about 5 minutes.
- In a bowl, combine the olive oil, Cajun seasoning, garlic powder, paprika, and cayenne pepper (if using). Mix well.
- Add the shrimp to the bowl and toss until they are coated evenly with the seasoning mixture.
- Thread the seasoned shrimp onto skewers.
- Lightly coat the air fryer basket with cooking spray to prevent sticking.
- Place the shrimp skewers in the air fryer basket, making sure they are not overcrowded.
- Air fry the shrimp skewers for 6-8 minutes, flipping halfway through, until the shrimp are pink and cooked through.
- Remove the shrimp skewers from the air fryer and let them cool for a few minutes before serving.
- Serve the spicy Cajun shrimp skewers as a delicious and protein-rich appetizer or main course.

Garlic Herb Air-Fried Tilapia

INGREDIENTS:

(Calories: 130 / Carbs: 1g / Proteins: 26g / Fats: 1g)

- 4 ounces tilapia fillet, 1 teaspoon olive oil
- 1/2 teaspoon minced garlic
- 1/2 teaspoon dried parsley
- 1/4 teaspoon dried thyme
- 1/4 teaspoon dried oregano
- Salt and pepper to taste
- Lemon wedges for serving (optional)

Cooking time: 12 minutes / servings: 1
Preparation time: 5 minutes

INSTRUCTIONS FOR COOKING:

- Preheat your air fryer to 400°F (200°C) for about 5 minutes.
- Pat dry the cod fillet with a paper towel to remove excess moisture.
- In a small bowl, mix together the olive oil, lemon zest, lemon pepper seasoning, garlic powder, and salt to create a flavorful marinade.
- Brush the marinade onto both sides of the cod fillet, ensuring it is evenly coated.
- Lightly coat the air fryer basket with cooking spray to prevent sticking.
- Place the marinated cod fillet in the air fryer basket.
- Air fry the cod for 10-12 minutes, flipping halfway through, until it is cooked through and flakes easily with a fork.
- Remove the cod from the air fryer and let it rest for a few minutes before serving.
- Serve the lemon pepper air fried cod with lemon wedges for a tangy and refreshing twist.

Lemon Pepper Air-Fried Cod

INGREDIENTS:

(Calories: 200 / Carbs: 0g / Proteins: 26g / Fats: 1g)

- 4 ounces cod fillet
- 1 teaspoon olive oil
- 1/2 teaspoon lemon zest
- 1/2 teaspoon lemon pepper seasoning
- 1/4 teaspoon garlic powder
- Salt to taste
- Lemon wedges for serving (optional)

Cooking time: 12 minutes / servings: 1
Preparation time: 5 minutes

INSTRUCTIONS FOR COOKING:

- Preheat your air fryer to 400°F (200°C) for about 5 minutes.
- Pat dry the cod fillet with a paper towel to remove excess moisture.
- In a small bowl, mix together the olive oil, lemon zest, lemon pepper seasoning, garlic powder, and salt to create a flavorful marinade.
- Brush the marinade onto both sides of the cod fillet, ensuring it is evenly coated.
- Lightly coat the air fryer basket with cooking spray to prevent sticking.
- Place the marinated cod fillet in the air fryer basket.
- Air fry the cod for 10-12 minutes, flipping halfway through, until it is cooked through and flakes easily with a fork.
- Remove the cod from the air fryer and let it rest for a few minutes before serving.
- Serve the lemon pepper air fried cod with lemon wedges for a tangy and refreshing twist.

Teriyaki Glazed Air-Fried Salmon

INGREDIENTS:

(Calories: 200 / Carbs: 6g / Proteins: 24g / Fats: 8g)

- 4 ounces salmon fillet
- 1 tablespoon low-sodium soy sauce, 1 tablespoon water
- 1/2 tablespoon honey (or a sugar substitute suitable for diabetics)
- 1/2 teaspoon minced garlic
- 1/2 teaspoon grated ginger
- 1/4 teaspoon cornstarch (optional, to thicken the sauce)
- Sesame seeds and green onions for garnish (optional)

Cooking time: 10 minutes / servings: 1
Preparation time: 5 minutes

INSTRUCTIONS FOR COOKING:

- Preheat your air fryer to 400°F (200°C) for about 5 minutes.
- In a small bowl, whisk together the soy sauce, water, honey (or sugar substitute), minced garlic, grated ginger, and cornstarch (if using) to create the teriyaki glaze.
- Place the salmon fillet in a shallow dish or zip-top bag and pour the teriyaki glaze over it. Let it marinate for 10-15 minutes.
- Lightly coat the air fryer basket with cooking spray to prevent sticking.
- Remove the salmon from the marinade, allowing any excess to drip off, and place it in the air fryer basket.
- Air fry the salmon for 10 minutes, or until it is cooked to your desired level of doneness.
- If desired, during the last 2 minutes of cooking, brush the salmon with any remaining teriyaki glaze for a flavorful glaze on top.
- Once cooked, remove the salmon from the air fryer and let it rest for a few minutes before serving.

Blackened Air-Fried Catfish

INGREDIENTS:

(Calories: 200 / Carbs: 1g / Proteins: 30g / Fats: 7g)

- 4 ounces catfish fillet, 1/2 teaspoon paprika
- 1/4 teaspoon garlic powder, 1/4 teaspoon onion powder
- 1/4 teaspoon dried thyme, 1/4 teaspoon dried oregano
- 1/8 teaspoon cayenne pepper (adjust according to spice preference)
- Salt and pepper to taste
- Lemon wedges for serving (optional)

Cooking time: 10 minutes / servings: 1
Preparation time: 5 minutes

INSTRUCTIONS FOR COOKING:

- Preheat your air fryer to 400°F (200°C) for about 5 minutes.
- In a small bowl, mix together the paprika, garlic powder, onion powder, dried thyme, dried oregano, cayenne pepper, salt, and pepper to create the blackened seasoning.
- Lightly coat the catfish fillet with cooking spray to help the seasoning adhere.
- Sprinkle the blackened seasoning evenly on both sides of the catfish fillet, pressing it gently to ensure it sticks.
- Lightly coat the air fryer basket with cooking spray to prevent sticking.
- Place the seasoned catfish fillet in the air fryer basket.
- Air fry the catfish for 10 minutes, flipping halfway through, until it is cooked through and crispy on the outside.
- Once cooked, remove the catfish from the air fryer and let it rest for a few minutes.
- Serve the blackened air fried catfish with lemon wedges on the side, if desired.

Herb-Crusted Air-Fried Halibut

INGREDIENTS:

(Calories: 220 / Carbs: 2g / Proteins: 30g / Fats: 9g)

- 4 ounces halibut fillet
- 1 tablespoon almond flour
- 1 tablespoon grated Parmesan cheese
- 1/2 teaspoon dried parsley
- 1/2 teaspoon dried basil
- 1/4 teaspoon garlic powder
- Salt and pepper to taste
- Lemon wedges for serving (optional)

Cooking time: 12 minutes / servings: 1
Preparation time: 10 minutes

INSTRUCTIONS FOR COOKING:

- Preheat your air fryer to 400°F (200°C) for about 5 minutes.
- In a shallow bowl, mix together the almond flour, grated Parmesan cheese, dried parsley, dried basil, garlic powder, salt, and pepper.
- Lightly coat the halibut fillet with cooking spray to help the herb crust adhere.
- Dip the halibut fillet into the herb mixture, pressing it gently to ensure the coating sticks.
- Lightly coat the air fryer basket with cooking spray to prevent sticking.
- Place the coated halibut fillet in the air fryer basket.
- Air fry the halibut for 12 minutes, or until it is cooked through and the coating is golden and crispy.
- Once cooked, remove the halibut from the air fryer and let it rest for a few minutes.
- Serve the herb-crusted air fried halibut with lemon wedges on the side, if desired.

Chili Lime Air-Fried Shrimp

INGREDIENTS:

(Calories: 150 / Carbs: 2g / Proteins: 18g / Fats: 8g)

- 4 ounces shrimp, peeled and deveined
- 1 tablespoon olive oil, 1/2 teaspoon chili powder
- 1/4 teaspoon garlic powder
- 1/4 teaspoon paprika
- 1/4 teaspoon cumin
- 1/4 teaspoon lime zest
- Salt and pepper to taste
- Lime wedges for serving (optional)

Cooking time: 8 minutes / servings: 1
Preparation time: 10 minutes

INSTRUCTIONS FOR COOKING:

- Preheat your air fryer to 400°F (200°C) for about 5 minutes.
- In a bowl, combine the olive oil, chili powder, garlic powder, paprika, cumin, lime zest, salt, and pepper.
- Add the shrimp to the bowl and toss to coat evenly with the seasoning mixture.
- Lightly coat the air fryer basket with cooking spray to prevent sticking.
- Place the seasoned shrimp in the air fryer basket.
- Air fry the shrimp for 8 minutes, shaking the basket halfway through, until the shrimp are pink and cooked through.
- Once cooked, remove the shrimp from the air fryer and let them cool for a minute.
- Serve the chili lime air fried shrimp with lime wedges on the side, if desired.

Mediterranean Herb Air-Fried Swordfish

INGREDIENTS:

(Calories: 230 / Carbs: 1g / Proteins: 28g / Fats: 13g)

- 4 ounces swordfish steak
- 1 tablespoon olive oil
- 1/2 teaspoon dried oregano
- 1/2 teaspoon dried thyme
- 1/4 teaspoon garlic powder
- 1/4 teaspoon onion powder
- Salt and pepper to taste
- Lemon wedges for serving (optional)

Cooking time: 10 minutes / servings: 1
Preparation time: 10 minutes

INSTRUCTIONS FOR COOKING:

- Preheat your air fryer to 400°F (200°C) for about 5 minutes.
- Brush the swordfish steak with olive oil on both sides.
- In a small bowl, mix together the dried oregano, dried thyme, garlic powder, onion powder, salt, and pepper.
- Sprinkle the herb mixture evenly over the swordfish steak, pressing it gently to adhere.
- Lightly coat the air fryer basket with cooking spray to prevent sticking.
- Place the seasoned swordfish steak in the air fryer basket.
- Air fry the swordfish for 10 minutes, or until it is cooked through and flakes easily with a fork.
- Once cooked, remove the swordfish from the air fryer and let it rest for a few minutes.
- Serve the Mediterranean herb air fried swordfish with lemon wedges on the side, if desired.

Parmesan Crusted Air-Fried Scallops

INGREDIENTS:

(Calories: 180 / Carbs: 2g / Proteins: 21g / Fats: 9g)

- 4 ounces scallops
- 1 tablespoon olive oil
- 1/4 cup grated Parmesan cheese
- 1/4 teaspoon garlic powder
- 1/4 teaspoon paprika
- Salt and pepper to taste
- Lemon wedges for serving (optional)

Cooking time: 8 minutes / servings: 1
Preparation time: 10 minutes

INSTRUCTIONS FOR COOKING:

- Preheat your air fryer to 400°F (200°C) for about 5 minutes.
- Pat the scallops dry with a paper towel.
- Drizzle the scallops with olive oil and toss to coat.
- In a shallow dish, mix together the grated Parmesan cheese, garlic powder, paprika, salt, and pepper.
- Dip each scallop into the Parmesan mixture, pressing it gently to adhere.
- Lightly coat the air fryer basket with cooking spray to prevent sticking.
- Place the coated scallops in the air fryer basket.
- Air fry the scallops for 8 minutes, shaking the basket halfway through, until they are golden and cooked through.
- Once cooked, remove the scallops from the air fryer and let them cool for a minute.
- Serve the Parmesan crusted air fried scallops with lemon wedges on the side, if desired.

Dijon Mustard Glazed Air-Fried Trout

INGREDIENTS:

(Calories: 180 / Carbs: 2g / Proteins: 24g / Fats: 8g)

- 4 ounces trout fillet
- 1 tablespoon Dijon mustard
- 1/2 tablespoon lemon juice
- 1/2 teaspoon dried dill
- Salt and pepper to taste
- Lemon wedges for serving (optional)

Cooking time: 10 minutes / servings: 1
Preparation time: 10 minutes

INSTRUCTIONS FOR COOKING:

- Preheat your air fryer to 400°F (200°C) for about 5 minutes.
- In a small bowl, mix together the Dijon mustard, lemon juice, dried dill, salt, and pepper.
- Pat the trout fillet dry with a paper towel.
- Spread the Dijon mustard mixture evenly over the trout fillet, coating both sides.
- Lightly coat the air fryer basket with cooking spray to prevent sticking.
- Place the glazed trout fillet in the air fryer basket.
- Air fry the trout for 10 minutes, or until it is cooked through and flakes easily with a fork.
- Once cooked, remove the trout from the air fryer and let it rest for a few minutes.
- Serve the Dijon mustard glazed air fried trout with lemon wedges on the side, if desired.

Sesame Ginger Air-Fried Tuna Steaks

INGREDIENTS:

(Calories: 220 / Carbs: 2g / Proteins: 29g / Fats: 10g)

- 4 ounces tuna steak
- 1 tablespoon low-sodium soy sauce
- 1/2 tablespoon sesame oil
- 1/2 tablespoon grated ginger
- 1/2 tablespoon sesame seeds
- Salt and pepper to taste
- Green onions for garnish (optional)

Cooking time: 8 minutes / servings: 1
Preparation time: 10 minutes

INSTRUCTIONS FOR COOKING:

- Preheat your air fryer to 400°F (200°C) for about 5 minutes.
- In a small bowl, mix together the low-sodium soy sauce, sesame oil, grated ginger, sesame seeds, salt, and pepper.
- Pat the tuna steak dry with a paper towel.
- Brush the sesame ginger mixture over both sides of the tuna steak.
- Lightly coat the air fryer basket with cooking spray to prevent sticking.
- Place the marinated tuna steak in the air fryer basket.
- Air fry the tuna for 8 minutes, or until it is cooked to your desired level of doneness.
- Once cooked, remove the tuna from the air fryer and let it rest for a few minutes.
- Garnish the sesame ginger air fried tuna steaks with chopped green onions, if desired.

Greek Air-Fried Sea Bass

INGREDIENTS:

(Calories: 350 / Carbs: 28g / Proteins: 32g / Fats: 10g)

- 4 ounces boneless, skinless chicken breast
- 1/4 cup sugar-free BBQ sauce
- 1 ear of corn
- 2 cups mixed salad greens
- 1/4 cup cherry tomatoes, halved
- 1/4 cup cucumber, sliced
- 1 tablespoon red onion, finely chopped
- 2 tablespoons low-fat ranch dressing (sugar-free or reduced-fat)

Cooking time: 25 minutes / servings: 1
Preparation time: 15 minutes

INSTRUCTIONS FOR COOKING:

- Preheat the air fryer to 400°F (200°C).
- Season the chicken breast with salt and pepper. Place it in the air fryer basket and cook for 10 minutes, flipping halfway through.
- Brush the chicken breast with the sugar-free BBQ sauce and continue cooking for another 5 minutes, or until the internal temperature reaches 165°F (74°C).
- While the chicken is cooking, prepare the grilled corn. Remove the husk and silk from the corn and lightly brush it with olive oil. Place it in the air fryer basket and cook for 10 minutes, turning occasionally, until lightly charred. Let it cool slightly, then cut the kernels off the cob.
- In a large salad bowl, combine the mixed salad greens, cherry tomatoes, cucumber, and red onion. Toss to mix well.
- Slice the cooked chicken breast into thin strips.
- Add the sliced chicken and grilled corn kernels to the salad bowl. Drizzle with low-fat ranch dressing and toss gently to coat all the ingredients.

Cajun Shrimp Po' Boys

INGREDIENTS:

(Calories: 320 / Carbs: 31g / Proteins: 28g / Fats: 9g)

- 4 ounces shrimp, peeled and deveined
- 1/2 tablespoon Cajun seasoning
- 1/2 tablespoon olive oil
- 1 whole wheat roll or baguette
- Lettuce leaves6 Sliced tomatoes
- Sliced pickles
- Low-fat mayonnaise (optional)

Cooking time: 10 minutes / servings: 1
Preparation time: 15 minutes

INSTRUCTIONS FOR COOKING:

- Preheat your air fryer to 400°F (200°C) for about 5 minutes.
- In a bowl, toss the shrimp with Cajun seasoning and olive oil, ensuring they are well coated.
- Lightly coat the air fryer basket with cooking spray to prevent sticking.
- Place the seasoned shrimp in the air fryer basket.
- Air fry the shrimp for 10 minutes, or until they are cooked through and crispy.
- While the shrimp is cooking, slice the whole wheat roll or baguette in half lengthwise.
- Layer the bottom half of the roll with lettuce leaves, sliced tomatoes, and sliced pickles.
- Once the shrimp is cooked, arrange them on top of the prepared roll
- Optionally, spread some low-fat mayonnaise on the top half of the roll before placing it on the shrimp.
- Press the top and bottom halves of the roll together to form a sandwich.
- Slice the po' boy sandwich in half and serve.

Lemon Garlic Air-Fried Mahi-Mahi

INGREDIENTS:

(Calories: 150 / Carbs: 1g / Proteins: 29g / Fats: 3g)

- 4 ounces mahi mahi fillet
- 1 tablespoon lemon juice
- 1 clove garlic, minced
- 1/2 teaspoon dried parsley
- Salt and pepper to taste
- Lemon wedges for serving (optional)

Cooking time: 10 minutes / servings: 1
Preparation time: 10 minutes

INSTRUCTIONS FOR COOKING:

- Preheat your air fryer to 400°F (200°C) for about 5 minutes.
- In a small bowl, mix together the lemon juice, minced garlic, dried parsley, salt, and pepper.
- Pat the mahi mahi fillet dry with a paper towel.
- Brush the lemon garlic mixture over both sides of the mahi mahi fillet.
- Lightly coat the air fryer basket with cooking spray to prevent sticking.
- Place the marinated mahi mahi fillet in the air fryer basket.
- Air fry the mahi mahi for 10 minutes, or until it is cooked through and flakes easily with a fork.
- Once cooked, remove the mahi mahi from the air fryer and let it rest for a few minutes.
- Serve the lemon garlic air fried mahi mahi with lemon wedges on the side, if desired.

Spicy Buffalo Air-Fried Shrimp

INGREDIENTS:

(Calories: 160 / Carbs: 1g / Proteins: 29g / Fats: 3g)

- 4 ounces shrimp, peeled and deveined
- 1 tablespoon hot sauce
- 1/2 tablespoon olive oil
- 1/2 teaspoon paprika
- 1/4 teaspoon garlic powder
- Salt and pepper to taste
- Celery sticks for serving (optional)
- Low-fat blue cheese dressing for dipping (optional)

Cooking time: 8 minutes / servings: 1
Preparation time: 15 minutes

INSTRUCTIONS FOR COOKING:

- Preheat your air fryer to 400°F (200°C) for about 5 minutes.
- In a bowl, toss the shrimp with hot sauce, olive oil, paprika, garlic powder, salt, and pepper, ensuring they are well coated.
- Lightly coat the air fryer basket with cooking spray to prevent sticking.
- Place the seasoned shrimp in the air fryer basket.
- Air fry the shrimp for 8 minutes, flipping halfway through, or until they are cooked through and crispy.
- Once cooked, remove the shrimp from the air fryer.
- Serve the spicy buffalo air fried shrimp with celery sticks on the side, if desired.
- Optionally, serve with a side of low-fat blue cheese dressing for dipping.

Coconut Crusted Air-Fried Shrimp

INGREDIENTS:

(Calories: 190 / Carbs: 9g / Proteins: 19g / Fats: 9g)

- 4 ounces shrimp, peeled and deveined
- 2 tablespoons unsweetened shredded coconut
- 1 tablespoon whole wheat flour
- 1/2 teaspoon paprika
- 1/4 teaspoon garlic powder
- Salt and pepper to taste
- 1 egg, beaten
- Cooking spray

Cooking time: 8 minutes / servings: 1
Preparation time: 15 minutes

INSTRUCTIONS FOR COOKING:

- Preheat your air fryer to 400°F (200°C) for about 5 minutes.
- In a shallow bowl, mix together the shredded coconut, whole wheat flour, paprika, garlic powder, salt, and pepper.
- Dip each shrimp into the beaten egg, allowing any excess to drip off.
- Coat each shrimp in the coconut mixture, pressing gently to adhere.
- Lightly coat the air fryer basket with cooking spray to prevent sticking.
- Place the coated shrimp in the air fryer basket.
- Air fry the shrimp for 8 minutes, flipping halfway through, or until they are cooked through and the coconut coating is golden brown and crispy.
- Once cooked, remove the shrimp from the air fryer.
- Serve the coconut crusted air fried shrimp as is or with your favorite dipping sauce.

Herb-Marinated Air-Fried Mackerel

INGREDIENTS:

(Calories: 230 / Carbs: 1g / Proteins: 20g / Fats: 16g)

- 4 ounces mackerel fillet
- 1 tablespoon lemon juice
- 1 tablespoon olive oil
- 1/2 teaspoon dried herbs (such as thyme, oregano, or basil)
- 1/4 teaspoon garlic powder
- Salt and pepper to taste
- Lemon wedges for serving (optional)

Cooking time: 10 minutes / servings: 1
Preparation time: 10 minutes

INSTRUCTIONS FOR COOKING:

- Preheat your air fryer to 400°F (200°C) for about 5 minutes.
- In a small bowl, whisk together the lemon juice, olive oil, dried herbs, garlic powder, salt, and pepper.
- Pat the mackerel fillet dry with a paper towel.
- Place the mackerel fillet in a shallow dish and pour the herb marinade over it, ensuring it is evenly coated.
- Let the mackerel marinate for 5 minutes.
- Lightly coat the air fryer basket with cooking spray to prevent sticking.
- Place the marinated mackerel fillet in the air fryer basket.
- Air fry the mackerel for 10 minutes, or until it is cooked through and flakes easily with a fork.
- Once cooked, remove the mackerel from the air fryer and let it rest for a few minutes.
- Serve the herb marinated air fried mackerel with lemon wedges on the side, if desired.

Panko Crusted Crab Cakes

INGREDIENTS:

(Calories: 180 / Carbs: 7g / Proteins: 18g / Fats: 8g)

- 4 ounces lump crab meat
- 2 tablespoons whole wheat panko breadcrumbs
- 1 tablespoon chopped fresh parsley
- 1 tablespoon light mayonnaise, 1 teaspoon Dijon mustard
- 1/4 teaspoon Old Bay seasoning
- 1/4 teaspoon lemon zest
- Salt and pepper to taste
- Cooking spray

Cooking time: 12 minutes / servings: 1
Preparation time: 20 minutes

INSTRUCTIONS FOR COOKING:

- Preheat your air fryer to 400°F (200°C) for about 5 minutes.
- In a bowl, combine the crab meat, panko breadcrumbs, parsley, mayonnaise, Dijon mustard, Old Bay seasoning, lemon zest, salt, and pepper. Gently mix until well combined.
- Shape the mixture into a compact patty.
- Lightly coat the air fryer basket with cooking spray to prevent sticking.
- Place the crab cake patty in the air fryer basket.
- Air fry the crab cake for 12 minutes, flipping halfway through, or until it is golden brown and cooked through.
- Once cooked, remove the crab cake from the air fryer.
- Serve the panko crusted air fried crab cake with a side salad or your favorite dipping sauce.

Balsamic Glazed Air-Fried Salmon

INGREDIENTS:

(Calories: 220 / Carbs: 30g / Proteins: 25g / Fats: 12g)

- 4 ounces salmon fillet
- 1 tablespoon balsamic vinegar
- 1 teaspoon olive oil
- 1/2 teaspoon Dijon mustard
- 1/2 teaspoon honey (optional for added sweetness)
- Salt and pepper to taste
- Chopped fresh herbs (such as parsley or dill) for garnish (optional)

Cooking time: 10 minutes / servings: 1
Preparation time: 10 minutes

INSTRUCTIONS FOR COOKING:

- Preheat your air fryer to 400°F (200°C) for about 5 minutes.
- In a small bowl, whisk together the balsamic vinegar, olive oil, Dijon mustard, honey (if using), salt, and pepper.
- Pat the salmon fillet dry with a paper towel.
- Place the salmon fillet in a shallow dish and pour the balsamic glaze over it, ensuring it is evenly coated.
- Let the salmon marinate for 5 minutes.
- Lightly coat the air fryer basket with cooking spray to prevent sticking.
- Place the marinated salmon fillet in the air fryer basket.
- Air fry the salmon for 10 minutes, or until it is cooked through and flakes easily with a fork.
- Once cooked, remove the salmon from the air fryer and let it rest for a few minutes.
- Serve the balsamic glazed air fried salmon garnished with fresh herbs, if desired.

Parmesan Herb Air-Fried Scampi

INGREDIENTS:

(Calories: 170 / Carbs: 1g / Proteins: 24g / Fats: 7g)

- 4 ounces raw shrimp, peeled and deveined
- 1 tablespoon grated Parmesan cheese
- 1 tablespoon chopped fresh parsley
- 1/2 tablespoon olive oil
- 1/2 teaspoon minced garlic
- 1/2 teaspoon lemon juice
- Salt and pepper to taste

Cooking time: 8 minutes / servings: 1
Preparation time: 10 minutes

INSTRUCTIONS FOR COOKING:

- Preheat your air fryer to 400°F (200°C) for about 5 minutes.
- In a bowl, combine the grated Parmesan cheese, chopped parsley, olive oil, minced garlic, lemon juice, salt, and pepper. Mix well.
- Add the shrimp to the bowl and toss to coat them evenly with the Parmesan herb mixture.
- Lightly coat the air fryer basket with cooking spray to prevent sticking.
- Place the seasoned shrimp in the air fryer basket in a single layer.
- Air fry the shrimp for 8 minutes, shaking the basket halfway through to ensure even cooking.
- Once cooked, remove the scampi from the air fryer.
- Serve the Parmesan and herb air fried scampi with a side of steamed vegetables or a salad.

Soy-Glazed Air-Fried Salmon

INGREDIENTS:

(Calories: 250 / Carbs: 7g / Proteins: 25g / Fats: 14g)

- 4 ounces salmon fillet, 1 tablespoon low-sodium soy sauce
- 1 teaspoon honey (or a sugar substitute for a lower glycemic option)
- 1/2 teaspoon sesame oil
- 1/2 teaspoon sesame seeds
- 1/2 teaspoon minced garlic
- Salt and pepper to taste
- Sliced green onions for garnish (optional)

Cooking time: 10 minutes / servings: 1
Preparation time: 10 minutes

INSTRUCTIONS FOR COOKING:

- Preheat your air fryer to 400°F (200°C) for about 5 minutes.
- In a small bowl, whisk together the soy sauce, honey, sesame oil, sesame seeds, minced garlic, salt, and pepper.
- Pat the salmon fillet dry with a paper towel.
- Place the salmon fillet in a shallow dish and pour the soy glaze over it, ensuring it is evenly coated.
- Let the salmon marinate for 5 minutes.
- Lightly coat the air fryer basket with cooking spray to prevent sticking.
- Place the marinated salmon fillet in the air fryer basket.
- Air fry the salmon for 10 minutes, or until it is cooked through and flakes easily with a fork.
- Once cooked, remove the salmon from the air fryer and let it rest for a few minutes.
- Garnish with sliced green onions, if desired, and serve the soy glazed air fried sesame salmon with a side of steamed vegetables or brown rice.

Garlic Herb Air-Fried Scallops

INGREDIENTS:

(Calories: 170 / Carbs: 1g / Proteins: 24g / Fats: 7g)

- 4 ounces raw shrimp, peeled and deveined
- 1 tablespoon grated Parmesan cheese
- 1 tablespoon chopped fresh parsley
- 1/2 tablespoon olive oil
- 1/2 teaspoon minced garlic
- 1/2 teaspoon lemon juice
- Salt and pepper to taste

Cooking time: 8 minutes / servings: 1
Preparation time: 10 minutes

INSTRUCTIONS FOR COOKING:

- Preheat your air fryer to 400°F (200°C) for about 5 minutes.
- In a bowl, combine the grated Parmesan cheese, chopped parsley, olive oil, minced garlic, lemon juice, salt, and pepper. Mix well.
- Add the shrimp to the bowl and toss to coat them evenly with the Parmesan herb mixture.
- Lightly coat the air fryer basket with cooking spray to prevent sticking.
- Place the seasoned shrimp in the air fryer basket in a single layer.
- Air fry the shrimp for 8 minutes, shaking the basket halfway through to ensure even cooking.
- Once cooked, remove the scampi from the air fryer.
- Serve the Parmesan and herb air fried scampi with a side of steamed vegetables or a salad.

Lemon Basil Air-Fried Snapper

INGREDIENTS:

(Calories: 250 / Carbs: 7g / Proteins: 25g / Fats: 14g)

- 4 ounces salmon fillet, 1 tablespoon low-sodium soy sauce
- 1 teaspoon honey (or a sugar substitute for a lower glycemic option)
- 1/2 teaspoon sesame oil
- 1/2 teaspoon sesame seeds
- 1/2 teaspoon minced garlic
- Salt and pepper to taste
- Sliced green onions for garnish (optional)

Cooking time: 10 minutes / servings: 1
Preparation time: 10 minutes

INSTRUCTIONS FOR COOKING:

- Preheat your air fryer to 400°F (200°C) for about 5 minutes.
- In a small bowl, whisk together the soy sauce, honey, sesame oil, sesame seeds, minced garlic, salt, and pepper.
- Pat the salmon fillet dry with a paper towel.
- Place the salmon fillet in a shallow dish and pour the soy glaze over it, ensuring it is evenly coated.
- Let the salmon marinate for 5 minutes.
- Lightly coat the air fryer basket with cooking spray to prevent sticking.
- Place the marinated salmon fillet in the air fryer basket.
- Air fry the salmon for 10 minutes, or until it is cooked through and flakes easily with a fork.
- Once cooked, remove the salmon from the air fryer and let it rest for a few minutes.
- Garnish with sliced green onions, if desired, and serve the soy glazed air fried sesame salmon with a side of steamed vegetables or brown rice.

Cajun Catfish Nuggets

INGREDIENTS:

(Calories: 200 / Carbs: 15g / Proteins: 22g / Fats: 6g)

- 4 ounces catfish fillet, cut into bite-sized nuggets
- 1/4 cup whole wheat flour
- 1 teaspoon Cajun seasoning
- 1/4 teaspoon garlic powder
- 1/4 teaspoon paprika
- Salt and pepper to taste
- Cooking spray

Cooking time: 12 minutes / servings: 1
Preparation time: 15 minutes

INSTRUCTIONS FOR COOKING:

- Preheat your air fryer to 400°F (200°C) for about 5 minutes.
- In a shallow dish, combine the whole wheat flour, Cajun seasoning, garlic powder, paprika, salt, and pepper.
- Lightly coat the catfish nuggets with the flour mixture, shaking off any excess.
- Lightly coat the air fryer basket with cooking spray to prevent sticking.
- Arrange the catfish nuggets in a single layer in the air fryer basket.
- Air fry the catfish nuggets for 12 minutes, flipping them halfway through cooking.
- Once cooked, remove the catfish nuggets from the air fryer and let them cool for a few minutes before serving.

Mediterranean Herb Air-Fried Trout

INGREDIENTS:

(Calories: 180 / Carbs: 0g / Proteins: 25g / Fats: 8g)

- 4 ounces trout fillet, 1 tablespoon olive oil
- 1/2 teaspoon dried oregano
- 1/2 teaspoon dried basil
- 1/4 teaspoon garlic powder
- 1/4 teaspoon lemon zest
- Salt and pepper to taste
- Lemon wedges for serving (optional)

Cooking time: 10 minutes / servings: 1
Preparation time: 10 minutes

INSTRUCTIONS FOR COOKING:

- Preheat your air fryer to 400°F (200°C) for about 5 minutes.
- In a bowl, combine the olive oil, dried oregano, dried basil, garlic powder, lemon zest, salt, and pepper.
- Pat the trout fillet dry with a paper towel and place it in a shallow dish. Pour the Mediterranean herb mixture over the fillet, ensuring it is evenly coated.
- Lightly coat the air fryer basket with cooking spray to prevent sticking.
- Place the seasoned trout fillet in the air fryer basket.
- Air fry the trout for 10 minutes, or until it is cooked through and flakes easily with a fork.
- Once cooked, remove the trout from the air fryer and let it rest for a few minutes.
- Serve the Mediterranean herb air fried trout with lemon wedges on the side for squeezing over the fish, if desired.

Teriyaki Glazed Shrimp Skewers

INGREDIENTS:

(Calories: 130 / Carbs: 9g / Proteins: 14g / Fats: 3g)

- 6 large shrimp, peeled and deveined
- 1 tablespoon low-sodium soy sauce
- 1 tablespoon honey or sugar-free alternative
- 1 tablespoon water, 1/2 teaspoon minced garlic
- 1/2 teaspoon grated ginger
- 1/4 teaspoon sesame oil
- Pinch of red pepper flakes (optional)
- Skewers, soaked in water if using wooden skewers

Cooking time: 8 minutes / servings: 1
Preparation time: 15 minutes

INSTRUCTIONS FOR COOKING:

- Preheat your air fryer to 400°F (200°C) for about 5 minutes.
- In a small bowl, whisk together the soy sauce, honey (or sugar-free alternative), water, minced garlic, grated ginger, sesame oil, and red pepper flakes (if using).
- Thread the shrimp onto skewers, making sure they are secure and evenly spaced.
- Lightly coat the air fryer basket with cooking spray to prevent sticking.
- Place the shrimp skewers in the air fryer basket and brush them generously with the teriyaki glaze.
- Air fry the shrimp skewers for 4 minutes, then carefully flip them over and brush the other side with the glaze.
- Air fry for an additional 4 minutes, or until the shrimp are pink, opaque, and cooked through.
- Once cooked, remove the shrimp skewers from the air fryer and let them rest for a minute before serving.

Lemon Pepper Air-Fried Sole

INGREDIENTS:

(Calories: 120 / Carbs: 0g / Proteins: 23g / Fats: 3g)

- 4 ounces sole fillet
- 1 teaspoon olive oil
- 1/2 teaspoon lemon zest
- 1/2 teaspoon freshly ground black pepper
- 1/4 teaspoon garlic powder
- Salt to taste
- Lemon wedges for serving (optional)

Cooking time: 8 minutes / servings: 1
Preparation time: 10 minutes

INSTRUCTIONS FOR COOKING:

- Preheat your air fryer to 400°F (200°C) for about 5 minutes.
- Pat the sole fillet dry with a paper towel.
- In a small bowl, combine the olive oil, lemon zest, black pepper, garlic powder, and salt.
- Brush both sides of the sole fillet with the lemon pepper mixture.
- Lightly coat the air fryer basket with cooking spray to prevent sticking.
- Place the seasoned sole fillet in the air fryer basket.
- Air fry the sole for 8 minutes, or until it is cooked through and flakes easily with a fork.
- Once cooked, remove the sole from the air fryer and let it rest for a few minutes.
- Serve the lemon pepper air fried sole with lemon wedges on the side for squeezing over the fish, if desired.

Spicy Sriracha Air-Fried Calamari

INGREDIENTS:

(Calories: 150 / Carbs: 12g / Proteins: 15g / Fats: 5g)

- 4 ounces calamari rings, 1 tablespoon cornstarch
- 1 tablespoon sriracha sauce
- 1 tablespoon low-sodium soy sauce
- 1/2 teaspoon minced garlic
- 1/2 teaspoon grated ginger
- 1/4 teaspoon sesame oil
- Cooking spray

Cooking time: 10 minutes / servings: 1
Preparation time: 15 minutes

INSTRUCTIONS FOR COOKING:

- Preheat your air fryer to 400°F (200°C) for about 5 minutes.
- In a mixing bowl, combine the cornstarch, sriracha sauce, soy sauce, minced garlic, grated ginger, and sesame oil. Stir well to create a marinade.
- Add the calamari rings to the marinade and toss until they are evenly coated.
- Lightly coat the air fryer basket with cooking spray to prevent sticking.
- Place the marinated calamari rings in the air fryer basket, making sure they are spread out in a single layer.
- Air fry the calamari rings for 8-10 minutes, or until they are golden brown and crispy.
- Once cooked, remove the calamari rings from the air fryer and let them cool for a minute before serving.

Herb-Crusted Red Snapper

INGREDIENTS:

(Calories: 350 / Carbs: 28g / Proteins: 32g / Fats: 10g)

- 4 ounces boneless, skinless chicken breast
- 1/4 cup sugar-free BBQ sauce
- 1 ear of corn, 2 cups mixed salad greens
- 1/4 cup cherry tomatoes, halved
- 1/4 cup cucumber, sliced
- 1 tablespoon red onion, finely chopped
- 2 tablespoons low-fat ranch dressing (sugar-free or reduced-fat)

Cooking time: 12 minutes / servings: 1
Preparation time: 10 minutes

INSTRUCTIONS FOR COOKING:

- Preheat the air fryer to 400°F (200°C).
- Season the chicken breast with salt and pepper. Place it in the air fryer basket and cook for 10 minutes, flipping halfway through.
- Brush the chicken breast with the sugar-free BBQ sauce and continue cooking for another 5 minutes, or until the internal temperature reaches 165°F (74°C).
- While the chicken is cooking, prepare the grilled corn. Remove the husk and silk from the corn and lightly brush it with olive oil. Place it in the air fryer basket and cook for 10 minutes, turning occasionally, until lightly charred. Let it cool slightly, then cut the kernels off the cob.
- In a large salad bowl, combine the mixed salad greens, cherry tomatoes, cucumber, and red onion. Toss to mix well.
- Slice the cooked chicken breast into thin strips.
- Add the sliced chicken and grilled corn kernels to the salad bowl. Drizzle with low-fat ranch dressing and toss gently to coat all the ingredients.

Chapter 9: Vegetarian recipes

- Crispy Tofu Nuggets
- Zucchini Feta Fritters
- Stuffed Portobello Mushrooms
- Eggplant Parmesan
- Air-Fried Veggie Spring Rolls
- Mediterranean Stuffed Peppers
- Cauliflower Buffalo Bites
- Air-Fried Falafel
- Sweet Potato Veggie Burgers
- Caprese Stuffed Avocado
- Quinoa Stuffed Bell Peppers
- Crispy Zucchini Chips
- Spinach Feta Stuffed Mushrooms

- Greek Stuffed Tomatoes
- Crispy Parmesan Asparagus
- Caprese Skewers
- Sweet Potato Fries
- Chickpea Vegetable Curry
- Air-Fried Vegetable Tempura
- Mediterranean Eggplant Bake
- Quinoa Stuffed Peppers
- Air-Fried Brussels Sprouts
- Stuffed Portobello Mushrooms
- Sweet Potato Buddha Bowl
- Crispy Onion Rings

Chapter 9: Vegetarian recipes

Crispy Tofu Nuggets

INGREDIENTS:

(Calories: 120 / Carbs: 9g / Proteins: 10g / Fats: 5g)

- 4 ounces firm tofu, drained and pressed
- 1 tablespoon cornstarch
- 1/2 teaspoon garlic powder
- 1/2 teaspoon onion powder
- 1/4 teaspoon paprika
- Salt and pepper to taste
- Cooking spray

Cooking time: 15 minutes / servings: 1
Preparation time: 10 minutes

INSTRUCTIONS FOR COOKING:

- Preheat your air fryer to 400°F (200°C) for about 5 minutes.
- Cut the tofu into bite-sized nuggets.
- In a shallow bowl, combine the cornstarch, garlic powder, onion powder, paprika, salt, and pepper. Mix well.
- Toss the tofu nuggets in the cornstarch mixture until they are evenly coated.
- Lightly coat the air fryer basket with cooking spray to prevent sticking.
- Place the coated tofu nuggets in the air fryer basket, making sure they are spread out in a single layer.
- Air fry the tofu nuggets for 12-15 minutes, or until they are crispy and golden brown.
- Once cooked, remove the tofu nuggets from the air fryer and let them cool for a minute before serving.

Zucchini Feta Fritters

INGREDIENTS:

(Calories: 150 / Carbs: 9g / Proteins: 10g / Fats: 8g)

- 1 medium zucchini, grated and squeezed to remove excess moisture
- 1/4 cup crumbled feta cheese
- 2 tablespoons almond flour
- 1 egg, beaten, 1/2 teaspoon dried oregano
- 1/4 teaspoon garlic powder
- Salt and pepper to taste
- Cooking spray

Cooking time: 10 minutes / servings: 1
Preparation time: 15 minutes

INSTRUCTIONS FOR COOKING:

- Preheat your air fryer to 375°F (190°C) for about 5 minutes.
- In a mixing bowl, combine the grated zucchini, crumbled feta cheese, almond flour, beaten egg, dried oregano, garlic powder, salt, and pepper. Mix well to form a batter.
- Lightly coat the air fryer basket with cooking spray to prevent sticking.
- Spoon the zucchini and feta batter into the air fryer, forming small fritters. Make sure they are evenly spaced.
- Air fry the fritters for 8-10 minutes, or until they are golden brown and crispy on the outside.
- Once cooked, remove the fritters from the air fryer and let them cool for a minute before serving.

Stuffed Portobello Mushrooms

INGREDIENTS:

(Calories: 150 / Carbs: 9g / Proteins: 8g / Fats: 10g)

- 2 large Portobello mushrooms
- 1 cup fresh spinach, chopped
- 2 tablespoons grated Parmesan cheese
- 1 tablespoon olive oil
- 1 clove garlic, minced
- Salt and pepper to taste

Cooking time: 15 minutes / servings: 1
Preparation time: 15 minutes

INSTRUCTIONS FOR COOKING:

- Preheat your air fryer to 375°F (190°C) for about 5 minutes.
- Remove the stems from the Portobello mushrooms and scrape out the gills using a spoon.
- In a small bowl, combine the chopped spinach, grated Parmesan cheese, minced garlic, olive oil, salt, and pepper. Mix well.
- Fill each Portobello mushroom cap with the spinach and cheese mixture, pressing it down gently.
- Lightly coat the air fryer basket with cooking spray to prevent sticking.
- Place the stuffed Portobello mushrooms in the air fryer basket, ensuring they are evenly spaced.
- Air fry the mushrooms for 12-15 minutes, or until the mushrooms are tender and the cheese is melted and golden.
- Once cooked, remove the mushrooms from the air fryer and let them cool for a minute before serving.

Eggplant Parmesan

INGREDIENTS:

(Calories: 180 / Carbs: 22g / Proteins: 7g / Fats: 7g)

- 1 small eggplant, sliced into rounds
- 1/4 cup whole wheat breadcrumbs
- 2 tablespoons grated Parmesan cheese
- 1/4 teaspoon dried oregano
- 1/4 teaspoon dried basil
- 1/4 teaspoon garlic powder
- Salt and pepper to taste
- 1/2 cup fresh tomato sauce

Cooking time: 20 minutes / servings: 1
Preparation time: 20 minutes

INSTRUCTIONS FOR COOKING:

- Preheat your air fryer to 375°F (190°C) for about 5 minutes.
- In a shallow bowl, combine the whole wheat breadcrumbs, grated Parmesan cheese, dried oregano, dried basil, garlic powder, salt, and pepper. Mix well.
- Dip each eggplant slice into the breadcrumb mixture, pressing it down to coat both sides.
- Lightly coat the air fryer basket with cooking spray to prevent sticking.
- Place the breaded eggplant slices in the air fryer basket, making sure they are evenly spaced.
- Air fry the eggplant slices for 10 minutes, then flip them over and air fry for an additional 10 minutes, or until they are crispy and golden.
- Once cooked, remove the eggplant slices from the air fryer and let them cool for a minute.
- Serve the crispy eggplant slices with fresh tomato sauce on top.

Air-Fried Veggie Spring Rolls

INGREDIENTS:

(Calories: 160 / Carbs: 26g / Proteins: 4g / Fats: 4g)

- 2 spring roll wrappers
- 1/2 cup shredded cabbage
- 1/4 cup shredded carrots
- 1/4 cup sliced bell peppers
- 2 tablespoons chopped green onions
- 1 tablespoon low-sodium soy sauce
- 1 teaspoon sesame oil
- 1/2 teaspoon grated ginger
- Cooking spray

Cooking time: 10 minutes / servings: 1
Preparation time: 15 minutes

INSTRUCTIONS FOR COOKING:

- In a mixing bowl, combine the shredded cabbage, shredded carrots, sliced bell peppers, chopped green onions, soy sauce, sesame oil, and grated ginger. Mix well to coat the vegetables evenly.
- Preheat your air fryer to 375°F (190°C) for about 5 minutes.
- Place a spring roll wrapper on a clean surface. Spoon a portion of the vegetable mixture onto the center of the wrapper.
- Fold the sides of the wrapper over the filling and roll it tightly, tucking in the edges as you go.
- Lightly coat the air fryer basket with cooking spray to prevent sticking.
- Place the spring rolls in the air fryer basket, making sure they are evenly spaced.
- Air fry the spring rolls for 8-10 minutes, or until they are crispy and golden.
- Once cooked, remove the spring rolls from the air fryer and let them cool for a minute before serving.

Mediterranean Stuffed Peppers

INGREDIENTS:

(Calories: 180 / Carbs: 25g / Proteins: 7g / Fats: 6g)

- 1 large bell pepper, 1/4 cup cooked quinoa
- 2 tablespoons crumbled feta cheese
- 2 tablespoons chopped Kalamata olives
- 1 tablespoon chopped fresh parsley
- 1 tablespoon chopped fresh mint
- 1/2 teaspoon lemon zest, Salt and pepper to taste
- Cooking spray

Cooking time: 25 minutes / servings: 1
Preparation time: 20 minutes

INSTRUCTIONS FOR COOKING:

- Preheat your air fryer to 375°F (190°C) for about 5 minutes.
- Cut the bell pepper in half lengthwise and remove the seeds and membranes.
- In a mixing bowl, combine the cooked quinoa, crumbled feta cheese, chopped Kalamata olives, chopped fresh parsley, chopped fresh mint, lemon zest, salt, and pepper. Mix well.
- Fill each bell pepper half with the quinoa mixture, pressing it down gently.
- Lightly coat the air fryer basket with cooking spray to prevent sticking.
- Place the stuffed bell peppers in the air fryer basket, making sure they are evenly spaced.
- Air fry the bell peppers for 20-25 minutes, or until the peppers are tender and the filling is heated through.
- Once cooked, remove the bell peppers from the air fryer and let them cool for a minute before serving.

Cauliflower Buffalo Bites

INGREDIENTS:

(Calories: 120 / Carbs: 9g / Proteins: 4g / Fats: 8g)

- 1 cup cauliflower florets, 1 tablespoon olive oil
- 1/4 teaspoon garlic powder
- 1/4 teaspoon paprika
- 1/4 teaspoon cayenne pepper (adjust to taste)
- Salt and pepper to taste
- 2 tablespoons hot sauce (sugar-free)
- 2 tablespoons Greek yogurt
- 1 tablespoon chopped fresh parsley (optional)

Cooking time: 15 minutes / servings: 1
Preparation time: 10 minutes

INSTRUCTIONS FOR COOKING:

- Preheat your air fryer to 375°F (190°C) for about 5 minutes.
- In a mixing bowl, toss the cauliflower florets with olive oil, garlic powder, paprika, cayenne pepper, salt, and pepper until well coated.
- Place the seasoned cauliflower florets in the air fryer basket, making sure they are evenly spaced.
- Air fry the cauliflower for 12-15 minutes, shaking the basket halfway through, until they are crispy and golden brown.
- In a separate bowl, mix the hot sauce and Greek yogurt to make the dip.
- Once cooked, remove the cauliflower bites from the air fryer and toss them in the hot sauce mixture until well coated.
- Garnish with chopped fresh parsley (optional) and serve with the Greek yogurt dip.

Air-Fried Falafel

INGREDIENTS:

(Calories: 260 / Carbs: 22g / Proteins: 8g / Fats: 17g)

- 1/2 cup canned chickpeas, drained and rinsed
- 2 tablespoons chopped fresh parsley
- 1 tablespoon chopped fresh cilantro
- 1/4 small onion, finely chopped
- 1 clove garlic, minced, 1/2 teaspoon ground cumin
- 1/4 teaspoon ground coriander, 1/4 teaspoon baking powder
- Salt and pepper to taste, 1 tablespoon olive oil
- 2 tablespoons tahini, 1 tablespoon lemon juice
- Water (as needed)
- Chopped fresh parsley for garnish (optional)

Cooking time: 15 minutes / servings: 1
Preparation time: 15 minutes

INSTRUCTIONS FOR COOKING:

- Preheat your air fryer to 375°F (190°C) for about 5 minutes.
- In a food processor, combine the chickpeas, fresh parsley, fresh cilantro, onion, garlic, cumin, coriander, baking powder, salt, and pepper. Pulse until well combined but still slightly chunky.
- Shape the mixture into small falafel patties or balls.
- Lightly brush the falafel patties with olive oil.
- Place the falafel patties in the air fryer basket, making sure they are evenly spaced.
- Air fry the falafel for 12-15 minutes, flipping them halfway through, until they are crispy and golden brown.
- In a small bowl, whisk together tahini, lemon juice, and water until you reach a desired sauce consistency.
- Once cooked, remove the falafel from the air fryer and serve with tahini sauce.
- Garnish with chopped fresh parsley, if desired.

Sweet Potato Veggie Burgers

INGREDIENTS:

(Calories: 300 / Carbs: 54g / Proteins: 13g / Fats: 5g)

- 1/2 cup cooked sweet potato, mashed
- 1/2 cup canned black beans, rinsed and drained
- 1/4 small onion, finely chopped
- 1/4 cup whole wheat breadcrumbs
- 1/4 teaspoon ground cumin
- 1/4 teaspoon paprika, salt and pepper to taste
- 1 teaspoon olive oil, mhole wheat burger bun
- Lettuce, tomato slices, and onion slices for topping (optional)

Cooking time: 25 minutes / servings: 1
Preparation time: 20 minutes

INSTRUCTIONS FOR COOKING:

- Preheat your air fryer to 375°F (190°C) for about 5 minutes.
- In a mixing bowl, combine the mashed sweet potato, black beans, onion, breadcrumbs, cumin, paprika, salt, and pepper. Mix well to combine all the ingredients.
- Shape the mixture into a patty, making sure it is firm and holds its shape.
- Brush the patty with olive oil on both sides to promote browning.
- Place the patty in the air fryer basket and cook for 12-15 minutes, flipping halfway through, until it is crispy on the outside.
- While the patty is cooking, lightly toast the whole wheat burger bun.
- Once cooked, remove the patty from the air fryer and assemble it on the bun. Add lettuce, tomato slices, and onion slices if desired.

Caprese Stuffed Avocado

INGREDIENTS:

(Calories: 360 / Carbs: 18g / Proteins: 9g / Fats: 30g)

- 1 ripe avocado
- 4-6 cherry tomatoes, halved
- 2-3 small mozzarella balls, cut into small pieces
- Fresh basil leaves, torn
- Balsamic glaze
- Salt and pepper to taste

Cooking time: 0 minutes / servings: 1
Preparation time: 10 minutes

INSTRUCTIONS FOR COOKING:

- Cut the avocado in half and remove the pit. Scoop out a little extra flesh from each half to create a hollow space for the filling.
- Season the avocado halves with salt and pepper.
- Stuff each avocado half with cherry tomatoes, mozzarella pieces, and torn basil leaves.
- Drizzle the stuffed avocado halves with balsamic glaze.
- Serve the caprese stuffed avocado immediately.

Quinoa Stuffed Bell Peppers

INGREDIENTS:

(Calories: 250 / Carbs: 45g / Proteins: 12g / Fats: 2g)

- 1 bell pepper, 1/4 cup cooked quinoa
- 1/4 cup canned black beans, rinsed and drained
- 2 tablespoons diced tomatoes
- 2 tablespoons diced onion
- 2 tablespoons diced bell pepper (from the top of the bell pepper)
- 1/2 teaspoon chili powder
- Salt and pepper to taste
- Optional toppings: shredded cheese, chopped cilantro

Cooking time: 25 minutes / servings: 1
Preparation time: 15 minutes

INSTRUCTIONS FOR COOKING:

- Preheat your air fryer to 375°F (190°C) for about 5 minutes.
- Cut off the top of the bell pepper and remove the seeds and membranes. Reserve the diced bell pepper from the top for later use.
- In a mixing bowl, combine the cooked quinoa, black beans, diced tomatoes, diced onion, diced bell pepper, chili powder, salt, and pepper. Mix well to combine all the ingredients.
- Stuff the bell pepper with the quinoa and black bean mixture.
- Place the stuffed bell pepper in the air fryer basket and cook for 20-25 minutes, or until the bell pepper is tender and the filling is heated through.
- Optional: Sprinkle shredded cheese on top of the stuffed bell pepper during the last few minutes of cooking for a cheesy topping.
- Once cooked, remove the stuffed bell pepper from the air fryer and let it cool for a few minutes.
- Garnish with chopped cilantro if desired, and serve the quinoa and black bean stuffed bell pepper.

Crispy Zucchini Chips

INGREDIENTS:

(Calories: 120 / Carbs: 12g / Proteins: 8g / Fats: 4g)

- 1 medium zucchini
- 1/4 cup whole wheat breadcrumbs
- 1/4 cup grated Parmesan cheese
- 1/2 teaspoon dried Italian seasoning
- 1/4 teaspoon garlic powder
- 1/4 teaspoon salt
- 1/8 teaspoon black pepper
- Cooking spray (olive oil or non-stick)

Cooking time: 15 minutes / servings: 1
Preparation time: 10 minutes

INSTRUCTIONS FOR COOKING:

- Preheat the air fryer to 400°F (200°C) for 5 minutes.
- Wash the zucchini thoroughly and cut it into thin round slices, about 1/8 inch thick.
- cheese, Italian seasoning, garlic powder, salt, and black pepper. Mix well.
- Spray the air fryer basket with cooking spray to prevent sticking.
- Take a few zucchini slices at a time and coat them with the breadcrumb mixture. Press gently to ensure the coating sticks to the slices.
- Place the coated zucchini slices in a single layer in the air fryer basket. Avoid overcrowding, and cook in batches if necessary.
- Lightly spray the coated zucchini slices with cooking spray to help them crisp up.
- Air fry the zucchini chips at 400°F (200°C) for 10-12 minutes, flipping them halfway through the cooking time.
- Once the zucchini chips are golden brown and crispy, remove them from the air fryer and transfer to a serving plate.

Spinach Feta Stuffed Mushrooms

INGREDIENTS:

(Calories: 80 / Carbs: 6g / Proteins: 5g / Fats: 4g)

- 2 large mushrooms
- 1 cup fresh spinach, chopped
- 1/4 cup crumbled feta cheese
- 1/4 teaspoon garlic powder
- 1/4 teaspoon dried oregano
- Salt and pepper to taste
- Cooking spray (olive oil or non-stick)

Cooking time: 12 minutes / servings: 1
Preparation time: 15 minutes

INSTRUCTIONS FOR COOKING:

- Preheat the air fryer to 375°F (190°C) for 5 minutes.
- Remove the stems from the mushrooms and set them aside for another use.
- In a bowl, combine the chopped spinach, crumbled feta cheese, garlic powder, dried oregano, salt, and pepper. Mix well.
- Spoon the spinach and feta mixture into the mushroom caps, filling them generously.
- Lightly spray the air fryer basket with cooking spray to prevent sticking.
- Place the stuffed mushroom caps in a single layer in the air fryer basket.
- Air fry the stuffed mushrooms at 375°F (190°C) for 10-12 minutes until the mushrooms are tender and the filling is heated through.
- Once cooked, remove the stuffed mushrooms from the air fryer and let them cool for a few minutes before serving.

Greek Stuffed Tomatoes

INGREDIENTS:

(Calories: 40 / Carbs: 18g / Proteins: 6g / Fats: 5g)

- 2 medium tomatoes
- 1/4 cup cooked quinoa
- 2 tablespoons crumbled feta cheese
- 2 tablespoons chopped Kalamata olives
- 1 tablespoon chopped fresh parsley
- 1/2 tablespoon lemon juice
- 1/2 teaspoon dried oregano
- Salt and pepper to taste
- Cooking spray (olive oil or non-stick)

Cooking time: 15 minutes / servings: 1
Preparation time: 20 minutes

INSTRUCTIONS FOR COOKING:

- Preheat the air fryer to 375°F (190°C) for 5 minutes.
- Cut off the top part of each tomato and scoop out the pulp and seeds, leaving a hollow tomato shell. Save the pulp for other use if desired.
- In a bowl, combine the cooked quinoa, crumbled feta cheese, chopped Kalamata olives, chopped parsley, lemon juice, dried oregano, salt, and pepper. Mix well.
- Stuff each tomato with the quinoa mixture, filling them generously.
- Lightly spray the air fryer basket with cooking spray to prevent sticking.
- Place the stuffed tomatoes in a single layer in the air fryer basket.
- Air fry the stuffed tomatoes at 375°F (190°C) for 12-15 minutes until the tomatoes are tender and the filling is heated through.
- Once cooked, remove the stuffed tomatoes from the air fryer and let them cool for a few minutes before serving.

Crispy Parmesan Asparagus

INGREDIENTS:

(Calories: 100 / Carbs: 6g / Proteins: 10g / Fats: 4g)

- 8-10 asparagus spears, 1/4 cup grated Parmesan cheese
- 2 tablespoons almond flour (or whole wheat flour)
- 1/2 teaspoon garlic powder
- 1/4 teaspoon paprika
- Salt and pepper to taste
- Cooking spray (olive oil or non-stick)

Cooking time: 8 minutes / servings: 1
Preparation time: 10 minutes

INSTRUCTIONS FOR COOKING:

- Preheat the air fryer to 400°F (200°C) for 5 minutes.
- Wash the asparagus spears and trim off the tough ends.
- In a shallow dish, combine the grated Parmesan cheese, almond flour (or whole wheat flour), garlic powder, paprika, salt, and pepper. Mix well.
- Lightly spray the air fryer basket with cooking spray to prevent sticking.
- Take a few asparagus spears at a time and coat them with the Parmesan mixture. Press gently to ensure the coating sticks to the asparagus.
- Place the coated asparagus spears in a single layer in the air fryer basket. Avoid overcrowding, and cook in batches if necessary.
- Lightly spray the coated asparagus spears with cooking spray to help them crisp up.
- Air fry the asparagus at 400°F (200°C) for 7-8 minutes until they are tender-crisp and the coating is golden brown.
- Once cooked, remove the asparagus from the air fryer and transfer to a serving plate.

Caprese Skewers

INGREDIENTS:

(Calories: 150 / Carbs: 4g / Proteins: 12g / Fats: 9g)

- 6-8 cherry tomatoes
- 2 ounces fresh mozzarella cheese, cut into small cubes
- Fresh basil leaves
- Balsamic glaze (optional)
- Salt and pepper to taste

Cooking time: 0 minutes / servings: 1
Preparation time: 10 minutes

INSTRUCTIONS FOR COOKING:

- Wash the cherry tomatoes and pat them dry. Cut them in half.
- Cut the fresh mozzarella cheese into small cubes.
- Take a toothpick or a small skewer and thread a cherry tomato half onto it, followed by a cube of mozzarella cheese and a basil leaf. Repeat until all the ingredients are used.
- Season the caprese skewers with a pinch of salt and pepper.

Sweet Potato Fries

INGREDIENTS:

(Calories: 200 / Carbs: 25g / Proteins: 5g / Fats: 8g)

- 1 medium-sized sweet potato
- 1 tablespoon olive oil
- 1/2 teaspoon paprika
- 1/4 teaspoon garlic powder
- Salt and pepper, to taste
- Cooking spray (optional)
- 2 tablespoons plain Greek yogurt
- 1/2 teaspoon lemon juice
- 1/4 teaspoon dried dill
- Pinch of salt

Cooking time: 20 minutes / servings: 1
Preparation time: 10 minutes

INSTRUCTIONS FOR COOKING:

- Preheat the air fryer to 400°F (200°C).
- Wash and scrub the sweet potato. Cut it into thin strips resembling fries.
- In a bowl, combine the olive oil, paprika, garlic powder, salt, and pepper. Toss the sweet potato fries in the mixture until they are evenly coated.
- If desired, lightly spray the air fryer basket with cooking spray to prevent sticking. Place the seasoned sweet potato fries in the air fryer basket in a single layer, making sure they are not overcrowded.
- Cook the fries in the air fryer for approximately 15-20 minutes, shaking the basket halfway through the cooking process to ensure even browning. The fries should be crispy and golden brown.
- While the fries are cooking, prepare the yogurt dipping sauce. In a small bowl, mix together the Greek yogurt, lemon juice, dried dill, and a pinch of salt.
- Once the sweet potato fries are done, remove them from the air fryer and let them cool slightly. Serve them with the yogurt dipping sauce on the side.

Chickpea Vegetable Curry

INGREDIENTS:

(Calories: ~300 / Carbs: 50g / Proteins: 12g / Fats: 5g)

- 1/2 cup cooked chickpeas, 1/2 small onion, diced
- 1 clove garlic, minced, 1/2 teaspoon curry powder
- 1/4 teaspoon ground cumin, 1/4 teaspoon ground turmeric
- Pinch of cayenne pepper (optional, for heat), 1/2 cup diced tomatoes
- 1/2 cup chopped mixed vegetables (e.g., bell peppers, carrots, zucchini)
- 1/2 cup vegetable broth, salt and pepper, to taste
- 1/4 cup cooked basmati rice, fresh cilantro, for garnish

Cooking time: 20 minutes / servings: 1
Preparation time: 15 minutes

INSTRUCTIONS FOR COOKING:

- Heat a non-stick skillet over medium heat. Add a small amount of cooking oil, then add the diced onion and minced garlic. Sauté until the onion becomes translucent.
- Add the curry powder, ground cumin, ground turmeric, and cayenne pepper (if using) to the skillet. Stir well to coat the onions and garlic with the spices.
- Add the diced tomatoes and mixed vegetables to the skillet. Cook for a few minutes until the vegetables begin to soften.
- Stir in the cooked chickpeas and vegetable broth. Season with salt and pepper to taste. Simmer for 10-15 minutes, allowing the flavors to meld together.
- While the curry is simmering, reheat the cooked basmati rice.
- Once the curry is ready, serve it over the heated basmati rice. Garnish with fresh cilantro.

Air-Fried Vegetable Tempura

INGREDIENTS:

(Calories: 150 / Carbs: 30g / Proteins: 5g / Fats: 1g)

- 1/2 cup assorted vegetables (e.g., zucchini, bell peppers, broccoli florets)
- 1/4 cup whole wheat flour
- 1/4 cup sparkling water
- 1/2 teaspoon baking powder
- 1/4 teaspoon salt
- Cooking spray
- Low-sodium soy sauce or ponzu sauce (for dipping)

Cooking time: 15 minutes / servings: 1
Preparation time: 15 minutes

INSTRUCTIONS FOR COOKING:

- Preheat the air fryer to 400°F (200°C).
- Wash and prepare the vegetables by cutting them into bite-sized pieces.
- In a bowl, whisk together the whole wheat flour, sparkling water, baking powder, and salt until the batter is smooth.
- Dip the vegetables into the batter, ensuring they are coated evenly.
- Lightly spray the air fryer basket with cooking spray. Place the battered vegetables in a single layer in the air fryer basket.
- Cook the vegetable tempura in the air fryer for approximately 10-12 minutes, flipping them halfway through the cooking time for even browning. They should be crispy and golden brown.
- Once done, remove the vegetable tempura from the air fryer and serve with low-sodium soy sauce or ponzu sauce for dipping.

Mediterranean Eggplant Bake

INGREDIENTS:

(Calories: 180 / Carbs: 20g / Proteins: 11g / Fats: 5g)

- 1 small eggplant, sliced into rounds
- 1 small tomato, sliced
- 1/4 small onion, thinly sliced
- 1 clove garlic, minced, 1 tablespoon olive oil
- 1/2 teaspoon dried basil, 1/2 teaspoon dried oregano
- Salt and pepper, to taste
- 1 tablespoon grated Parmesan cheese (optional)
- Fresh basil leaves, for garnish

Cooking time: 30 minutes / servings: 1
Preparation time: 10 minutes

INSTRUCTIONS FOR COOKING:

- Preheat the air fryer to 375°F (190°C).
- In a bowl, toss the eggplant slices with olive oil, minced garlic, dried basil, dried oregano, salt, and pepper.
- Place the seasoned eggplant slices in a single layer in the air fryer basket. Cook for approximately 10 minutes, flipping the slices halfway through.
- Remove the eggplant from the air fryer and set it aside. Layer the sliced tomato, onion, and cooked eggplant in a small baking dish.
- Sprinkle grated Parmesan cheese (if using) over the top.
- Bake the Mediterranean eggplant and tomato dish in a preheated oven at 375°F (190°C) for about 15-20 minutes or until the vegetables are tender and the flavors have melded.
- Once done, remove from the oven and garnish with fresh basil leaves before serving.

Quinoa Stuffed Peppers

INGREDIENTS:

(Calories: 200 / Carbs: 30g / Proteins: 7g / Fats: 5g)

- 1 bell pepper (any color), halved and seeded
- 1/4 cup cooked quinoa
- 1/4 cup grilled mixed vegetables (e.g., zucchini, eggplant, bell peppers)
- 1/4 small onion, diced, 1 clove garlic, minced
- 1/2 teaspoon dried basil, 1/2 teaspoon dried oregano
- Salt and pepper, to taste, 1 tablespoon grated Parmesan cheese (optional)
- Fresh parsley, for garnish

Cooking time: 30 minutes / servings: 1
Preparation time: 20 minutes

INSTRUCTIONS FOR COOKING:

- Preheat the air fryer to 375°F (190°C).
- In a bowl, combine the cooked quinoa, grilled mixed vegetables, diced onion, minced garlic, dried basil, dried oregano, salt, and pepper.
- Stuff the halved bell pepper with the quinoa and vegetable mixture, pressing it down gently.
- Place the stuffed peppers in the air fryer basket. Cook for approximately 25-30 minutes until the peppers are tender and the filling is heated through.
- If desired, sprinkle grated Parmesan cheese over the top of the stuffed peppers during the last few minutes of cooking.
- Once done, remove the stuffed peppers from the air fryer and garnish with fresh parsley before serving.

Air-Fried Brussels Sprouts

INGREDIENTS:

(Calories: 150 / Carbs: 15g / Proteins: 5g / Fats: 8g)

- 1 cup Brussels sprouts, trimmed and halved
- 1 tablespoon olive oil
- Salt and pepper, to taste
- 1 tablespoon balsamic vinegar
- 1/2 teaspoon honey or a sugar substitute (optional)

Cooking time: 15 minutes / servings: 1
Preparation time: 10 minutes

INSTRUCTIONS FOR COOKING:

- Preheat the air fryer to 400°F (200°C).
- In a bowl, toss the Brussels sprouts with olive oil, salt, and pepper until they are well coated.
- Place the Brussels sprouts in the air fryer basket in a single layer. Cook for approximately 12-15 minutes, shaking the basket halfway through, until they are crispy and lightly browned.
- While the Brussels sprouts are cooking, prepare the balsamic glaze. In a small saucepan, heat the balsamic vinegar over medium heat. If using honey or a sugar substitute, add it to the vinegar and stir until dissolved. Simmer the mixture for a few minutes until it thickens slightly.
- Once the Brussels sprouts are done, remove them from the air fryer and drizzle the balsamic glaze over them.
- Toss the Brussels sprouts gently to coat them with the glaze.

Stuffed Portobello Mushrooms

INGREDIENTS:

(Calories: 150 / Carbs: 10g / Proteins: 8g / Fats: 10g)

- 2 large portobello mushrooms
- 1 cup fresh spinach, chopped
- 2 tablespoons crumbled goat cheese
- 1 clove garlic, minced
- 1 tablespoon olive oil
- Salt and pepper, to taste
- Fresh parsley, for garnish

Cooking time: 20 minutes / servings: 1
Preparation time: 15 minutes

INSTRUCTIONS FOR COOKING:

- Preheat the air fryer to 375°F (190°C).
- Remove the stems from the portobello mushrooms and gently scrape out the gills with a spoon.
- In a bowl, combine the chopped spinach, crumbled goat cheese, minced garlic, olive oil, salt, and pepper.
- Stuff the spinach and goat cheese mixture into the portobello mushrooms, pressing it down gently.
- Place the stuffed mushrooms in the air fryer basket. Cook for approximately 15-20 minutes until the mushrooms are tender and the filling is heated through.
- Once done, remove the stuffed mushrooms from the air fryer and garnish with fresh parsley before serving.

Sweet Potato Buddha Bowl

INGREDIENTS:

(Calories: 350 / Carbs: 45g / Proteins: 10g / Fats: 15g)

- 1 small sweet potato, peeled and cubed
- 1/2 cup cooked chickpeas
- 1 cup mixed greens (e.g., spinach, kale, arugula)
- 1/4 cup cherry tomatoes, halved
- 1/4 small red onion, thinly sliced
- 1 tablespoon tahini, 1 tablespoon lemon juice
- 1 tablespoon water, Salt and pepper, to taste
- Sprinkle of sesame seeds, for garnish

Cooking time: 25 minutes / servings: 1
Preparation time: 15 minutes

INSTRUCTIONS FOR COOKING:

- Preheat the air fryer to 400°F (200°C).
- Toss the cubed sweet potato with a drizzle of olive oil, salt, and pepper. Place it in the air fryer basket and cook for approximately 20-25 minutes until the sweet potato is tender and lightly browned.
- In a bowl, combine the cooked chickpeas, mixed greens, cherry tomatoes, and red onion.
- In a separate small bowl, whisk together the tahini, lemon juice, water, salt, and pepper to make the dressing.
- Once the sweet potato is done, assemble the Buddha bowl by arranging the mixed greens and chickpea mixture in a bowl. Top it with the air-fried sweet potato cubes.
- Drizzle the tahini dressing over the bowl and sprinkle sesame seeds on top.

Crispy Onion Rings

INGREDIENTS:

(Calories: 180 / Carbs: 32g / Proteins: 9g / Fats: 2g)

- 1 medium onion, cut into rings
- 1/2 cup whole wheat flour
- 1/2 teaspoon paprika
- 1/4 teaspoon garlic powder
- 1/4 teaspoon salt
- 1/8 teaspoon black pepper
- 1/2 cup unsweetened almond milk (or any milk of your choice)
- Cooking spray
- 1/4 cup plain Greek yogurt
- 1/2 teaspoon lemon juice
- 1/4 teaspoon dried dill
- Salt and pepper, to taste

Cooking time: 12 minutes / servings: 1
Preparation time: 15 minutes

INSTRUCTIONS FOR COOKING:

- Preheat the air fryer to 400°F (200°C).
- In a shallow dish, combine the whole wheat flour, paprika, garlic powder, salt, and black pepper.
- Dip the onion rings into the almond milk and then into the flour mixture, ensuring they are coated evenly.
- Lightly spray the air fryer basket with cooking spray. Place the coated onion rings in a single layer in the air fryer basket.
- Cook the onion rings in the air fryer for approximately 10-12 minutes, flipping them halfway through the cooking time for even browning. They should be crispy and golden brown.
- While the onion rings are cooking, prepare the Greek yogurt dip. In a small bowl, mix together the plain Greek yogurt, lemon juice, dried dill, salt, and pepper.
- Once the onion rings are done, remove them from the air fryer and serve them hot with the Greek yogurt dip

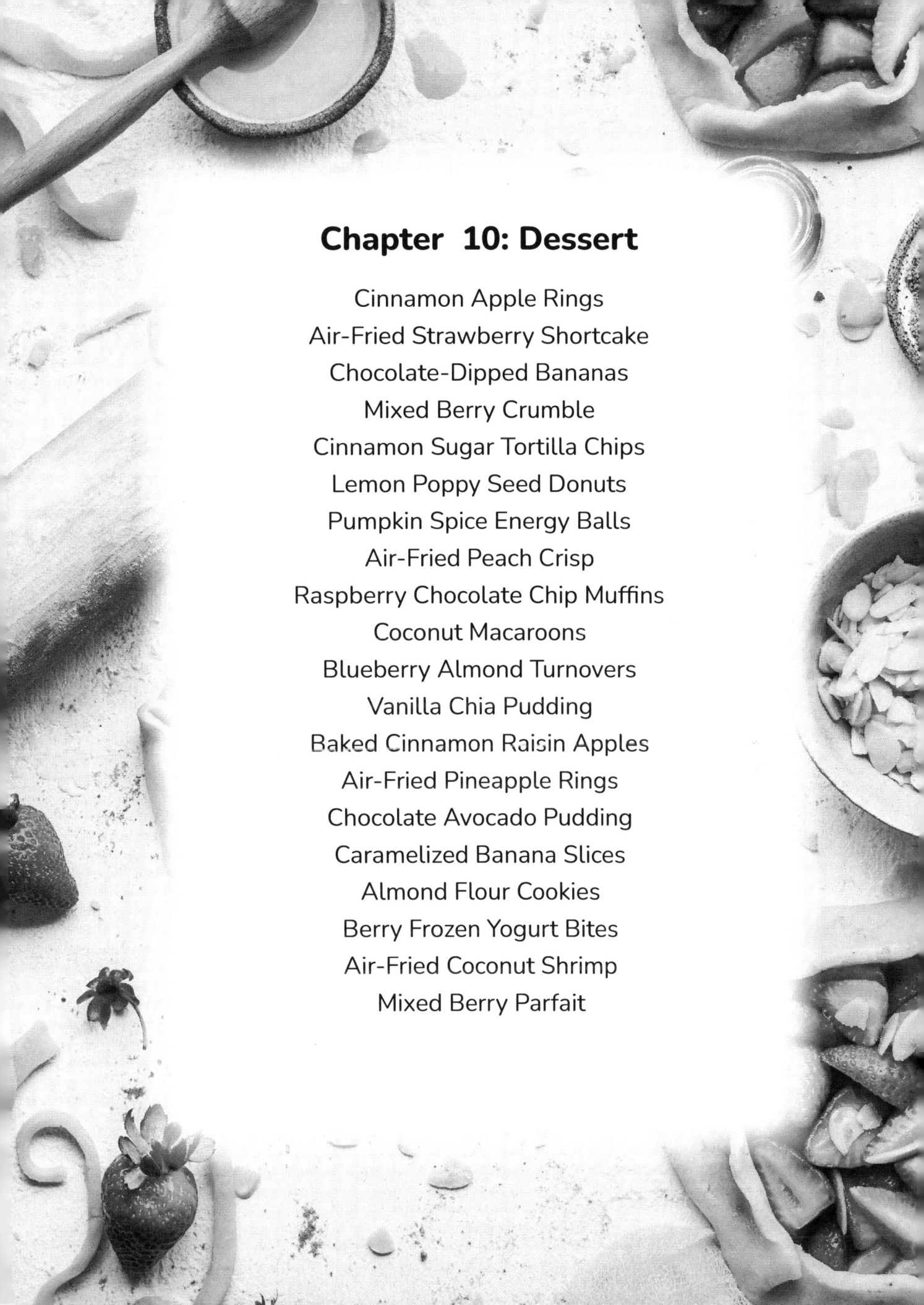

Chapter 10: Dessert

Cinnamon Apple Rings
Air-Fried Strawberry Shortcake
Chocolate-Dipped Bananas
Mixed Berry Crumble
Cinnamon Sugar Tortilla Chips
Lemon Poppy Seed Donuts
Pumpkin Spice Energy Balls
Air-Fried Peach Crisp
Raspberry Chocolate Chip Muffins
Coconut Macaroons
Blueberry Almond Turnovers
Vanilla Chia Pudding
Baked Cinnamon Raisin Apples
Air-Fried Pineapple Rings
Chocolate Avocado Pudding
Caramelized Banana Slices
Almond Flour Cookies
Berry Frozen Yogurt Bites
Air-Fried Coconut Shrimp
Mixed Berry Parfait

Chapter 10: Dessert

Cinnamon Apple Rings

INGREDIENTS:

(Calories: ~100 / Carbs: 20g / Proteins: 6g / Fats: 0g)

- 1 medium apple, 1 tablespoon lemon juice
- 1/2 teaspoon ground cinnamon
- 1/4 teaspoon nutmeg (optional)
- Cooking spray, 1/4 cup plain Greek yogurt
- 1/2 teaspoon honey or a sugar substitute (optional)
- 1/4 teaspoon vanilla extract

Cooking time: 10 minutes / servings: 1
Preparation time: 15 minutes

INSTRUCTIONS FOR COOKING:

- Preheat the air fryer to 375°F (190°C).
- Core the apple and cut it into rings about 1/4-inch thick. Place the apple rings in a bowl and toss them with lemon juice to prevent browning.
- In a separate bowl, mix together the ground cinnamon and nutmeg.
- Lightly spray the air fryer basket with cooking spray. Dip each apple ring into the cinnamon and nutmeg mixture, making sure to coat both sides.
- Arrange the coated apple rings in a single layer in the air fryer basket. Cook for approximately 8-10 minutes until the apple rings are tender and lightly browned.
- While the apple rings are cooking, prepare the Greek yogurt dip. In a small bowl, mix together the plain Greek yogurt, honey or sugar substitute (if using), and vanilla extract.
- Once the apple rings are done, remove them from the air fryer and serve them hot with the Greek yogurt dip.

Air-Fried Strawberry Shortcake

INGREDIENTS:

(Calories: ~120 / Carbs: 20g / Proteins: 5g / Fats: 2g)

- 1 slice whole wheat bread
- Cooking spray
- 1/4 cup sliced strawberries
- 1/4 cup low-fat whipped cream or Greek yogurt
- Fresh mint leaves, for garnish (optional)

Cooking time: 10 minutes / servings: 1
Preparation time: 10 minutes

INSTRUCTIONS FOR COOKING:

- Preheat the air fryer to 375°F (190°C).
- Cut the slice of whole wheat bread into small squares or circles to create bite-sized pieces for the shortcake.
- Lightly spray the air fryer basket with cooking spray. Place the bread pieces in the air fryer basket in a single layer.
- Cook the bread pieces in the air fryer for approximately 5-7 minutes until they are crispy and golden brown, shaking the basket occasionally for even browning.
- While the bread pieces are cooking, slice the strawberries and set them aside.
- Once the bread pieces are done, remove them from the air fryer and let them cool slightly.
- To assemble the shortcake, layer the crispy bread pieces, sliced strawberries, and low-fat whipped cream or Greek yogurt in a serving dish.
- Garnish with fresh mint leaves (if desired) and serve immediately.

Chocolate-Dipped Bananas

INGREDIENTS:

(Calories: ~150 / Carbs: 20g / Proteins: 2g / Fats: 8g)

- 1 ripe banana
- 1 ounce dark chocolate, chopped
- 1/2 teaspoon coconut oil
- Optional toppings: chopped nuts, shredded coconut, or sprinkles (choose sugar-free options)

Cooking time: 10 minutes / servings: 1
Preparation time: 10 minutes

INSTRUCTIONS FOR COOKING:

- Preheat the air fryer to 375°F (190°C).
- Peel the banana and cut it into 1-inch thick slices.
- In a microwave-safe bowl, combine the chopped dark chocolate and coconut oil. Microwave in 20-second intervals, stirring in between, until the chocolate is melted and smooth.
- Dip each banana slice halfway into the melted chocolate and place them on a parchment-lined tray.
- Place the tray with the chocolate-dipped banana slices in the air fryer basket. Cook for approximately 6-8 minutes until the chocolate is set and the bananas are slightly softened.
- Remove the tray from the air fryer and let the chocolate-dipped bananas cool for a few minutes.
- Optional: Sprinkle the dipped bananas with chopped nuts, shredded coconut, or sprinkles for added flavor and texture.

Mixed Berry Crumble

INGREDIENTS:

(Calories: ~180 / Carbs: 15g / Proteins: 4g / Fats: 12g)

- 1/2 cup mixed berries (such as blueberries, raspberries, and strawberries)
- 1/4 teaspoon lemon juice, 1 tablespoon almond flour
- 1 tablespoon rolled oats
- 1 tablespoon unsalted butter, melted
- 1 tablespoon granulated sweetener of your choice (choose a sugar-free option)
- 1/4 teaspoon ground cinnamon, Pinch of salt
- Optional: Sugar-free whipped cream or Greek yogurt for serving

Cooking time: 25 minutes / servings: 1
Preparation time: 15 minutes

INSTRUCTIONS FOR COOKING:

- Preheat the air fryer to 375°F (190°C).
- In a small bowl, toss the mixed berries with lemon juice to enhance the flavors.
- In another bowl, combine the almond flour, rolled oats, melted butter, sweetener, ground cinnamon, and salt. Mix well until the ingredients are evenly combined and form a crumbly texture.
- Lightly grease a ramekin or oven-safe dish that fits in the air fryer basket. Place the mixed berries in the ramekin, then sprinkle the almond flour topping over the berries.
- Place the ramekin in the air fryer basket. Cook for approximately 20-25 minutes until the berries are bubbling and the topping is golden brown and crispy.
- Remove the ramekin from the air fryer and let it cool for a few minutes.
- Optional: Serve the mixed berry crumble warm with a dollop of sugar-free whipped cream or Greek yogurt.

Cinnamon Sugar Tortilla Chips

INGREDIENTS:

(Calories: ~120 / Carbs: 26g / Proteins: 2g / Fats: 1g)

- 1 small whole wheat tortilla
- Cooking spray, 1/2 teaspoon ground cinnamon
- 1/2 teaspoon granulated sweetener of your choice (choose a sugar-free option)
- 1/4 cup diced mixed fruits (such as strawberries, kiwi, and pineapple)
- 1 tablespoon finely chopped fresh mint leaves
- 1/2 teaspoon lime juice

Cooking time: 8 minutes / servings: 1
Preparation time: 10 minutes

INSTRUCTIONS FOR COOKING:

- Preheat the air fryer to 375°F (190°C).
- Cut the whole wheat tortilla into triangle-shaped chips.
- Lightly spray the air fryer basket with cooking spray. Arrange the tortilla chips in a single layer in the air fryer basket.
- Cook the tortilla chips in the air fryer for approximately 6-8 minutes until they are crispy and lightly golden brown.
- While the tortilla chips are cooking, prepare the fruit salsa. In a small bowl, combine the diced mixed fruits, chopped mint leaves, and lime juice. Toss gently to mix well.
- In another small bowl, combine the ground cinnamon and granulated sweetener.
- Once the tortilla chips are done, remove them from the air fryer and immediately sprinkle them with the cinnamon sugar mixture.
- Serve the cinnamon sugar tortilla chips with the fruit salsa on the side.

Lemon Poppy Seed Donuts

INGREDIENTS:

(Calories: ~160 / Carbs: 10g / Proteins: 6g / Fats: 12g)

- 1/4 cup almond flour, 1 tablespoon coconut flour
- 1/2 teaspoon baking powder, 1/2 teaspoon poppy seeds
- 1 tablespoon granulated sweetener of your choice (choose a sugar-free option)
- Zest of 1/2 lemon, 1 tablespoon lemon juice
- 1 tablespoon unsweetened almond milk (or any milk of your choice)
- 1/4 teaspoon vanilla extract, 1/2 teaspoon melted coconut oil
- Cooking spray, optional: Powdered sweetener for dusting

Cooking time: 8 minutes / servings: 1
Preparation time: 15 minutes

INSTRUCTIONS FOR COOKING:

- Preheat the air fryer to 350°F (175°C).
- In a bowl, whisk together the almond flour, coconut flour, baking powder, poppy seeds, granulated sweetener, and lemon zest.
- In a separate bowl, combine the lemon juice, almond milk, vanilla extract, and melted coconut oil. Whisk until well combined.
- Add the wet ingredients to the dry ingredients and mix until a smooth batter forms.
- Lightly grease the air fryer basket with cooking spray. Spoon the batter into a donut mold or shape the batter into small donut shapes using your hands.
- Place the donuts in the air fryer basket and cook for approximately 6-8 minutes until they are golden brown and cooked through.
- Remove the donuts from the air fryer and let them cool for a few minutes.
- Optional: Dust the cooled donuts with powdered sweetener for extra sweetness.

Pumpkin Spice Energy Balls

INGREDIENTS:

(Calories: ~150 / Carbs: 10g / Proteins: 4g / Fats: 10g)

- 1/4 cup canned pumpkin puree, 1/4 cup almond flour
- 2 tablespoons ground flaxseed
- 2 tablespoons unsweetened shredded coconut
- 1 tablespoon chopped walnuts
- 1 tablespoon honey or sweetener of your choice (choose a sugar-free option)
- 1/2 teaspoon pumpkin spice mix
- Optional: Extra shredded coconut for rolling

Cooking time: 15 minutes / servings: 1 (~ 4 energy balls) / preparation time: 15 minutes

INSTRUCTIONS FOR COOKING:

- In a mixing bowl, combine the pumpkin puree, almond flour, ground flaxseed, shredded coconut, chopped walnuts, honey or sweetener, and pumpkin spice mix. Mix well until all ingredients are evenly combined.
- Take small portions of the mixture and roll them into small balls between your palms. If desired, roll the energy balls in extra shredded coconut for added texture.
- Place the energy balls on a plate or tray and refrigerate for at least 30 minutes to firm up.
- Once chilled, the pumpkin spice energy balls are ready to be enjoyed. Store any leftovers in an airtight container in the refrigerator for up to a week.

Air-Fried Peach Crisp

INGREDIENTS:

(Calories: ~250 / Carbs: 30g / Proteins: 5g / Fats: 14g)

- 1 ripe peach, sliced, 1/4 cup rolled oats
- 1 tablespoon almond flour
- 1 tablespoon chopped almonds
- 1 tablespoon unsweetened shredded coconut
- 1 tablespoon melted coconut oil
- 1 tablespoon honey or sweetener of your choice (choose a sugar-free option)
- 1/2 teaspoon ground cinnamon

Cooking time: 20 minutes / servings: 1
Preparation time: 10 minutes

INSTRUCTIONS FOR COOKING:

- Preheat the air fryer to 375°F (190°C).
- In a bowl, combine the rolled oats, almond flour, chopped almonds, shredded coconut, melted coconut oil, honey or sweetener, and ground cinnamon. Mix well until the mixture resembles a crumbly texture.
- Place the sliced peaches in an air fryer-safe dish or ramekin. Sprinkle the oat topping evenly over the peaches.
- Place the dish in the preheated air fryer and cook for approximately 15-20 minutes until the peaches are tender and the topping is golden brown and crispy.
- Carefully remove the dish from the air fryer and let it cool for a few minutes.
- Serve the air fried peach crisp warm. You can enjoy it as is or pair it with a dollop of unsweetened Greek yogurt or a sprinkle of cinnamon for added flavor.

Raspberry Chocolate Chip Muffins

INGREDIENTS:

(Calories: ~200 / Carbs: 10g / Proteins: 20g / Fats: 8g)

- 1/4 cup almond flour
- 1/4 cup vanilla protein powder (low-sugar or sugar-free)
- 1/4 teaspoon baking powder, pinch of salt
- 1/4 cup unsweetened almond milk (or any milk of your choice)
- 1 tablespoon unsweetened applesauce, 1/2 teaspoon vanilla extract
- 1/4 cup fresh raspberries
- 1 tablespoon sugar-free dark chocolate chips

Cooking time: 20 minutes / servings: 1 (2 muffins)
Preparation time: 15 minutes

INSTRUCTIONS FOR COOKING:

- Preheat the air fryer to 350°F (175°C).
- In a mixing bowl, combine the almond flour, protein powder, baking powder, and salt. Mix well.
- Add the almond milk, applesauce, and vanilla extract to the dry ingredients. Stir until just combined, being careful not to overmix.
- Gently fold in the fresh raspberries and dark chocolate chips.
- Line a muffin tin with paper liners. Divide the batter equally among the muffin cups.
- Place the muffin tin in the preheated air fryer and cook for approximately 18-20 minutes until the muffins are set and golden brown.
- Remove the muffins from the air fryer and let them cool before serving.

Coconut Macaroons

INGREDIENTS:

(Calories: ~130 / Carbs: 9g / Proteins: 4g / Fats: 9g)

- 4 ounces boneless, skinless chicken breast
- 1/4 cup sugar-free BBQ sauce
- 1 ear of corn
- 2 cups mixed salad greens
- 1/4 cup cherry tomatoes, halved
- 1/4 cup cucumber, sliced
- 1 tablespoon red onion, finely chopped
- 2 tablespoons low-fat ranch dressing (sugar-free or reduced-fat)

Cooking time: 10 minutes / servings: 1 (2 macaroons) / preparation time: 10 minutes

INSTRUCTIONS FOR COOKING:

- Preheat the air fryer to 325°F (160°C).
- In a bowl, combine the shredded coconut, coconut flour, and sugar-free sweetener.
- In a separate bowl, whisk the egg white until frothy. Add the vanilla extract and mix well.
- Pour the egg white mixture into the dry ingredients. Stir until well combined and a sticky dough forms.
- Shape the dough into 2 small macaroons and place them on a greased air fryer tray or in an air fryer-safe dish.
- Place the tray or dish in the preheated air fryer and cook for approximately 8-10 minutes until the macaroons are golden brown.
- While the macaroons are cooling, melt the sugar-free dark chocolate chips in the microwave or on the stovetop.
- Drizzle the melted dark chocolate over the cooled macaroons.

Blueberry Almond Turnovers

INGREDIENTS:

(Calories: ~300 / Carbs: 30g / Proteins: 5g / Fats: 18g)

- 1 sheet of puff pastry, thawed
- 1/4 cup fresh blueberries
- 1 tablespoon almond flour
- 1 tablespoon sugar-free sweetener (such as erythritol or stevia)
- 1/4 teaspoon almond extract
- 1 egg, beaten (for egg wash)
- Optional: Powdered sugar substitute for dusting (choose a sugar-free option)

Cooking time: 10 minutes / servings: 1 (2 turnovers)
Preparation time: 20 minutes

INSTRUCTIONS FOR COOKING:

- Preheat the air fryer to 375°F (190°C).
- In a bowl, combine the fresh blueberries, almond flour, sugar-free sweetener, and almond extract. Mix well to coat the blueberries.
- Roll out the puff pastry sheet on a lightly floured surface. Cut it into 4 equal squares.
- Place a spoonful of the blueberry mixture onto one half of each square. Fold the other half over to create a triangle shape. Press the edges together to seal the turnovers.
- Brush the turnovers with the beaten egg wash.
- Place the turnovers in the preheated air fryer and cook for approximately 10 minutes or until they are golden brown and puffed up.
- Remove the turnovers from the air fryer and let them cool slightly before serving. Optional: Dust with powdered sugar substitute for added sweetness.

Vanilla Chia Pudding

INGREDIENTS:

(Calories: ~150 / Carbs: 12g / Proteins: 6g / Fats: 9g)

- 2 tablespoons chia seeds
- 1/2 cup unsweetened almond milk (or any milk of your choice)
- 1/4 teaspoon vanilla extract
- 1 tablespoon sugar-free sweetener (such as erythritol or stevia)
- Fresh berries (such as strawberries, blueberries, or raspberries) for topping

Cooking time: 5 minutes / servings: 1
Preparation time: 5 minutes (plus chilling time)

INSTRUCTIONS FOR COOKING:

- In a bowl, combine the chia seeds, unsweetened almond milk, vanilla extract, and sugar-free sweetener. Stir well to mix all the ingredients together.
- Let the mixture sit for 5 minutes, then stir again to prevent clumping. Repeat this process a few more times over the next 15 minutes to ensure the chia seeds are evenly distributed.
- Cover the bowl and refrigerate for at least 2 hours or overnight to allow the chia seeds to absorb the liquid and thicken into a pudding-like consistency.
- Once the chia pudding has chilled, give it a good stir to break up any clumps that may have formed.
- Transfer the chia pudding to a serving bowl or individual jars. Top with fresh berries of your choice.
- Serve the vanilla chia pudding with fresh berries chilled and enjoy as a healthy and satisfying dessert or breakfast option.

Baked Cinnamon Raisin Apples

INGREDIENTS:

(Calories: ~120 / Carbs: 25g / Proteins: 4g / Fats: 1g)

- 1 medium-sized apple (such as Granny Smith or Fuji), cored and sliced
- 1 tablespoon raisins
- 1/2 teaspoon ground cinnamon
- 1/2 teaspoon sugar-free sweetener (such as erythritol or stevia)
- 2 tablespoons plain Greek yogurt (low-fat or non-fat)

Cooking time: 20 minutes / servings: 1
Preparation time: 10 minutes

INSTRUCTIONS FOR COOKING:

- Preheat the air fryer to 350°F (175°C).
- In a bowl, toss the sliced apples with raisins, ground cinnamon, and sugar-free sweetener until well coated.
- Place the apple mixture in a small baking dish that fits inside the air fryer.
- Put the baking dish with the apple mixture into the preheated air fryer. Cook for approximately 20 minutes or until the apples are tender and slightly caramelized.
- Remove the baked apples from the air fryer and let them cool slightly.
- Serve the baked cinnamon raisin apples with a dollop of Greek yogurt on top.

Air-Fried Pineapple Rings

INGREDIENTS:

(Calories: ~150 / Carbs: 22g / Proteins: 2g / Fats: 8g)

- 2 pineapple rings (fresh or canned in juice, drained)
- Cooking spray or oil mist
- 2 tablespoons coconut cream (full-fat)
- Optional: Sugar-free sweetener (such as erythritol or stevia), to taste
- Optional: Shredded coconut, for garnish

Cooking time: 8 minutes / servings: 1
Preparation time: 5 minutes

INSTRUCTIONS FOR COOKING:

- Preheat the air fryer to 375°F (190°C).
- Lightly coat both sides of the pineapple rings with cooking spray or oil mist to prevent sticking.
- Place the pineapple rings in the preheated air fryer and cook for approximately 4 minutes per side, until they are golden brown and slightly caramelized.
- While the pineapple rings are cooking, prepare the coconut whipped cream. In a bowl, whisk the coconut cream until fluffy. Add sugar-free sweetener if desired.
- Once the pineapple rings are cooked, remove them from the air fryer and let them cool slightly.
- Serve the air fried pineapple rings with a dollop of coconut whipped cream on top. Optional: Sprinkle shredded coconut over the whipped cream for added flavor and texture.

Chocolate Avocado Pudding

INGREDIENTS:

(Calories: ~200 / Carbs: 15g / Proteins: 3g / Fats: 15g)

- 1 small ripe avocado
- 1 tablespoon unsweetened cocoa powder
- 1 tablespoon sugar-free sweetener (such as erythritol or stevia)
- 1/4 teaspoon vanilla extract
- 2-3 tablespoons unsweetened almond milk (or any non-dairy milk)
- Fresh berries (such as strawberries, blueberries, or raspberries), for topping

Cooking time: 0 minutes / servings: 1
Preparation time: 10 minutes

INSTRUCTIONS FOR COOKING:

- Cut the avocado in half, remove the pit, and scoop out the flesh into a blender or food processor.
- Add the cocoa powder, sugar-free sweetener, vanilla extract, and almond milk to the blender.
- Blend the ingredients until smooth and creamy, adding more almond milk if needed to achieve the desired consistency.
- Transfer the chocolate avocado pudding to a serving dish and refrigerate for at least 1 hour to chill and set.
- Before serving, top the pudding with fresh berries.

Caramelized Banana Slices

INGREDIENTS:

(Calories: ~100 / Carbs: 26g / Proteins: 0.5g / Fats: 1g)

- 1 ripe banana, peeled and sliced
- 1/2 teaspoon cinnamon
- 1/2 teaspoon sugar-free sweetener (such as erythritol or stevia)
- Cooking spray or oil mist

Cooking time: 8 minutes / servings: 1
Preparation time: 5 minutes

INSTRUCTIONS FOR COOKING:

- Preheat the air fryer to 375°F (190°C).
- In a bowl, combine the sliced banana, cinnamon, and sugar-free sweetener. Toss until the banana slices are evenly coated.
- Lightly coat the air fryer basket with cooking spray or oil mist to prevent sticking.
- Place the banana slices in a single layer in the air fryer basket.
- Air fry the banana slices for approximately 4 minutes, then flip them and cook for another 4 minutes, until they are caramelized and slightly crispy.
- Remove the caramelized banana slices from the air fryer and let them cool slightly before serving.

Almond Flour Cookies

INGREDIENTS:

(Calories: ~150 / Carbs: 6g / Proteins: 3g / Fats: 13g)

- 1/4 cup almond flour
- 1 tablespoon unsweetened coconut flour
- 1/4 teaspoon baking powder, pinch of salt
- 1 tablespoon unsalted butter, softened
- 1 tablespoon sugar-free sweetener (such as erythritol or stevia)
- 1/4 teaspoon vanilla extract
- 1 tablespoon sugar-free chocolate chips

Cooking time: 10-12 minutes / servings: 1
Preparation time: 10 minutes

INSTRUCTIONS FOR COOKING:

- Preheat the air fryer to 350°F (175°C).
- In a bowl, whisk together the almond flour, coconut flour, baking powder, and salt.
- In a separate bowl, cream together the softened butter, sugar-free sweetener, and vanilla extract until well combined.
- Gradually add the dry ingredients to the butter mixture, mixing until a dough forms.
- Fold in the sugar-free chocolate chips.
- Roll the dough into small balls and place them on a parchment-lined air fryer tray or in the air fryer basket.
- Air fry the cookies for 10-12 minutes until golden brown and slightly firm to the touch.
- Remove the cookies from the air fryer and let them cool completely before serving.

Berry Frozen Yogurt Bites

INGREDIENTS:

(Calories: ~70 / Carbs: 8g / Proteins: 8g / Fats: 0g)

- 1/2 cup plain Greek yogurt
- 1 tablespoon sugar-free sweetener (such as erythritol or stevia)
- 1/4 cup mixed berries (such as strawberries, blueberries, or raspberries)

Freezing time: 4 hours or overnight / servings: 1
Preparation time: 5 minutes

INSTRUCTIONS FOR COOKING:

- In a bowl, mix together the Greek yogurt and sugar-free sweetener until well combined.
- Spoon the yogurt mixture into small silicone molds or an ice cube tray, filling each cavity about halfway.
- Drop a few mixed berries into each cavity, pressing them gently into the yogurt.
- Place the molds or tray in the freezer and freeze for at least 4 hours or overnight until the yogurt bites are firm.
- Once frozen, remove the yogurt bites from the molds or tray and serve immediately.

Air-Fried Coconut Shrimp

INGREDIENTS:

(Calories: ~250 / Carbs: 16g / Proteins: 17g / Fats: 14g)

- 4 large shrimp, peeled and deveined
- 2 tablespoons unsweetened shredded coconut
- 2 tablespoons almond flour
- 1/2 teaspoon garlic powder
- Pinch of salt
- Pinch of black pepper
- 1 egg, beaten

Cooking time: 10 minutes / servings: 1
Preparation time: 15 minutes

INSTRUCTIONS FOR COOKING:

- Preheat the air fryer to 400°F (200°C).
- In a shallow bowl, mix together the shredded coconut, almond flour, garlic powder, salt, and black pepper.
- Dip each shrimp into the beaten egg, allowing any excess to drip off.
- Roll the shrimp in the coconut mixture, pressing gently to adhere the coating.
- Place the coated shrimp in the air fryer basket or on an air fryer tray.
- Air fry the shrimp for 8-10 minutes until golden brown and crispy, flipping halfway through cooking.
- Meanwhile, prepare the mango dipping sauce by blending the diced mango, Greek yogurt, lime juice, and honey (if using) until smooth.
- Serve the air-fried coconut shrimp with the mango dipping sauce on the side.

Mixed Berry Parfait

INGREDIENTS:

(Calories: ~200 / Carbs: 25g / Proteins: 17g / Fats: 6g)

- 1/2 cup plain Greek yogurt
- 1/4 cup mixed berries
  (such as strawberries, blueberries, and raspberries)
- 1 tablespoon sugar-free sweetener
  (such as erythritol or stevia)
- 2 tablespoons granola
  (choose a low-sugar or sugar-free option)

Cooking time: 10 minutes / servings: 1
Preparation time: 10 minutes

INSTRUCTIONS FOR COOKING:

- In a glass or bowl, layer half of the Greek yogurt.
- Add half of the mixed berries on top of the yogurt.
- Sprinkle half of the sugar-free sweetener over the berries.
- Repeat the layers with the remaining Greek yogurt, mixed berries, and sweetener.
- Top the parfait with the granola.

Chapter 11: Week-meal plan 30 days

DAY 1:
- Breakfast: Crustless Vegetable Quiche
- Snack: Air Fried Zucchini Fries
- Lunch: Chicken Salad
- Snack: Buffalo Cauliflower Bites
- Dinner: Grilled Balsamic Chicken

DAY 2:
- Breakfast: Spinach and Mushroom Egg Muffins
- Snack: Baked Parmesan Wings
- Lunch: Salmon with Lemon-Dill
- Snack: Mediterranean Stuffed Mushrooms
- Dinner: Lemon Dill Salmon

DAY 3:
- Breakfast: Low-Carb Omelette with Fresh Herbs
- Snack: Roasted Chickpeas
- Lunch: Quinoa Veggie Salad
- Snack: Caprese Skewers
- Dinner: Roasted Veggie Quinoa

DAY 4:
- Breakfast: Cinnamon Apple Air Fryer Pancakes
- Snack: Spicy Tofu Wraps
- Lunch: Greek Salad
- Snack: Spinach Artichoke Dip
- Dinner: Greek Feta Salad

DAY 5:
- Breakfast: Almond Flour Blueberry Muffins
- Snack: Zucchini Pizza Bites
- Lunch: Shrimp Avocado Salad
- Snack: Teriyaki Turkey Meatballs
- Dinner: Shrimp Avocado Wraps

DAY 6:
- Breakfast: Avocado and Tomato Breakfast Toast
- Snack: Smokey Eggplant Dip
- Lunch: Spinach Strawberry Salad
- Snack: Lemon Pepper Shrimp
- Dinner: Strawberry Spinach Salad

DAY 7:
- Breakfast: Almond Flour Blueberry Muffins
- Snack: Zucchini Pizza Bites
- Lunch: Shrimp Avocado Salad
- Snack: Teriyaki Turkey Meatballs
- Dinner: Shrimp Avocado Wraps

DAY 8:
- Breakfast: Avocado and Tomato Breakfast Toast
- Snack: Smokey Eggplant Dip
- Lunch: Spinach Strawberry Salad
- Snack: Lemon Pepper Shrimp
- Dinner: Strawberry Spinach Salad

DAY 9:
- Breakfast: Sweet Potato Hash Browns
- Snack: Cilantro Lime Shrimp Skewers
- Lunch: Tofu Stir-Fry
- Snack: Spinach Feta Mushrooms
- Dinner: Tofu Stir-Fry

DAY 10:
- Breakfast: Zucchini and Feta Fritters
- Snack: Greek Chicken Meatballs
- Lunch: Caprese salad
- Snack: Avocado Egg Salad Wraps
- Dinner: Caprese Skewers

DAY 11:
- Breakfast: Smoked Salmon and Cream Cheese Roll-Ups
- Snack: Buffalo Cauliflower Poppers
- Lunch: Tuna Lettuce Wraps
- Snack: Quinoa Stuffed Zucchini
- Dinner: Tuna Lettuce Wraps

DAY 12:
- Breakfast: Coconut Flour Banana Bread
- Snack: Asian Sesame Beef Skewers
- Lunch: Sesame Chicken Salad
- Snack: Garlic Parmesan Chicken Bites
- Dinner: Chickpea Cucumber Salad

DAY 13:
- Breakfast: Quinoa Breakfast Bowl with Mixed Berries
- Snack: Mediterranean Cucumber Roll-Ups
- Lunch: Chickpea Salad
- Snack: Stuffed Peppers
- Dinner: Zucchini Chickpea Fritters

DAY 14:
- Breakfast: Turkey Sausage and Vegetable Skewers
- Snack: Quinoa Stuffed Zucchini
- Lunch: Zucchini Falafel
- Snack: Stuffed Peppers
- Dinner: Zucchini Falafel

DAY 15:
- Breakfast: Mediterranean Eggplant and Tomato Breakfast Bake
- Snack: Turkey Kabobs
- Lunch: Cauliflower Rice Bowl
- Snack: Shrimp Caesar Salad
- Dinner: Mexican Cauli Bowl

DAY 16:
- Breakfast: Veggie Quiche
- Snack: Stuffed Bell Peppers
- Lunch: Kale Quinoa Salad
- Snack: Lentil Tahini Salad
- Dinner: Kale Butternut Salad

DAY 17:
- Breakfast: Spinach Egg Muffins
- Snack: Shrimp Caesar Salad
- Lunch: Teriyaki Salmon Salad
- Snack: Asian Chicken Noodle Salad
- Dinner: Teriyaki Salmon Bowl

DAY 18:
- Breakfast: Herbed Omelette
- Snack: Mushroom Spinach Salad
- Lunch: Chicken Pita Wraps
- Snack: Watermelon Feta Salad
- Dinner: Chicken Pita Wraps

DAY 19:
- Breakfast: Apple Pancakes
- Snack: Thai Beef Salad
- Lunch: Shrimp Lettuce Cups
- Snack: Lemon Caper Baked Cod
- Dinner: Shrimp Lettuce Cups

DAY 20:
- Breakfast: Zucchini and Feta Fritters
- Snack: Greek Chicken Meatballs
- Lunch: Caprese salad
- Snack: Avocado Egg Salad Wraps
- Dinner: Caprese Skewers

DAY 21:
- Breakfast: Avocado Toast
- Snack: Turkey Veggie Skewers
- Lunch: BBQ Chicken Salad
- Snack: Roasted Red Pepper Hummus
- Dinner: BBQ Chicken Ranch

DAY 22:
- Breakfast: Veggie Burritos
- Snack: Stuffed Bell Peppers
- Lunch: Mushroom Spinach Salad
- Snack: Buffalo Cauliflower Bites
- Dinner: Mushroom Spinach Salad

DAY 23:
- Breakfast: Greek Yogurt Parfait with Berries and Nuts
- Snack: Quinoa Sushi Rolls
- Lunch: Thai Beef Salad
- Snack: Lemon Pepper Shrimp
- Dinner: Thai Beef Salad

DAY 24:
- Breakfast: Smoked Salmon and Cream Cheese Roll-Ups
- Snack: Buffalo Cauliflower Poppers
- Lunch: Lentil Salad
- Snack: Stuffed Peppers
- Dinner: Lentil Salad

DAY 25:
- Breakfast: Zucchini and Feta Fritters
- Snack: Asian Sesame Beef Skewers
- Lunch: Tuna Salad
- Snack: Quinoa Stuffed Zucchini
- Dinner: Tuna Salad

DAY 26:
- Breakfast: Quinoa Breakfast Bowl with Mixed Berries
- Snack: Asian Sesame Beef Skewers
- Lunch: Watermelon Feta Salad
- Dinner: Lemon Caper Baked Cod

DAY 27:
- Breakfast: Almond Flour Blueberry Muffins
- Snack: Teriyaki Turkey Meatballs
- Lunch: Lemon Caper Baked Cod
- Snack: Caprese Skewers
- Dinner: Grilled Balsamic Chicken

DAY 28:
- Breakfast: Avocado and Tomato Breakfast Toast
- Snack: Smokey Eggplant Dip
- Lunch: Spinach Strawberry Salad
- Snack: Lemon Pepper Shrimp
- Dinner: Strawberry Spinach Salad

DAY 29:
- Breakfast: Sweet Potato Hash Browns
- Snack: Cilantro Lime Shrimp Skewers
- Lunch: Tofu Stir-Fry
- Snack: Spinach Feta Mushrooms
- Dinner: Tofu Stir-Fry

DAY 30:
- Breakfast: Avocado and Tomato Breakfast Toast
- Snack: Spicy Tofu Wraps
- Lunch: Grilled Shrimp Caesar
- Snack: Zucchini Pizza Bites
- Dinner: Mediterranean Cucumber Roll-Ups

Chapter 12: Measurement conversion

Volume Conversions:

1 teaspoon (tsp) = 5 milliliters (ml)
1 tablespoon (tbsp) = 15 milliliters (ml)
1 fluid ounce (fl oz) = 30 milliliters (ml)
1 cup = 240 milliliters (ml)
1 pint (pt) = 480 milliliters (ml) or 2 cups
1 quart (qt) = 960 milliliters (ml) or 4 cups
1 gallon (gal) = 3.8 liters (L) or 16 cups

Weight Conversions:

1 ounce (oz) = 28 grams (g)
1 pound (lb) = 454 grams (g)
1 kilogram (kg) = 2.2 pounds (lbs)
For smaller measurements, use fractions or decimals of ounces or grams (e.g., ½ oz or 15 g)

Temperature Conversions:

Fahrenheit (°F) to Celsius (°C): Subtract 32 from the Fahrenheit temperature, then multiply by 5/9.
Celsius (°C) to Fahrenheit (°F): Multiply the Celsius temperature by 9/5, then add 32.

Cup Equivalents for Common Ingredients:

Butter: 1 cup = 226 grams (g) or 2 sticks
Flour: 1 cup = 120 grams (g)
Sugar: 1 cup = 200 grams (g)
Brown Sugar: 1 cup = 220 grams (g)
Milk: 1 cup = 240 milliliters (ml)
Honey/Syrup: 1 cup = 340 grams (g)

Oven Temperature Equivalents:

Slow Oven: 300°F (150°C)
Moderate Oven: 350°F (180°C)
Moderate-Hot Oven: 375°F (190°C)
Hot Oven: 400°F (200°C)
Very Hot Oven: 450°F (230°C)

Chapter 13: INDEX

Almond flour
Apple Pancakes, 12
Blueberry Muffins, 12
Eggplant Mozzarella Stack, 32
Zucchini Chickpea Fritters, 39
Parmesan Chicken Tenders, 57

Almonds
Quinoa Bowl, 15
Strawberry Spinach Salad, 36

Apple
Apple Pancakes, 12
Assorted vegetables
Sesame Chicken Salad, 38
Chickpea Cucumber Salad, 39
Tuna Lettuce Wraps, 38

Avocado
Avocado Toast, 12
Shrimp Avocado Salad, 18
Cauliflower Rice Bowl, 22
Mexican Quinoa Bowl, 25
Southwest Quinoa Salad, 29
Shrimp Avocado Salad, 31
Turkey Taco Wraps, 31
Shrimp Avocado Wraps, 36
Mexican Chicken Bowl, 43
Southwest Chicken Salad, 47

Balsamic vinegar
Chicken Salad, 17
Mushroom Spinach Salad, 24
Grilled Balsamic Chicken, 35
Balsamic Glazed Salmon, 53

Banana
Banana Bread, 14

Basil pesto
Zucchini Noodle Salad, 33

Beef sirloin
Thai Beef Salad, 42
Teriyaki Beef Skewers, 54

Beet
Beet Goat Cheese Salad, 41
Bell pepper
Turkey Skewers, 15
Stuffed Peppers, 21
Quinoa Stuffed Peppers, 32
Stuffed Bell Peppers, 39
Turkey Veggie Skewers, 43
Stuffed Bell Peppers, 44

Quinoa Stuffed Peppers, 50
Herbed Omelette, 11
Black Bean Salad, 19
Turkey Kabobs, 25
Stuffed Bell Peppers, 26
Air-Fried Shrimp Cups, 41
Southwest Quinoa Bowl, 51

Black beans
Black Bean Salad, 19
Cauliflower Rice Bowl, 22
Quinoa Stuffed Peppers, 32
Southwest Quinoa Bowl, 33
Black Bean Corn Salad, 37
Stuffed Bell Peppers, 44
Southwest Quinoa Bowl, 51

Boneless, skinless chicken breast
BBQ Chicken Salad, 24
Mexican Quinoa Bowl, 25

Brown rice
Teriyaki Salmon Bowl, 40

Butternut squash
Kale Quinoa Salad, 22
Kale Butternut Salad, 40

Cajun seasoning
Cajun Grilled Chicken, 55

Canned black beans
Stuffed Bell Peppers, 39
Mexican Cauli Bowl, 40

Canned chickpeas
Chickpea Cucumber Salad, 39
Zucchini Chickpea Fritters, 39

Canned tuna
Tuna Salad, 25
Tuna Lettuce Wraps, 38

Capers
Lemon-Caper Baked Cod, 45

Cauliflower florets
Mexican Cauli Bowl, 40

Cauliflower rice
Cauliflower Rice Bowl, 22

Cayenne pepper
Spicy Shrimp Skewers, 56

Cherry tomatoes
Caprese Skewers, 28

Greek Orzo Salad, 28
Mediterranean Pasta Salad, 30
Zucchini Noodle Salad, 33
Caprese Skewers, 38
Mushroom Spinach Salad, 42
Caprese Skewers, 46
Zucchini Noodle Salad, 51

Chicken breast
Caesar Salad, 19
Sesame Chicken Salad, 20
Chicken Pita Wraps, 23
Southwest Quinoa Salad, 29
Stuffed Chicken Breast, 30
Grilled Chicken Salad, 32
Grilled Balsamic Chicken, 35
Light Caesar Chicken, 37
Sesame Chicken Salad, 38
Chicken Pita Wraps, 41
BBQ Chicken Ranch, 42
Mexican Chicken Bowl, 43
Asian Chicken Noodle Salad, 45
Southwest Chicken Salad, 47
Spinach Stuffed Chicken, 48
Lemon Herb Grilled Chicken, 50
Grilled Lemon Chicken, 53
Mediterranean Chicken, 54
Cajun Grilled Chicken, 55
Parmesan Chicken Tenders, 57

Chicken thigh
Roasted Chicken Thighs, 55

Chicken wings
Air-Fried Chicken Wings, 55

Chickpeas
Chickpea Salad, 21
Zucchini Falafel, 21
Falafel Salad, 29

Cod fillet
Baked Cod, 27
Chicken Lettuce Wraps, 28
Lemon-Caper Baked Cod, 45

Cooked quinoa
Mexican Quinoa Bowl, 25
Stuffed Bell Peppers, 39

Corn
Black Bean Salad, 19
Black Bean Corn Salad, 37

Cream cheese
Salmon Roll-Ups, 14

Cucumber
Chickpea Salad, 21
Greek Orzo Salad, 28
Chickpea Cucumber Salad, 39
Greek Orzo Salad, 46

Diced tomatoes
Mexican Cauli Bowl, 40
Mediterranean Pasta Salad, 48

Diced vegetables
Quinoa Stuffed Peppers, 50

Dijon mustard
Grilled Chicken Salad, 32
Grilled Balsamic Chicken, 35
Honey Mustard Pork Tenderloin, 56

Dried dill
Lemon-Dill Salmon, 35

Dried herbs
Lemon Herb Grilled Chicken, 50
Grilled Lamb Chops, 56
Roasted Turkey Breast, 53

Edamame beans
Asian Tofu Salad, 49

Eggplant
Eggplant Bake, 15
Eggplant Mozzarella Stack, 32
Eggplant Mozzarella Stack, 50

Eggs
Veggie Quiche, 11
Spinach Egg Muffins, 11
Herbed Omelette, 11
Veggie Burritos, 13

Falafel balls
Air-Fried Falafel Salad, 47

Feta cheese
Zucchini Fritters, 14
Eggplant Bake, 15
Greek Salad, 18
Chickpea Salad, 21
Watermelon Feta Salad, 27
Mediterranean Pasta Salad, 30
Roasted Veggie Quinoa, 35
Greek Feta Salad, 36
Watermelon Feta Salad, 45
Greek Orzo Salad, 46
Air-Fried Falafel Salad, 47
Spinach Stuffed Chicken, 48

Firm tofu
Sesame Tofu Salad, 31
Black Bean Corn Salad, 37
Asian Tofu Salad, 49

Fresh basil
Caprese Salad, 20
Caprese Skewers, 28
Zucchini Noodle Salad, 51

Fresh basil leaves
Caprese Skewers, 38
Caprese Skewers, 46
Fresh blueberries
Blueberry Muffins, 12

Fresh dill
Salmon with Lemon-Dill, 17
Salmon Roll-Ups, 14

Fresh mozzarella
Eggplant Mozzarella Stack, 50
Caprese Skewers, 38
Caprese Skewers, 46

Garlic
Roasted Chicken Thighs, 55
Grilled Lamb Chops, 56

Goat cheese
Spinach Strawberry Salad, 18
Beet Goat Cheese Salad, 23
Beet Goat Cheese Salad, 41

Greek yogurt
Yogurt Parfait, 13
Chicken Pita Wraps, 23
Turkey Kabobs, 25
Chicken Pita Wraps, 41

Grilled chicken
Southwest Quinoa Bowl, 33
Chicken Salad, 17
Noodle Salad, 27

Ground turkey
Turkey Taco Wraps, 31
Turkey Taco Lettuce Wraps, 49

Honey
Honey Mustard Pork Tenderloin, 56
Honey Sriracha Salmon, 57

Shrimp
Shrimp Lettuce Cups, 23

Hummus
Falafel Salad, 29

Kalamata olives
Greek Salad, 18
Tuna Salad, 25
Greek Feta Salad, 36
Mediterranean Tuna Salad, 43

Kale
Kale Quinoa Salad, 22
Kale Butternut Salad, 40

Lemon juice
Lemon-Dill Salmon, 35
Lemon-Caper Baked Cod, 45
Lemon Herb Grilled Chicken, 50
Grilled Lemon Chicken, 53
Grilled Shrimp, 54
Mediterranean Chicken, 54

Lettuce
Shrimp Lettuce Cups, 23
Thai Beef Wraps, 30
Turkey Taco Wraps, 31
Thai Beef Lettuce Wraps, 48
Turkey Taco Lettuce Wraps, 49

Lettuce leaves
Tuna Lettuce Wraps, 38
Chicken Lettuce Wraps, 46

Low-sodium soy sauce
Black Bean Corn Salad, 37
Chicken Lettuce Wraps, 46
Zucchini Pad Thai, 47

Mixed berries
Yogurt Parfait, 13
Quinoa Bowl, 15
Teriyaki Salmon Salad, 22
Mixed salad greens
Chicken Salad, 17
Greek Salad, 18
Sesame Chicken Salad, 20
Thai Beef Salad, 24
Falafel Salad, 29
Shrimp Avocado Salad, 31
Grilled Chicken Salad, 32
Greek Feta Salad, 36
Sesame Chicken Salad, 38
Thai Beef Salad, 42
Mediterranean Tuna Salad, 43
Lentil Tahini Salad, 44
Asian Chicken Noodle Salad, 45
Watermelon Feta Salad, 45
Air-Fried Falafel Salad, 47
Southwest Chicken Salad, 47

Asian Tofu Salad, 49
Grilled Shrimp Salad, 49

Mixed vegetables
Veggie Burritos, 13
Quinoa Veggie Salad, 17
Tofu Stir-Fry, 19
Tuna Lettuce Wraps, 20
Noodle Salad, 27
Baked Cod, 27
Roasted Veggie Quinoa, 35
Black Bean Corn Salad, 37

Mozzarella cheese
Caprese Salad, 20
Caprese Skewers, 28

Mushrooms
Spinach Egg Muffins, 11
Stuffed Chicken Breast, 30
Mushroom Spinach Salad, 42

Olive oil
Grilled Lemon Chicken, 53
Roasted Turkey Breast, 53
Balsamic Glazed Salmon, 53
Mediterranean Chicken, 54

Onion
Sweet Potato Hash, 13

Orzo pasta
Greek Orzo Salad, 28

Paprika
Cajun Grilled Chicken, 55
Spicy Shrimp Skewers, 56

Parmesan cheese
Grilled Shrimp Caesar, 44
Parmesan Chicken Tenders, 57

Quinoa
Quinoa Bowl, 15
Quinoa Veggie Salad, 17
Stuffed Peppers, 21
Kale Quinoa Salad, 22
Stuffed Bell Peppers, 26
Baked Cod, 27
Chicken Lettuce Wraps, 28
Southwest Quinoa Salad, 29
Quinoa Stuffed Peppers, 32
Southwest Quinoa Bowl, 33
Roasted Veggie Quinoa, 35
Mexican Chicken Bowl, 43
Stuffed Bell Peppers, 44
Quinoa Stuffed Peppers, 50
Southwest Quinoa Bowl, 51

Red bell pepper
Black Bean Corn Salad, 37
Thai Beef Salad, 42

Red onion
Tuna Salad, 25
Turkey Veggie Skewers, 43

Romaine lettuce
Caesar Salad, 19
Shrimp Caesar Salad, 26
Lentil Salad, 26
Light Caesar Chicken, 37
Grilled Shrimp Caesar, 44

Salmon fillet
Salmon with Lemon-Dill, 17
Teriyaki Salmon Salad, 22
Lemon-Dill Salmon, 35
Teriyaki Salmon Bowl, 40
Balsamic Glazed Salmon, 53
Honey Sriracha Salmon, 57

Shrimp
Shrimp Avocado Salad, 18
Shrimp Caesar Salad, 26
Lentil Salad, 26
Zucchini Pad Thai, 29
Shrimp Avocado Salad, 31
Shrimp Avocado Wraps, 36
Grilled Shrimp Caesar, 44
Grilled Shrimp Salad, 49
Grilled Shrimp, 54
Spicy Shrimp Skewers, 56

Soy-ginger sauce
Tofu Stir-Fry, 19
Tuna Lettuce Wraps, 20

Spinach
Spinach Egg Muffins, 11
Spinach Strawberry Salad, 18
Stuffed Bell Peppers, 26
Stuffed Chicken Breast, 30
Mushroom Spinach Salad, 42
Spinach Stuffed Chicken, 48

Spinach leaves
Mushroom Spinach Salad, 24
Strawberry Spinach Salad, 36

Sugar-free BBQ sauce
BBQ Chicken Salad, 24
BBQ Chicken Ranch, 42

Tahini
Zucchini Falafel, 21
Lentil Tahini Salad, 44

Tofu
Tofu Stir-Fry, 19
Tuna Lettuce Wraps, 20

Tomato
Avocado Toast, 12
Eggplant Bake, 15
Caprese Salad, 20
Eggplant Mozzarella Stack, 50

Turkey breast
Turkey Kabobs, 25
Roasted Turkey Breast, 53

Walnuts
Beet Goat Cheese Salad, 23
Kale Butternut Salad, 40
Beet Goat Cheese Salad, 41
Banana Bread, 14

Watermelon
Watermelon Feta Salad, 27
Watermelon Feta Salad, 45
Whole wheat croutons
Shrimp Caesar Salad, 26
Lentil Salad, 26

Whole wheat pasta
Mediterranean Pasta Salad, 30
Mediterranean Pasta Salad, 48

Zucchini
Zucchini Fritters, 14
Turkey Skewers, 15
Zucchini Falafel, 21
Stuffed Peppers, 21
Zucchini Pad Thai, 29
Zucchini Noodle Salad, 33
Zucchini Chickpea Fritters, 39
Turkey Veggie Skewers, 43
Zucchini Pad Thai, 47
Zucchini Noodle Salad, 51

Chapter 14: Conclusion

In conclusion, the "Diabetic Air Fryer Cookbook" is your friendly companion in the kitchen, providing a wealth of delicious recipes and helpful tips to support your diabetes management journey. With this cookbook, you can enjoy flavorful meals without compromising your health.

We understand that living with diabetes can be challenging, especially when it comes to finding tasty yet diabetes-friendly recipes. That's why we've carefully crafted a collection of breakfast, snack, lunch, and dinner options that are both nutritious and satisfying. From crispy vegetable quiches to mouthwatering buffalo cauliflower bites, our recipes are designed to tantalize your taste buds while keeping your blood sugar levels in check.

What sets this cookbook apart is our focus on the incredible versatility of air fryers. By using this handy kitchen appliance, you can enjoy the crispy goodness of fried foods with a fraction of the oil. Air frying allows you to savor the flavors and textures you love while maintaining a healthy lifestyle.

In addition to the delicious recipes, we provide practical advice to support your diabetes management. We guide you on portion control, understanding the glycemic index, and making mindful choices when it comes to carbohydrates, fats, and sugars. Our aim is to empower you to make informed decisions about your meals and take control of your health.

Whether you're a seasoned chef or a kitchen novice, the "Diabetic Air Fryer Cookbook" is designed to make your cooking experience enjoyable and stress-free. With easy-to-follow recipes and helpful tips, you can create wholesome meals that are tailored to your dietary needs and preferences.

We hope that this cookbook becomes your go-to resource, inspiring you to explore new flavors, experiment with ingredients, and embrace a healthy and flavorful lifestyle. Managing diabetes doesn't mean sacrificing taste, and with the "Diabetic Air Fryer Cookbook," you can savor every bite while nourishing your body.

Remember, you're not alone on this journey. We're here to support you every step of the way. So, grab your apron, fire up your air fryer, and get ready to embark on a delicious and health-conscious culinary adventure with the "Diabetic Air Fryer Cookbook."

Printed in Great Britain
by Amazon

efbd1060-bd88-4d19-9a29-e5f4c3aedffcR01